T0296023

Competence, Conduct, and Billion Dollar Consequences

This practical guide to understanding how regulators build insight and form judgements will help organisations to develop their strategy and approach to engagement and to improve their regulatory outcomes.

From robot-assisted surgery and advances in stem cell technology, the explosion in use of social media and advances in computing power to the development of autonomous vehicles and digital environments such as the metaverse, these exciting developments present questions, invite debate, and have implications. These rapid new developments also join a world described as being increasingly VUCA (volatile, uncertain, complex, and ambiguous), making industry-regulator relationships more important than ever to prevent consumer harm and to configure business success. This book is written for those who wish to build positive and progressive relationships with their regulators in these exciting times of rapid advancement. From developing their strategy, through to the practicalities of how to prepare and engage with regulators, readers are navigated through an ecosystem of insight to help build an understanding of what informs their regulator's opinion and judgements. Underpinned with real-world experiences and examples, this book shows that, through clearer strategic focus and more effective relationships, organisations can refine their approach and build their relationships to drive mutually beneficial regulatory relationships that avoid negative consequences and unnecessary costs.

Board members, executives, senior leaders, risk, compliance, legal professionals, regulators, and students of business, finance, and law will refer to this book again and again to guide holistic thinking about regulatory relationships and use the insights these can provide to help them calibrate their actions, activities, and progress.

Dr. Nigel Somerset is an independent consultant focused on transforming the performance, risk, and compliance of businesses. His experience includes accountability for leading portfolios valued in billions sterling through economic cycles, including the Global Financial Crisis, shaping and influencing industry strategy, and supporting organisations and executives on regulatory matters spanning day-to-day supervision, regulatory challenge, through to sanction.

Nigel also serves as executive in residence at the A.A.C.S.B.-accredited Sheffield Business School, is an Associate of The London Institute of Banking & Finance, and holds a D.B.A., M.B.A., and B.A. (Hons) in Financial Services.

"An excellent guide to developing positive and mutually beneficial relationships with regulators, based on significant experience. From strategy, to the practicalities of delivering what regulators require, it provides excellent insights, new ideas, and pitfalls to avoid. A must read for all who deal with the demands of regulators".

Prof. Nigel Garrow, *Sheffield Hallam University and former international food industry C.E.O.*

"Diligently researched and well written, this is a thought-provoking book with interesting insights and practical examples of the kind rarely seen in regulatory textbooks. The significance of regulatory context is particularly well handled, as is the importance of the relationship between the regulator and the regulated. Definitely worth a read".

Maggie Craig, *Former Head of Devolved Nations & Communications at the Financial Conduct Authority*

COMPETENCE, CONDUCT, AND BILLION DOLLAR CONSEQUENCES

HOW REGULATORY STRATEGY AND RELATIONSHIPS CAN IMPROVE ORGANISATIONAL OUTCOMES

Nigel P. Somerset

Routledge
Taylor & Francis Group

NEW YORK AND LONDON

Designed cover image: © Peshkova/Getty Images

First published 2023
by Routledge
605 Third Avenue, New York, NY 10158

and by Routledge
4 Park Square, Milton Park, Abingdon, Oxon, OX14 4RN

Routledge is an imprint of the Taylor & Francis Group, an informa business

Library of Congress Cataloging-in-Publication Data
Names: Somerset, Nigel P., author.
Title: Competence, conduct & billion dollar consequences : how regulatory
   strategy & relationships can improve organisational outcomes / Nigel P. Somerset.
Other titles: Competence, conduct and billion dollar consequences
Description: New York, NY : Routledge, 2023. | Includes bibliographical
   references and index.
Identifiers: LCCN 2022036642 | ISBN 9781032286778 (hardback) | ISBN
   9781032286761 (paperback) | ISBN 9781003297963 (ebook)
Subjects: LCSH: Corporate governance. | Industrial management. |
   Uncertainty. | COVID-19 Pandemic, 2020---Economic aspects.
Classification: LCC HD2741 .S7223 2023 | DDC 658.4--dc23/eng/20221209
LC record available at https://lccn.loc.gov/2022036642

ISBN: 978-1-032-28677-8 (hbk)
ISBN: 978-1-032-28676-1 (pbk)
ISBN: 978-1-003-29796-3 (ebk)

DOI: 10.4324/9781003297963

Typeset in Palatino Lt Std
by KnowledgeWorks Global Ltd.

TABLE OF CONTENTS

DETAILED TABLE OF CONTENTS

FIGURES

PREFACE

THESE ARE INCREDIBLE TIMES...

We live in incredible times. Even a momentary pause to consider the world around us reveals a fascinating array of exciting and challenging developments.

Consider for a moment some of the changes and events we have and continue to experience in our time; whether we think about the way we communicate and share our lives through social media connecting the world like never before; capture and store our often considerable catalogue of data with organisations and platforms we use; take our music, news, films, television, and books with us in our mobile devices; shop and conduct our banking whilst on the move; see the benefits of medical advances unfold, such as mapping the genome, developments in stem cell technology, medical device implants, and robotic surgical machines; experience the largest Global Financial Crisis in capitalist history that unfolded devastating consequences across the globe; or respond to a global pandemic that put the brakes on the world and locked it down in a way we have never experienced in our lifetimes, these truly are times of opportunity and challenge. Now, look forward and consider what may be on the horizon. Here, we see the green shoots of further truly amazing opportunities that not so long ago would have been considered science fiction, such as the arrival of advanced robotics[1], technologies that enable organ growth from cells, autonomous vehicles that allow us to change their colour at the touch of a button[2], through to the creation of the metaverse and nonfungible tokens to enable our digital lives.

The list could go on and on, yet all these developments have implications in terms of the way we need to think about how organisations harness new capability and conduct themselves as they develop. They also raise potential implications for regulation and regulators in terms of the need to adapt to accommodate such change. Most importantly, they have potential implications both in short and long-term outcomes for those who trust, utilise, and consume them. Those exciting developments present questions, they invite debate, and they require industries and regulators to engage in order that they can successfully navigate a way forward that continues to promote progressive developments whilst ensuring appropriate safeguards exist to prevent detriment or harm.

A BILLION DOLLAR HISTORY OF CONSEQUENCES ... WE CAN DO BETTER THAN THIS

Against the backdrop of such amazing opportunity and advancement, we have also faced challenges. Over the last decade, we have seen the practices of some of the world's largest industries and organisations called into question, at a cost of billions of dollars for those concerned. Failures that, as we will see, can at times be attributed to many aspects of how organisations are built and navigated, and call into question some aspect of competence or conduct that led to devastating consequences.

The practices of organisations have impacted whole economies, industries, and societies, with devastating effect, whilst for the organisations themselves, they have resulted in complete failure, record fines from regulators, have left brands and reputations in tatters, and led to the destruction of shareholder value on a huge scale.

These same practices have also undermined trust and confidence and driven an increased focus on the questions surrounding the role, importance, and level of protection afforded to consumers, resulting in new regulations and greater powers for regulators. As a result of this shift in power toward regulators across many industries, organisations have often experienced greater scrutiny and challenge, along with increased enforcement and sanction.

Against this backdrop, leaders have a balancing act to undertake as they think carefully about how their organisations are invested in and configured for success (build competence), how they are driven and controlled (conduct), how they assure positive outcomes for all stakeholders (consequences), as well as how they navigate critical relationships such as those with their regulator. How they perform this balancing act, as we shall see, has a critical impact on how trust and confidence will develop, how questions of protection, regulation, and the role of regulators are answered, and how relationships with regulators unfold.

INSIGHT FROM ACROSS INDUSTRIES THAT PROVIDE CHALLENGES AND LESSONS

Throughout the book, we take illustrative insight and examples from different industries, different organisations of varied size, and look at situations across a range of scale and complexity to demonstrate such situations can arise across a whole array of scenarios.

Whilst we take insight and examples from across industries to illustrate the situation described here throughout the book, recent history has provided one event from which much can be learned. As one of the most significant global events of the last 100 years, the Global Financial Crisis (G.F.C.) provides compelling examples upon which to reflect and take learnings from, and, as such, is used as a backcloth to many of the subjects and discussions throughout this text given the number of examples it has provided.

Although history in the financial services sector has provided many lessons regarding the importance of regulatory relationships, financial services are not alone or unique, and given the progress made in financial services since the G.F.C., there are interesting emerging challenges in other industries to transplant learnings to. We only need to consider some of the significant advancements noted above to realise these times of rapid technological change present exciting challenges on many fronts that pose new questions for how organisations and regulators work together for the good of their common beneficiaries. Take the example of the explosion of social media in recent years, which has connected individuals across the world in a way not seen before, whilst at the same time being criticised as an industry for its lack of content screening and the tragic stories of misuse leading to calls for greater protection. So, throughout the chapters ahead, we tap into other industries such as social media, pharmaceuticals, and aviation and consider some of the challenges and lessons they provide for how we build organisations, navigate organisations, and engage with regulators to improve outcomes for all stakeholders.

GREATER THAN THE SUM OF THE PARTS IS THE AIM

As many organisations have experienced a shift in power toward regulators, felt their scrutiny intensify, observed the significant impact their interventions or enforcement has had on their performance and reputations where they have fallen short of the required standard, so regulatory relationships across many industries have become a major focus.

This book is written with the aim of helping those who wish to improve their approach and understanding of how to build positive, proactive, and progressive relationships with their regulators. It is for those who wish to understand how those relationships can help them challenge and calibrate how they build their capability, how they navigate their organisation, and how they scrutinise the outcomes they generate for all stakeholders in terms of the consequences they drive. In other words, this book discusses how your strategy and approach to regulatory engagement can help you improve your outcomes and ensure you are not a contributor to the billion-dollar club of consequences. *In short, how more can be achieved when we work together.*

THE BOOK'S CENTRAL TENET IS TRANSFERRABLE

Whilst the focus is on regulatory relationships, what this book covers is applicable to how many critical relationships can be understood and appropriately nurtured…as much of what you will read will be transferrable to other situations. Where the stakes are high and the relationship critical to success, understanding the relationship and *ecosystem* of influences that drive its development is key and a central tenet of the book.

Appealing to professionals of all levels, and students in disciplines such as risk, compliance, audit, management, and organisational behaviour, the book introduces a new perspective on how to think about critical relationships in a broader context. It provides insights to help everyone from the Board to the individual colleague understand the drivers of their relationships and how to improve their strategy to effectively navigate them.

WHAT THE BOOK PROVIDES

The reader will explore how to identify, consider, and understand the various systems of interaction (the *ecosystem*) that surround their regulatory relationships. In doing so, they will consider what influences and shapes their development, how they can be used to better calibrate the activities of the organisation, inform regulatory opinion, and help steer toward better organisational outcomes. In taking this broader perspective, we see how it enables a deeper consideration of how to develop regulatory strategies to drive positive and mutually beneficial relationships with regulators.

The insights are drawn from across the plains of practice and theory and draw on a cumulative experience that runs into hundreds of years. They are based on academic research and the experience of Board, the C-Suite, and senior management professionals from across different industries and disciplines who have sat on both sides of the regulatory relationship. Furthermore, their engagements have covered a whole array of regulatory situations, from the day-to-day interactions of regulatory relationships, defining and establishing regulatory capability, through to sanction and enforcement.

The aim is to provide insight into areas that will interest all who engage in regulatory relationships (whichever side of the table they sit) and along the way provide practical insight from those that have been there, seen it, and done it at the most senior levels. Whether your view is from the Board table, a seasoned professional who frequently interacts with regulators, or you are yet to experience your first engagement, the book provides plenty of food for thought and examples for all to reflect upon. You'll read how Board and senior management choices and behaviours fundamentally underpin and drive your organisation's regulatory relationship strategy and approach. In addition, you will consider the activities and actions necessary for successful formal engagements and appreciate how even the most basic practicalities are crucial to get right. The book will be a source of new ideas to consider, useful insights and experiences to reflect upon, helpful reminders of the simple things often forgotten at great cost, through to uncomfortable real-life examples of fundamental pitfalls and errors to avoid. All of which provide insights to consider and feed your regulatory relationship strategy.

If you want to understand the *ecosystem* that surrounds your organisation's regulatory relationship and feeds your regulator, understand how that may influence your engagements and outcomes, and help you consider how you can adapt your approach to a more effective relationship underpinned with trust and confidence, then this book is for you.

PANDEMIC: THE POWER OF RELATIONSHIPS

Finally, as the writing of this book was drawing toward a close, the world saw the arrival of its latest crisis that would challenge societies across the globe, Covid-19. At that point (March 2020), a significant proportion of the world population had its liberty restricted as the globe faced the fight against the virus. The fight is a global effort to save lives.

Even in those early days in the fight against Covid-19, what became clear was that nations and industries across the globe were responding to the crisis to do whatever it took to save lives and arrest the pandemic sweeping the globe. As they did, relationships of all kinds, including regulatory, were bound in a common cause, with new relationships developing, existing ones being tested, and old ones being rekindled. A pandemic by its very nature is time critical, testing conventional timelines for regulatory endeavour and resulting in a necessary challenge and adjustment to theory, practice, and convention. The regulatory, organisational, and individual focus on saving lives, necessitated a re-think on the operation of regulation, regulatory oversight, and regulatory relationships to facilitate success by whatever means necessary. Covid-19 presented us with a stark lesson in adaptation that is covered with examples throughout, and in more detail in Chapter 2 and Chapter 8. In Chapter 2, we consider what a regulatory relationship is, its purpose, importance, what it entails, how stakeholders influence it, and how this latest crisis demonstrates how important relationships are at the point you need to respond. Chapter 8 provides a reflexive look at what the crisis has meant to regulatory responses and relationships and how, in crisis, relationships are key to your response. Overall, it has provided a live example for how our systems of regulatory engagement perform in crisis with some excellent results.

THE END AS A BEGINNING

The objective is that you will find many aspects of what this book covers useful and transferrable to the regulatory relationships you may have. Whether you are a seasoned professional used to regular interaction or new to such regulatory engagements, plenty of food for thought is the order of the day given the rapidly changing times. That food for thought will cover the basics that are often forgotten at some cost to more complex considerations of the way regulatory relationships are developing in such a dynamic and changing global environment.

Whatever your experience to date, the hope is that you find this book informs you, surprises and entertains you, reminds you, and most of all challenges you to consider what we can do as professional communities around our customers, patients, colleagues, constituents, families, and friends to deliver these exciting new opportunities in safe and secure ways.

By the end of the book, you will have reviewed a significant breadth of insight, examples, and subject areas that influence the building of effective regulatory relationships. Each of those subjects will have their own extensive literature base and useful examples to explore in greater detail should your interest be piqued (captured in chapter end notes and references). In addition, there is also a broad selection of literature in the bibliography that has been used in the foundation research for the book. These, it is hoped, will provide good entry points for further reading across the many subjects covered and an opportunity to begin exploring new avenues around the subject.

NOTES

1. See Sophia as an example of current advances in robotics at https://www.hansonrobotics.com/sophia/
2. See Younis, O. (2022), "Change your car's colour with an app: BMW unveils colour-changing car".

REFERENCES

Hanson Robotics, (2022), 'Sophia', [online], 2022, available: https://www.hanson-robotics.com/sophia/

Younis, O. (2022), 'Change Your Car's Colour With an App: BMW Unveils Colour-Changing Car', [online], Reuters, 7 January 2022, available: https://www.reuters.com/business/autos-transportation/change-your-cars-colour-with-an-app-bmw-unveils-colour-changing-car-2022-01-07/

ROUTE MAP OF THE BOOK

This section explains how the book is organised and introduces the framework used throughout the book to help the reader.

This framework is provided next, and we step through each chapter and illustrate where in that overall framework each item fits. In addition, throughout the book, chapter headings and illustrations will be accompanied by a *picture tile* of the overall framework as a constant reference point as to where that subject sits in relation to the framework.

THE FRAMEWORK

The overall concept of the book is that organisations have the opportunity to achieve significant improvements in their regulatory relationships, their regulator's view, and regulatory outcomes for the organisation by thinking about regulatory relationships from a more holistic perspective and using the insights the relationship can provide to help them calibrate their actions, activities, and progress.

That opportunity arises due to thinking differently across a wide variety of areas we explore throughout the chapters. However, at the highest level, these can fundamentally be categorised into two broad themes that impact and influence the outcome you achieve in terms of the regulator's view of your organisation and the relationship you enjoy with them.

Thinking in terms of these two broad themes allows us to build an illustration of our overall framework (see Figure A), the components of which we expand upon progressively throughout the book:

Theme 1: How you engage with your regulatory *ecosystem*

Theme 2: How you *engage* with your regulator

Outcome: *The regulatory view*, relationship you enjoy, outcomes you achieve

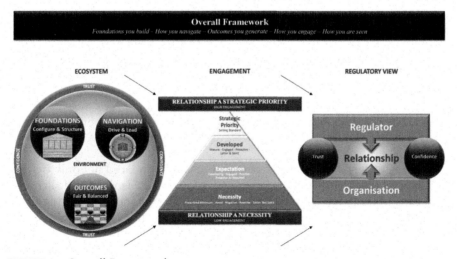

FIGURE A   Overall Framework

Theme 1 explores how organisations can understand their regulatory *ecosystem* from a broader perspective and how it can impact their regulator's view of the organisation. Theme 2 is focused on an organisation's strategy for *engagement*, the practicalities of engaging, and the drivers and emerging themes that may result in changes in the way relationships are conducted in the future.

Finally, throughout the text, we consider how each of these themes impacts the regulatory view, the relationship you enjoy and the outcomes you achieve.

As you can see from Figure A, these high-level broad categories contain many different elements that form their building blocks, each of which unfold as we progress through the chapters.

To start, we look at each element of our framework and map them to the chapters in which they are explored, along with a brief overview of the chapter. As we do, we show how the picture progressively builds as the chapters unfold and cover the core building blocks that help ensure your regulator's view is well informed and in line with what you aspire to achieve in terms of your relationship with them.

CHAPTER 1 – HOW DO ORGANISATIONS THINK ABOUT REGULATORY RELATIONSHIP STRATEGIES?

Chapter 1 describes how organisations in general have tended to think about regulatory relationships, what such relationships can entail, and why they are so important. It considers how organisations define their strategy, what that can involve, and how it may be shaped. In understanding how relationships work, it also explores how relationships can operate in different *modes*, how stakeholders can influence the relationship, and what some of the drivers of change are that we are seeing.

In terms of our roadmap, this chapter acts as the background from which our formal framework starts to build. It seeks to illustrate the many and varied influences on our relationships and the need for a way for organisations to make sense of the complex array of influences on the relationships they have.

CHAPTER 2 – A FRAMEWORK FOR BUILDING MORE EFFECTIVE RELATIONSHIPS

Chapter 2 introduces the first theme of our framework and describes the opportunity for organisations to take a *new perspective* on their regulatory relationship strategy.

That new perspective introduces the concept of the *regulatory ecosystem* and the benefits it has for keeping regulators better informed, allowing organisations to better calibrate their activities and lay the foundations for improved relationships.

It explores how regulatory relationships are influenced not only by that which the organisation directly drives and informs, but also by a wide array of sources of information fed by an organisation's ecosystem. In exploring these influences, it highlights the importance of the regulatory relationship as the key conduit between an organisation and its regulator, and underscores this with a brief overview of theories that support and demonstrate the importance of relationship building.

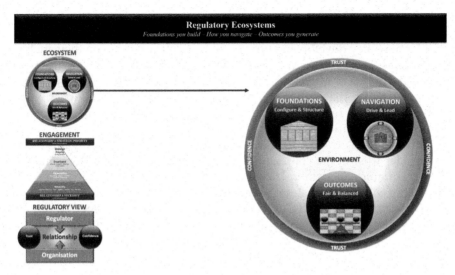

FIGURE B   Regulatory Ecosystems

Given any relationship must have a catalyst for its creation, it also introduces the concept of the *emergent regulatory relationship*, and how organisations can use their ecosystem to ensure relationships develop well at embryonic stages.

Finally, it considers the case for taking a new broader perspective of the regulatory relationship and introduces the components of the regulatory ecosystem.

CHAPTER 3 – THE ROLE OF TRUST IN REGULATORY RELATIONSHIP STRATEGIES

In Chapter 3, we begin our exploration of each element of the regulatory ecosystem, beginning with that which wraps around all other elements and forms the lifeblood of regulatory relationships – the building of trust and confidence.

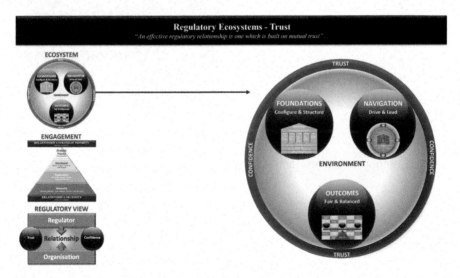

FIGURE C   Regulatory Ecosystems – Trust

Here, we explore what we mean by trust and its role and importance in regulatory relationships. As we explore the role of trust and confidence, we consider how they develop and build and the implications when they are lost. Using a series of examples, we focus in on the implications of losing trust and some of the dramatic impacts this can have. Examples illustrate how our trust is sensitive to the risks involved, and how a loss of trust can impact whole industries, destroy reputations and value, and be driven, at times, by events beyond an organisation's control.

In positioning trust as a fundamental foundation stone for organisations, we consider trust in the context of ethical and moral considerations and use further examples to demonstrate how these connected considerations can impact the building of trust with stakeholders.

Reflecting on research and real examples, we demonstrate the centrality of trust to a positive and productive relationship, highlighting the many dimensions it operates across and how trust forms as a picture that is built based on a body of evidence over time.

CHAPTER 4 – FOUNDATIONS: ESTABLISHING TRUST IN WHAT YOU BUILD

At this point, we start to consider how the fundamental foundations of how organisations set themselves up and operate can have a significant influence on how regulatory relationships take shape and operate.

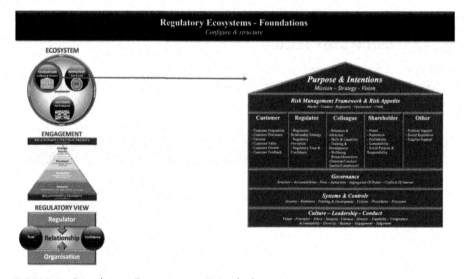

FIGURE D   Regulatory Ecosystems – Foundations

We explore each of the building blocks that typically form the construct of an organisation and highlight how each can be of interest to the regulator.

From an organisation's objectives and purpose, the strategy it follows, and the culture it creates, we see how such items are fundamental in shaping how an organisation approaches and engages in regulatory relationships. In addition, we systematically work our way through key aspects where regulators have a growing interest, such as an organisation's risk management approach and appetite for risk, how organisations manage their stakeholders, and their governance, systems, and controls.

In considering the importance of how organisations set themselves up and how they drive their business, we begin to understand how these decisions shape the outcomes regulators see, and therefore, how more and more regulators have become increasingly interested in an organisation's make up.

CHAPTER 5 – NAVIGATION: ESTABLISHING TRUST IN STRATEGY, CULTURE, LEADERSHIP AND CONDUCT

Chapter 5 explores how regulators are increasingly interested in how Board and leadership teams drive and lead their organisations. In broad terms, how the organisation is navigated and *wired up* to achieve the right outcomes.

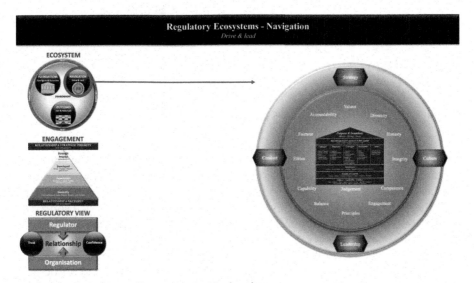

FIGURE E   Regulatory Ecosystems – Navigation

We look at how regulators consider the strategies, culture, leadership, and conduct of organisations as key barometers against which to consider the risk an organisation may pose to its objectives.

In addition, we explore the importance of the *human factor* and its influence on how the organisation may be driven and led. Here, we look at how such factors can influence both organisational outcomes and regulatory perception. In exploring this, we delve into areas such as animal spirits and dominant personalities and consider some of the dangers they can present and how some regulators monitor and assess for such characteristics.

CHAPTER 6 – OUTCOMES: THE ECOSYSTEM INFORMING REGULATORY OPINION

Having established the importance of the foundations regarding how organisations set themselves up and drive their business, this chapter moves on to explore the final element of our first theme, that being, the outcomes the organisation produces. Here we explore the *ecosystem* of information and insight that flows to your regulator as your organisation drives forward.

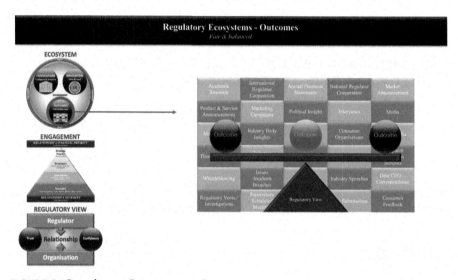

FIGURE F   Regulatory Ecosystems – Outcomes

We consider how the availability of data, information, and insight has expanded in terms of breadth of source and accelerated in its immediacy of availability. Furthermore, we see how regulators use this broader palette to help them shape their opinion and form judgements. Given this rich source of information is no longer under the direct control of organisations, we see how regulators are in a perfect position to triangulate insights and build a rich picture of the impact organisations have in terms of the outcomes they drive. In this respect, we demonstrate how the relationship is being fed and argue that taking the approach of considering all such information as part of the relationship provides the best chance of being able to keep your regulator fully and proactively informed, so that all they see is placed in context and understood. That is, think about the *ecosystem* as the basis of your relationship and key to proactive and effective engagement.

CHAPTER 7 – ENGAGEMENT: THE PRACTICAL CONSIDERATIONS WHEN INTERACTING WITH REGULATORS

In this chapter, we turn to the second theme in our framework where we explore the practical considerations of engagement.

We begin with the importance of understanding your regulator's objectives and establishing the context in which engagements are taking place.

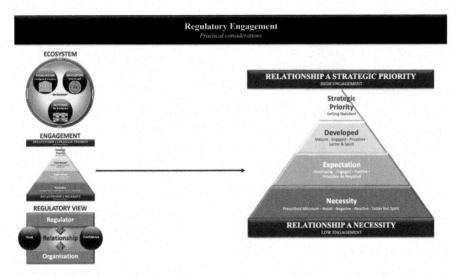

FIGURE G   Regulatory Engagement

Having established the context of engagements, we move on to under-standing the most fundamental of principles that underpin relationships and the importance of conduct and behaviour in building effective relationships. Here, we explore how the basics matter and how they are often overlooked. Exploring etiquette, considering examples where simple errors have nega-tively impacted engagements, and reflecting upon how this *human factor* can be so important reminds us that fundamentally relationships involve people and people form judgements that are influenced by their engagements.

Having considered the context and nature of engagements, we move into the more practical considerations of how to prepare and deliver on your com-mitments, from the fundamentals of accountabilities and planning, the rigour of appropriate preparation, the art of communication, to the robustness of delivery and step through some of the more critical steps that often make the difference in engagements.

CHAPTER 8 – PANDEMIC CRISIS: RELATIONSHIPS MATTER!

Chapter 8 sees us take the opportunity to pause as the world faced an incred-ible challenge. As the unfolding challenge of a global pandemic faced us, we looked in on the world of regulatory relationships and how they have and continue to adapt to the challenges.

Here, we consider the response using elements of the frameworks we have used throughout the book. We consider how, in times of crisis, rules, convention, and practice, can be rewritten. In addition, we see how such times can fundamentally change how relationships work as all become focussed on a common objective.

As we observe the impact, we see how useful the regulatory ecosystem approach can be in identifying multiple impacts across the field of regulatory relationships. To highlight the impact, we look at examples of how the eco-system lit up. Here, we see impacts across many fronts, from how the *mode* of operation shifted, how the importance of trust suddenly elevated, how

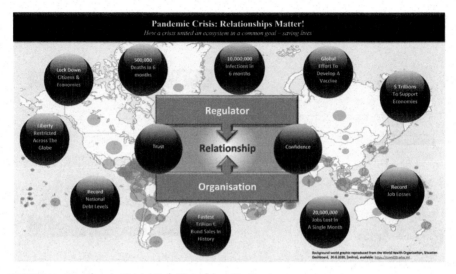

FIGURE H   Pandemic Crisis: Relationships Matter!

stakeholder focus rapidly changed, and, ultimately, how the regulatory relationships responded with pace and increased proactiveness, creativity, and flexibility.

CONCLUSIONS – AREAS FOR FUTURE FOCUS

As we draw together what can be concluded, the opportunity is taken to recap the salient ground we have covered in our journey and the key points from each chapter.

In this regard, we briefly review what has been seen in the past that we can take lessons from, what we are experiencing in the present in terms of the pandemic and how regulatory relationships have responded, before turning

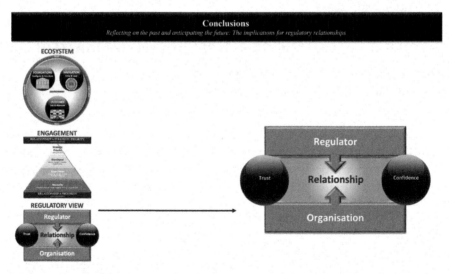

FIGURE I   Conclusions

our attention to the future in terms of what we can conclude are likely to be the key areas of future focus. In considering that future, areas are suggested as key focal points for organisations to consider, representing items that may warrant greater focus, items covered that appear likely to acquire a new level of importance given trends and advances we are seeing, and items that may arise given the challenges the globe now finds itself in.

APPENDIX I – AN INTRODUCTION TO REGULATORY THEORY

To provide a little context to what we discuss, we consider a couple of example regulatory theories and consider how they seek to explain how regulation operates and influences organisations and markets.

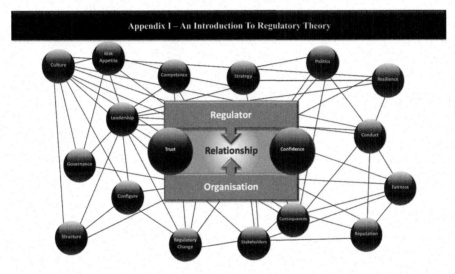

APPENDIX I

Here, we seek to introduce regulatory theory using brief examples to highlight that there is a whole body of insight covering theories of how regulation is influenced and created. Whilst a detailed consideration of regulatory theory is beyond the scope of this book, its introduction as an appendix aims to act as a pointer to this further body of literature should the reader wish understand more about the workings and drivers of regulation and its formation.

ACKNOWLEDGEMENTS

My fascination with regulatory engagement was sparked by both practical experience and the constant flow of regulatory findings across industries that led to a simple question… "surely there is a more effective way for the parties to operate, learn from each other, and engage to avoid some of this?"

That journey really commenced with some of the most turbulent times in capitalist history during the Global Financial Crisis, and interactions with regulators that were challenging, fascinating, and inspiring. I owe a debt of gratitude to all I have engaged with on matters of regulatory interest, who all played a part to inspire this work.

In parallel, I also began observing and discussing with colleagues, competitors, regulators, and associates from across different industries about their experiences, and, again, my thanks go out to all I have *harassed* over the years for their insight, reflection, and input. Your help and support has, and continues to be, much appreciated.

Special thanks also go to Dr. Murray Clarke and Professor Nigel Garrow of Sheffield Business School at Sheffield Hallam University. Their guidance, support, and assistance over the many years have encouraged, guided, and helped me navigate the process of developing academic work into a publication.

This work would never have been completed without the support and encouragement of my family. My love and thanks go, especially, to my amazing wife Katherine and to our fantastic children Oliver and Leah, who ground me, ensure I have balance, encourage and support me, and put a smile on my face every day. I watch in awe at their capacity to make everyone around them feel supported, encouraged, and loved. It also goes to my parents and sisters, who, over the years, provided a perfect balance of drive, support, and guidance to ensure the paths I followed were productive and full of fun along the way. My determination, persistence, and resilience are in no small way down to their examples.

Finally, my thanks also go to all those who gave up their time over the years to help and provide their expertise and experience, you know who you are. There are so many of you, that I would no doubt fail in any attempt to name you all. However, every minute of that time was valuable and your help has been greatly appreciated along this journey. I hope we can keep the conversations going and I hope the insight captured here inspires others to join the conversation and further develop professional practice in the field of regulatory relationships and engagement. *After all, more is achieved when we work together.*

ABOUT THE AUTHOR

Dr. Nigel Somerset has spent his career focusing on transforming the risk, compliance, and commercial performance of businesses, whilst helping to shape industry strategy. Leading through some of the most difficult economic environments and challenging organisational situations, he has engaged with regulators and executive teams across a breadth of situations, from day-to-day engagement, through to matters that have been subject to regulatory investigation and sanction.

Having graduated in Sheffield (U.K.) with a degree in Financial Services in 1993, he went on to achieve professional accreditation from the Chartered Institute of Bankers in 1995, an M.B.A. in 2002, and a Doctorate in 2016. Throughout his studies, he has focused on seeking better ways for industry to operate and progress in critical areas for the benefit of all stakeholders.

In 2017, he established himself as an independent consultant to pursue opportunities to improve outcomes for organisations facing significant issues, that often had attracted the attention of their regulators. Whether helping organisations to arrest and turn around performance, correct historic issues, face the challenges of the pandemic, prepare for regulatory engagement, or help individual executives satisfy regulatory requirements and commitments, Nigel assists them in finding appropriate solutions that satisfy both organisational and regulatory objectives in a collegiate, constructive, and transparent way.

In addition to consulting, Nigel is an executive in residence at Sheffield Business School in the United Kingdom, where he continued to study throughout his career. Sheffield Business School is accredited by the Association to Advance Collegiate Schools of Business (A.A.C.S.B.), placing it within the top 5% of business schools globally.

CHAPTER 1

How Do Organisations Think About Regulatory Relationship Strategies?

CHAPTER SUMMARY

This chapter explores how organisations think about regulatory strategy and considers what regulatory relationships can entail and why they are important.

We consider how organisations define their strategy, what we mean by a regulatory relationship strategy, and what organisations may consider in shaping it.

As regulatory relationships can operate in different contexts, we consider their differing *modes* of operation and how they are influenced by stakeholders.

Finally, we consider some of the drivers of change that we see influencing the direction of regulatory relationships and what the changing picture means for regulatory relationship strategies, in particular, the need for a new perspective with regard to how we approach them, which we pick up in the next chapter.

First, let's start with how organisations can be seen to go about establishing their regulatory relationship strategy.

HOW DO ORGANISATIONS ARTICULATE THEIR REGULATORY RELATIONSHIP STRATEGY?

Regulatory strategy is an important strategic choice that organisations should make. As part of their overall regulatory strategy, defining what their approach will be toward their regulatory relationships and what the regulatory relationship incorporates doesn't seem to be as easy as you might expect. What strategy will be followed, how the relationship is defined, and the level of commitment to making it work can vary significantly across industries and from organisation to organisation. Approaches differ, with some formally setting about defining their strategy and clearly setting out how the relationship will be approached, while others allow their strategy to form incrementally as they progress and as their relationship develops over time. Some at the other

DOI: 10.4324/9781003297963-1

extreme have no formal relationship strategy defined at all, which we cover in Chapter 5 (see Figure 5.2). In fact, for some, the notion of having a regulatory relationship strategy may not have been considered. Instead, their primary focus has been more on the fact there is a rulebook to be followed. The fundamental flaw in this view is that the rulebook will only ever form one part of a regulatory relationship. As we shall come on to see, regulatory relationships are a function of a much wider set of considerations that help regulators form their judgements on any organisation.

Having a regulatory relationship strategy and thinking through carefully how that will be set up for success is a crucial foundation stone in building a constructive and productive regulatory relationship for any organisation regardless of size and complexity.

For those organisations that do set out to define how they will approach and engage in their regulatory relationship, a variety of factors are often considered. First, for example, there is the obvious starting point of exploring the objectives and expectations of the regulators themselves. Regulators often set out their objectives, expectations, and their approach to supervision in clear documents, an example of which are those outlined by the Financial Conduct Authority (see Figures 1.1–1.3) for Financial Services in the United Kingdom (U.K.).

Our strategic objective is to ensure that the relevant markets function well, and our operational objectives are to:

1. *Protect consumers – We secure an appropriate degree of protection for consumers*
2. *Protect financial markets – We protect and enhance the integrity of the U.K. financial system*
3. *Promote competition – We promote effective competition in the interests of consumers*

FIGURE 1.1   Financial Conduct Authority Objectives (F.C.A. 2022)

The overall approach in the F.C.A. supervision model is based on the following principles:

1. *Forward-looking*
2. *A focus on strategy and business models*
3. *A focus on culture and governance*
4. *A focus on individual as well as firm accountability*
5. *Proportionate and risk-based*
6. *Two-way communication*
7. *Co-ordinated*
8. *Put right systemic harm that has occurred and stop it happening again*

FIGURE 1.2   Financial Conduct Authority Supervision Model Principles (F.C.A. 2021b)

Here, the Financial Conduct Authority (F.C.A.) clearly sets out the objectives and principles its supervisory approach is based on and what it expects of organisations in the conduct of their business, which includes expectations surrounding engaging with regulators (see Figure 1.3 (11)).

1. *Integrity – A firm must conduct its business with integrity*
2. *Skill, care, and diligence – A firm must conduct its business with due skill, care, and diligence*
3. *Management and control – A firm must take reasonable care to organise and control its affairs responsibly and effectively, with adequate risk management systems*
4. *Financial prudence – A firm must maintain adequate financial resources*
5. *Market conduct – A firm must observe proper standards of market conduct*
6. *Customers' interests – A firm must pay due regard to the interests of its customers and treat them fairly*
7. *Communications with clients – A firm must pay due regard to the information needs of its clients, and communicate information to them in a way which is clear, fair, and not misleading*
8. *Conflicts of interest – A firm must manage conflicts of interest fairly, both between itself and its customers and between a customer and another client*
9. *Customers: relationships of trust – A firm must take reasonable care to ensure the suitability of its advice and discretionary decisions for any customer who is entitled to rely upon its judgment*
10. *Clients' assets – A firm must arrange adequate protection for clients' assets when it is responsible for them*
11. *Relations with regulators – A firm must deal with its regulators in an open and cooperative way and must disclose to the F.C.A. appropriately anything relating to the firm of which that regulator would reasonably expect notice*

FIGURE 1.3   Financial Conduct Authority Principles for Businesses (F.C.A. 2018b)

In addition to considering the objectives and expectations of regulators, organisations will consider the underpinning laws that form the foundation of the regulator's objectives and provide good insight into what the regulator seeks to achieve and the powers they have at their disposal. The combination of a particular regulator's rules and expectations along with the underpinning legislation allows an organisation to build a picture of what could be perceived as a minimum requirement an organisation could choose to achieve.

The organisation then has its own choices to make in terms of the nature of the relationship it wishes to build with its regulator. This will often involve the Board setting their expectation and regulatory risk appetite and the executive adhering to these expectations, determining their strategy, and making it clear across the organisation what type of relationship they wish to pursue with regulators. It is at this point where organisations begin to define how they intend to engage with their regulator, what success looks like, and how they will track their progress.

The Traditional View of the Regulatory Relationship – A Partial View?

As organisations define these aspects, what can often result is a relatively narrow view of what could be construed as the regulatory relationship, comprised largely of what organisations can control and measure. Often practitioners describe the regulatory relationship in terms that reflect meeting minimum or fundamental regulatory requirements, such as the practicalities of meetings or discussions between organisational and regulatory contact points, the mandated submissions, or responses to requests and items they are compelled to disclose or keep regulators informed of. However, throughout this book we challenge the efficacy of this perspective and explore the opportunity beyond that traditional (often narrow) view. We consider that whilst the traditional fundamental aspects of relationships remain critical, they now form part of a much wider system of insight and information that feeds and influences the regulator. Within this system, regulators enjoy new and growing sources of insight, greater availability of data, and a real-time view of organisational impact. As regulators gather and assimilate information, their ability to create a rich picture of insight, form judgements, and build their opinions improves. It is a system the organisation must increasingly understand, positively influence, and proactively engage with and navigate as part of its regulatory relationship.

Having reflected on how some organisations articulate their regulatory relationship strategy, and what a regulatory relationship entails, let's start to consider the regulatory relationship in broader terms. In the coming sections, we consider its purpose, importance, how it may operate, where its boundaries may be, and who the key stakeholders are. This helps us build out the regulatory relationship picture and understand it across several dimensions, as well as begin to appreciate the dynamic nature and breadth of influence that surrounds it.

WHAT DO WE MEAN BY A REGULATORY RELATIONSHIP STRATEGY?

Having a clear understanding of what your strategy toward your regulator will be, is crucial if you are to ensure the organisation is clear on what you are trying to achieve with your regulator and appropriately align the organisation to deliver that.

Whilst organisations approach this in a variety of ways as noted above, the definition opposite provides a useful high-level view of how organisations can consider what a regulatory relationship strategy entails. In addition, Figure 1.4 provides areas an organisation may consider and work through in order to create a clear position in terms of its regulator.

> **Regulatory Relationship Strategy**
> The overall objective, scope, planning and directing of activities, resources, and approach dedicated to the regulatory relationship

As different industries have different regulatory frameworks, regulators have different powers, and organisations operate across different markets and environments, there will be no *one best way* in terms of a strategy that will work for all, but there will be areas worthy of consideration by all, even if that consideration leads to a conclusion that a particular aspect is not applicable to their business given its scale and complexity. We briefly consider this area next.

Vision or Strategic Intent – Organisations should consider how they paint the picture for the organisation in terms of how they see their future relationship with their regulator. Their aspiration should be clear, as should why the organisation considers this important in the context of the organisation, its objectives, and its stakeholders.

Objectives – Organisations should consider what the objectives are and articulate them in terms that make clear the outcome(s) they are setting out to achieve for their regulatory relationships and over what timescale. This, in conjunction with the vision, will combine to be a powerful focal point for the organisation and will fundamentally affect how the regulatory relationship is approached by those across the organisation. Being clear on what future relationship you envision and the key outcomes you wish to see in bringing that vision to life is critical to steering the right action and behaviour.

Posture – Organisations should consider what their expectations are in terms of posture toward their regulatory relationships. Sending clear messages in terms of the importance of the regulatory relationship, and how regulatory requirements are to be dealt with and prioritised. In addition, it should be clear regarding what approach they expect individuals to take with regulators and what attitude toward regulatory delivery and engagement they expect to see, all of which are critical in setting the correct tone around the regulatory relationship.

Scope – Organisations should consider what they deem to be the scope of the regulatory relationship. As we have seen above, the approach to thinking about the relationship strategy and what is deemed in scope can vary significantly, from the relationship being thought of in terms of a minimum requirement based upon regulatory expectation or broadened in line with the organisation's appetite to keep their regulator well informed and updated.

Scope is a key ingredient of a regulatory relationship strategy for organisations to consider, indeed, in terms of what defines a relationship, we encourage a broad view as we discuss in later chapters. Scope therefore can be thought of in many terms, from that which you must do as a minimum, to encompassing in scope all that informs your regulator's opinion.

Plan – Developing a comprehensive plan for your regulatory relationships is crucial in ensuring the organisation is well aligned, well prepared, and able to effectively manage relationships (including clear accountabilities being mapped). Plans should be crafted in the context of the organisation, its environment, and the regulatory relationship strategy it is following.

Policies – Organisations should consider how they capture in policies the areas that are key in steering activities and actions in line with their objectives. Policies could incorporate matters such as expectations on posture, approach, and the process for coordinating engagement.

Resources – Given the strategic significance of regulatory relationships, organisations should consider how resources (financial cost of compliance, human resources deployed, etc.) will be made available and organised to deliver on both regulatory requirements and the organisation's strategy. Many factors will need to be considered, not least the size and complexity of the organisation and its operations, and the regulatory environment it operates in. However, having sufficient skilled resources to deliver on your commitments will be key to being able to deliver your desired strategic approach. From one extreme it may be a single point of contact as the main conduit to the regulator, at the other, it could be a whole regulatory liaison area dealing with multiple regulators,

FIGURE 1.4   Shaping Your Regulatory Relationship Strategy

across different disciplines, in different geographies. Being able to deliver on your commitments in an efficient and effective way will be key to developing your regulatory relationships.

Measures – Organisations should consider how they will assure themselves that the vision and objectives they have set out and the activities and actions they have put in place to achieve them, are progressing as expected. In realising the regulatory relationship strategy, measures that will track progress and outcomes will be important in ensuring the strategy is realised, the outcomes are in line with expectations, and progress can be seen and demonstrated in terms of how the regulatory relationship is progressing.

FIGURE 1.4   *(Continued)*

Scale and Complexity Are Important Considerations

Regulatory powers, scope, and the number of regulated organisations regulators are responsible for overseeing can vary enormously from one regulator to another.

This variety means that the regulators of any industry need to consider carefully how they will direct and focus their limited resources for best effect as they seek to achieve their regulatory objectives.

Given that regulated organisations can and do vary significantly in scale and complexity, these attributes are often used by regulators to determine how they will regulate any given organisation. In general terms, regulators seek to link the potential impact a regulated entity can have on their regulatory objectives to the level, intensity, and approach they adopt in their regulatory activities with that entity. The greater the potential impact, the greater the level of interest and interaction.

The implications of such linkages can mean large and complex organisations with potential for significant impact on a regulator's objectives will see the greatest levels of interest and interaction. This may involve being subject to the regulator's full suite of supervisory methods, from general market studies to detailed onsite investigations of practices. Whilst at the opposite end of the spectrum, the smaller and simpler organisations who pose limited risk to the regulator's objectives will still be subject to the same principles and rules but may see a lower level of direct interaction and scrutiny from their regulator. In fact, for some, all their interaction may be over channels that don't involve direct face-to-face interactions, for example, email requests for data, market studies, or requests for information due to concerns being raised with the regulator over some aspect of the organisation's activities.

Regardless of the scale and complexity of the organisation and its level of interest to its regulator, organisations should still consider the nature of the regulatory relationship they wish to have with their regulator, as doing so can have considerable benefits regardless of scale. For example, being clear on your vision, objectives, and posture may drive a commitment to action and activities, such as the importance of engaging in industry consultations. Furthermore, a clear focus on the importance of the regulatory relationship may send an important cultural signal regarding the importance of the regulator to the firm and compliance with its requirements. Regulatory relationship strategy is an important strategic choice, regardless of scale.

Whilst the above provides a useful framework of considerations in determining your regulatory relationship strategy, it must also be set in the context of the relationship you enjoy now. Where organisations seek to significantly change their strategy, they need to think carefully about how that change will be created. For example, if an organisation is to move from an approach to their regulatory relationship that could be described as adversarial, resulting from a strategy that focused on keeping a regulator at arms-length, to one where they aspire to be leading in proactive and positive regulatory engagement aimed at furthering industry developments, there will be wider considerations in bringing such a change about. Such considerations could for example be cultural, structural, and personal in nature in terms of whether organisations have the right leadership and people in key areas, are organised in the right way, and aligned to a culture that can facilitate such a change.

Having considered different approaches in how organisations articulate their regulatory relationship strategy and what they may consider when setting the overall regulatory relationship strategy, we move onto think about the regulatory relationship itself and take a brief look at its purpose and importance.

WHAT IS THE REGULATORY RELATIONSHIP AND WHY IS IT IMPORTANT?

The regulatory relationship is the conduit through which the regulator and the regulatee seek to understand each other's position vis-à-vis their respective objectives. As one senior regulator succinctly put it:

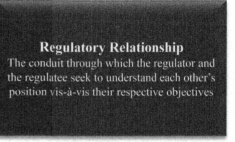

Regulatory Relationship
The conduit through which the regulator and the regulatee seek to understand each other's position vis-à-vis their respective objectives

"I think the regulatory relationship is about how the people in an organisation think about the story they wish to tell, interact on all levels with the regulator, and work for a common objective".

In this respect, its importance is in being the key part of the communication system between the parties. It will both help regulators form judgements on the organisation concerned, and the degree of regulatory oversight any organisation may need, whilst helping organisations form judgements on how effectively their regulatory relationship strategy is performing in meeting both the regulator's objectives and their own.

As much regulation, and the regulators that govern them, is focused on consumer protection, the more effective this mechanism proves to be at highlighting potentially problematic risks and challenges, the more proactive organisations and their regulators can be in addressing them. For the relationship to be effective in this regard, as we will discuss in later chapters, it demands a relationship that is open, transparent, proactive, and which promotes the surfacing of issues early and allows issues and challenges to be worked through in an orderly fashion.

The Relationship Is Not a *Silver Bullet* in Assuring Regulatory Objectives Are Met

The regulatory relationship is not, however, a whole solution to ensure the organisation is always on the right side of the regulator and regulatory objectives. The relationship sits as just one part of a whole system of organisational delivery and control incorporating how organisations set themselves up for success, how they navigate, how they lead and drive their organisations (which we explore later) as well as external constraints on them such as laws, regulations, rules, and accepted professional practice to name a few.

Given the purpose of the regulatory relationship is to be the conduit through which we understand each other's position vis-à-vis respective objectives, it is crucial that organisations gain a deep understanding of their regulator's objectives (just as regulators will be keen to understand the organisation's). Such an understanding can help organisations shape its regulatory relationship strategy, whilst also considering how their organisation is moving in concert with the regulator or runs the risk of being misaligned.

Across industries, the objectives of regulators may be articulated in a variety of ways, however, there are often common threads organisations will see, usually in the form establishing consumer protection and assurance via establishing and monitoring principles, standards, rules, and regulations[1]. Next are examples of the stated objectives and extracts from regulatory publications across industries to demonstrate the point.

As you read these extracts, consider how you might think about a regulatory relationship strategy for an organisation in each of these industries considering the items highlighted in Figure 1.4. For example, what vision do they have for how their future relationship should work, what objectives might you set for your regulatory relationship given the regulator's focus, and what would you define as the scope of your regulatory relationship? It's a useful exercise as you read these brief summaries to consider how some of the elements of a strategy can be informed by the regulatory objectives, focus, and approach the regulator is taking.

Objectives – Civil Aviation Authority Example

The Civil Aviation Authority (C.A.A.) is the aviation regulator in the U.K. Below in Figure 1.5 is a short summary from the Civil Aviation Authority website (C.A.A. 2022a–d) of the role, objectives, vision, and approach to performance-based regulation, in addition to a snapshot of some of the activities the C.A.A. undertakes to attempt to make interactions and the system of regulatory relationships as effective as possible.

The C.A.A. (2022b) goes onto provide organisations with a policy framework, details on how decisions are made, and what organisations need to consider in terms of the potential implications of decisions. In fact, that dialogue and relationship with organisations takes many forms, such as, formal meetings, an industry magazine focused on topical subjects (*Clued-up*), as well as *Airspace Squawks* focused on safety through collaboration, insight sharing, tips, and hints on a variety of subjects. The whole *system* of interaction

As the U.K.'s specialist aviation regulator, we work so that:

- *the aviation industry meets the highest safety standards*
- *consumers have choice, value for money, are protected and treated fairly when they fly*
- *through efficient use of airspace, the environmental impact of aviation on local communities is effectively managed and CO_2 emissions are reduced*
- *the aviation industry manages security risks effectively. (C.A.A. 2022a)*

The Civil Aviation Authority (C.A.A.) provides safety assurance to the public in accordance with its statutory duties. The C.A.A. also follows the principles of better regulation, which means that our interventions should be proportionate and targeted to achieve the desired safety benefit without imposing undue burdens on stakeholders. (C.A.A. 2022b)

Our vision:
To continue to work with industry to demonstrably reduce safety risk across the total aviation system. (C.A.A. 2022d)

Performance-Based Regulation:
Performance-based regulation means developing a comprehensive risk picture with the organisations we regulate and building our knowledge and data to make sure we target our regulation in the areas where it will make the biggest difference. (C.A.A. 2022d)

FIGURE 1.5   Civil Aviation Authority Role and Strategic Objectives
(C.A.A. 2022a/b/d)

focuses on the sum of the parts sharing as much insight as possible to lift the standards as an industry. On the part of organisations themselves, regulation has required the reporting of accidents and incidents and the implementation of cultural principles to allow such reporting to flow freely. As a result, people are not punished where their actions and decisions are in line with their experience and training but may have led to problems. The overarching objective of all involved is the prevention of such accidents and incidents and a culture that feels at ease reporting issues that provide the best chance of preventing repetition of such issues.

In addition, to try and ensure relationship interactions are as productive as possible, the C.A.A. provides details of what those engaging in regulatory relationship discussions should expect as captured in Figure 1.6 below.

Targeted safety risk conversations between Accountable Managers and the C.A.A. is what drives the benefits of the performance-based approach. (C.A.A. 2022d)

Accountable Manager Meetings (A.M.Ms.) are a regular part of our oversight process to ensure that the C.A.A. and the Accountable Manager have a similar perspective on the major risks facing each entity. (C.A.A. 2022d)

Accountable Managers are encouraged to use the guidance to get the most out of the A.M.M., ensuring there is a constructive two-way dialogue about the actions and outcomes needed to further enhance safety. The core questions are intended as a guide to the content of the conversations, not as a script or checklist. The key thing is that we have a constructive, two-way dialogue about the business context, safety risks, and desired outcomes and importantly have a record of the discussions. (C.A.A. 2022c)

FIGURE 1.6   Civil Aviation Authority – What to Expect (C.A.A. 2022c/d)

The C.A.A. extract provides good examples of proactive and engaging approaches, aimed at ensuring the culture and activities of the industry are focused on the key objectives and shared concerns in a way that promotes the proactive raising of issues, challenge of standards, and sharing of best practices. This is done in an open and transparent way (see Figure 1.7) in terms of how engagement takes place, with pre-positioning of the questions and requirements to attempt to make preparation and disclosure as productive as possible.

- *What are the main safety risks (current and future)?*
- *How were these safety risks identified and recorded? How does the Accountable Manager gain assurance that these are the main safety risks?*
- *What outcomes does the Accountable Manager want to see as a result of managing these safety risks?*
- *What actions are being taken to better control or remove the safety risks – and are relevant stakeholders involved?*
- *Are the outcomes achievable and measurable? How are they monitored? How are improvement actions checked for effectiveness? (Plan, Do, Check, Review)?*
- *What do you do as the Accountable Manager if your safety actions are not giving the desired outcome?*
- *How do you share knowledge and lessons learned across the entity?*

The core questions will be shared with Accountable Managers prior to the meeting so they are aware of what to expect. The meeting should also cover:

- *Progress against previously agreed safety actions*
- *Planned future oversight activity*
- *Sector safety risks and total safety risk trends and issues, where possible, any other issues raised by the entity.*

After the meeting:
The C.A.A. will produce a record of the meeting, including details of significant discussions, all agreed safety actions and who is responsible for completing them, and the expected outcomes and timeframes for them.

FIGURE 1.7   Civil Aviation Authority – Core Questions (C.A.A. 2017c)

In terms of helping us consider how to engage with regulators, there is plenty that the C.A.A. provides its stakeholders in terms of guidance (see also Gaffney 2015 for a similar example of guidance from the U.S. Food and Drug Administration [F.D.A.]). As you browse their statements, it is also notable that some of what the C.A.A. puts forward to help their stakeholders will seem obvious areas to explore, but as we shall see in later chapters, sometimes organisations fail to keep things simple, to read the signs, and to use the insights at their disposal to ensure good outcomes for their consumers. As such, regulators will often need to step in, when all too often those interventions could have been easily avoided.

What, Why, How – Financial Conduct Authority Example

The F.C.A. is the conduct regulator for 50,000 businesses in the U.K., and the prudential supervisor for over 48,000 firms.

Below in Figure 1.8 is a short summary from the F.C.A. website on their role in the financial services sector, which expands on the objectives (see Figure 1.1), including what they do, why they do it, and how.

Our role
Financial markets must be honest, fair, and effective so consumers get a fair deal. We work to ensure that these markets work well for individuals, for businesses, and for the economy as a whole.

Why we do it
Financial services play a critical role in the lives of everyone in the U.K., from junior I.S.As. to pensions, direct debits to credit cards, loans to investments.
How well financial markets work has a fundamental impact on us all.
U.K. financial services employ over 1.1 million people and contribute £75 billion in tax per year. Based on our policy and enforcement work, we estimate that we add at least £11 of benefits to consumers and small businesses for every pound we spend.
If U.K. markets work well, competitively, and fairly, they benefit customers, staff, and shareholders and maintain confidence in the U.K. as a major global financial hub.

How we operate
Our strategic objective is to make sure relevant markets function well. We've outlined how we will achieve this objective in our three-year strategy.

- *protect consumers from bad conduct*
- *protect the integrity of the U.K. financial system*
- *promote effective competition in the interests of consumers*

We're an independent public body funded entirely by the fees we charge regulated firms. Our role is defined by the Financial Services and Markets Act 2000 (FSMA) and we're accountable to the Treasury, which is responsible for the U.K.'s financial system, and to Parliament.
We work with consumer groups, trade associations, and professional bodies, domestic regulators, international partners, and a wide range of other stakeholders.
We have a large and growing remit, and use a proportionate approach to regulation. We do this by prioritising the areas and firms that pose a higher risk to our objectives.

FIGURE 1.8   Financial Conduct Authority (F.C.A. 2022)

As part of their transparent approach, the F.C.A. provides insight on how they make regulatory judgements, which is a very useful consideration for those engaged in regulatory relationships. As you will see, judgement will play more and more into regulatory relationships, and as such organisations need to be very clear that regulator interaction has a significant human factor.

The F.C.A. also provide insights on how they achieve and interpret their objectives, how they make regulatory decisions, and how they assess their impact and performance. As a regulator responsible for a wide and diverse market and participant population, their focus is not only on rule making but also on principle-based regulation with clear statements on what consumers and firms can expect.

Understanding your regulator's objectives is a key first step in being able to assess how your organisation's overall corporate strategy aligns and whether you pose any risk to those objectives. It allows you to think about what that position means in terms of your strategy going forward and how you can shape your regulatory relationship strategy to help you get where you want to be with your regulator in future. Just as your objectives are of great interest to your regulator as we shall see later, understanding your regulator's objectives is key to informing your strategy toward them as a key stakeholder in your business.

In the sections ahead we will see dramatic examples of why regulation and regulatory relationships are crucial to the operation of some markets. As with many things, balance is key, and in the exuberance of driving businesses forward, it is easy for things to be missed, ill considered, or be given insufficient weight in the decision-making process, which can lead to poor outcomes for consumers. It is at these points that a counterbalance can be of benefit to a business that is keen to avoid poor outcomes for its customers and the negative attention of a regulator. It is also why more and more regulators are delving into how businesses are set up, and how they are driven and governed to understand the potential risks and detriment that could result.

Let's not forget also that there are wider benefits from having good regulatory relationships. The regulator operates from a position of distance with access and insight on the operations of the market as a whole. In this respect, it has a unique opportunity to provide insight on areas that may be of concern along with areas of best practice. These *smoke signals* can provide directional indicators on how the regulator sees opportunity for organisations in meeting its objectives whilst working to prevent previously suffered pitfalls.

The regulatory relationship therefore is a key conduit, which can help organisations that engage in a positive and proactive way to achieve better balance in how they meet their regulatory obligations, through better engagement, enquiry, and use of regulatory insight.

MODES OF OPERATION

Having understood what we mean by a regulatory relationship strategy, what the regulatory relationship commonly entails, along with its purpose and importance, we move on to briefly consider how those relationships can operate in different *modes*, depending on what the regulator and regulatee are focused on.

Dame Deirdre Hutton (2015) refers to these different *modes of operation*, as differences in the interaction approach depending on the focus that the respective organisations have. To illustrate the potential for different modes of operation, Dame Deirdre Hutton provides useful example scenarios where the approach, given the circumstances, could well lead to a different mode of engagement by both an organisation and the regulator. These may not be exhaustive, but they provide a useful lens through which to consider which *mode of relationship* you are in, or at least consider how the way you engage with a regulator can take on a different feel and form depending on the circumstances. The scenarios identified are as follows:

"Co-working – when both the regulator and the industry are confronted with new problems that have not previously been explored. In the C.A.A. context, this might be the new field of space planes".

"Partnership – where, jointly with industry or consumers (or both), you are wrestling with a problem which you all have a joint interest in solving". In the events that unfolded in the Covid-19 pandemic, this could be, for example, airlines and regulators addressing specific problems that arose as a result.

"Regulator – or, finally, you might be acting as a stern objective regulator". In this mode however, there are of course flavours of interaction, for example these may be routine relationship interactions, they could be specific investigations, or maybe enforcement activities to name a few. The Australian Prudential Regulation Authority (2022), for example, notes four areas of responsibility in regulatory oversight of the Australian Financial Services industry, being licencing, prudential standards, supervision (the mainstay of its work), and enforcement.

Once you know the regulatory mode in which you are operating, you can begin to appreciate what course the relationship may take, as clearly each of the above examples could feel and operate very differently depending on the items being discussed and faced.

The mode of operation is a useful backdrop to understand as you frame your approach to engage with regulators. For example, should you find yourself in enforcement, it would be wholly inappropriate to expect your regulator to take a *partnership approach* in resolving issues of your own making.

As well as having different *modes* under which relationships may operate, organisations will also commonly have a wider spectrum of stakeholders who could influence the direction, intensity, and nature of their regulatory relationship. Indeed, these same stakeholders could fundamentally change the mode of operation of the regulatory relationship as recently demonstrated in the Covid-19 pandemic, where relationships in some industries rapidly moved from a traditional regulator arrangement, to having dimensions of co-working and partnership as governments called on industry and regulators to work together in the common fight against the virus.

Understanding who your key stakeholders are, their expectations of your organisation, and their relative power and importance can help organisations consider how stakeholders may impact and influence their regulatory relationship.

WHO ARE THE STAKEHOLDERS AND HOW DO THEY INFLUENCE?

So far, we have considered how organisations often approach defining their regulatory relationship and strategy, reviewed the purpose and importance of the relationship, and briefly considered how relationships can operate in different modes. At this point, it is worth adding to the picture the broad spectrum of stakeholders that exist around the regulatory ecosystem and understanding how they often interact and influence the ecosystem, and by extension, the regulatory relationship itself.

Who the stakeholders and influencers are around an industry or organisation, and how they impact the regulatory relationship can vary significantly. The industry situation, nature of the organisation, and the environment in which you are operating will all impact the relationship. However, there are a couple of principles worth considering when we think about stakeholders and a few examples next will demonstrate this.

First, there are those stakeholders directly involved in your regulatory relationship. This may be the regulator and the regulatee organisation at its simplest level. Or it may involve third parties, particularly in the case where organisations are in difficulty and either the organisation themselves or the regulator appoints third parties to assist the organisation in correcting the issues and resolving matters to their satisfaction.

Second, there are those indirectly involved. These may be suppliers, politicians, the world of social media, organisations that inform regulators of trends and insights regarding the operation of any market and the organisations within it.

Finally, there are the broader influencers such as consumer groups, trade and industry groups, and pressure groups.

Taken together, these direct and indirect stakeholder groups all have influence to differing degrees depending on the impact being felt by any group. The sentiment of how important the broader relationships are to the regulator and by extension the regulatory relationship, was demonstrated well by Dame Deirdre Hutton (2015) of the C.A.A., whose quote below captures the balancing act for regulators.

> *"Experience suggests to me that no matter how clear your objectives, or how expert your staff, none of that will suffice without the right relationships with that web of external interests".*

Like any ecosystem, over time, the stakeholders involved will see their position in that system shift. Shifts in the impact an organisation has on its stakeholders (e.g., consumers) or its environment (e.g., communities) can often trigger adjustments in the power, influence, engagement, and objectives of all stakeholders in the system. Who can forget the shifts in power and influence as the Global Financial Crisis unfolded and governments and regulators across the globe took control of the financial services agenda, exerting their power to drive necessary and swift actions they wished to see financial institutions complete? Similarly, in a different context, consider how the trajectory and velocity of attention have shifted on social media and technology companies regarding how they use data, what content they allow, and some of the negative outcomes users have experienced whilst using their services.

Stakeholders are often a diverse group, whose level of involvement and intervention in any relationship can shift over time depending on the activities of the organisation concerned. It is important, therefore, that organisations are *tuned-in* to the changing dynamics of their stakeholders and communicating appropriately with their audiences.

Next we look at some of these stakeholder groups and consider their role and influence in our regulatory ecosystem.

Consumer

Few organisations would disagree that the customer is central to their existence and their key stakeholder – without them, the organisation would not exist. Over the years, we have all seen the corporate claims that espouse the importance of the customer to the business or mission and vision statements proclaiming the customer as the central focus of an organisation's drive. No matter how pure those intentions set out to be, legislation, regulation, and regulators continue to have a crucial role in ensuring consumers are treated fairly and equitably when engaging with organisations. From a regulatory relationship perspective then, the customer unsurprisingly (and often the broader public) truly is the central stakeholder to the relationship. Regulations, legislation, and regulatory engagement are focused on protecting the interests of these stakeholders to provide a balance check for the wider objectives organisations often pursue.

WHAT DRIVES THIS NEED TO PROTECT CONSUMERS?   Regulators are increasingly interested in how organisations set themselves up and drive their outcomes. This interest is driven by an appreciation that such factors can have a significant impact on the outcomes for consumers. If there is a lack of control and governance, we can see failures directly impacting customers. Similarly, with the wrong leadership, culture, and incentivisation, we may see poor sales practices in pursuit of results. In this respect, consumers have an important ally as regulators keep a close eye on how industries and organisations deliver outcomes that are suitable for customer needs and help protect them against the potential for poor practice.

Consider, for example, the setting of organisational targets, which can often be broad and far reaching. Balancing customer outcomes with broader organisational aspirations, which may include items such as achieving returns for shareholders, driving growth and expansion, or the need to invest heavily in innovation and product development to survive competitive pressures, all involve judgements, compromise, and trade-offs. These objectives can incentivise activities that impact consumers (both short and long term, positively or negatively) and, as such, an important aspect of regulatory relationships becomes the function of a counterbalance to ensure activities remain fair, proportionate, and prevent customer detriment. A further example of the competing objectives organisations face and regulators are mindful of is the extent to which objectives can draw organisations toward the short-term outcomes the organisation achieves versus the long term. As regulators look to protect the consumer, they will often focus on the sustainability, resilience, and reliability of what organisations are putting in place, again a useful counterbalance. This may involve regulators questioning longer-term strategy and levels of investment in matters such as safety and maintenance (e.g., aviation, food production), or the long-term implications of products for consumers where the longevity of relationships can span over many decades (e.g., financial services). Here, regulatory focus can often be on using their insights to help organisations draw their gaze to the longer term and consider whether their strategy and plans have sufficient consideration of the potential longer-term risks of their businesses and whether sufficient action is being taken to assure a safe future for the end consumer.

History provides many examples of where a focus on the short term and a lack of proactive management of the long-term risks can have a significant impact on consumers.

Such examples remind us that the consumer as our key stakeholder needs considering throughout the cycle of our relationships with them, from the very start as we consider the services they may need and we should invest in developing, right through to the outcomes they achieve and whether they meet customer objectives.

Figure 1.9 provides a historic example, given it helps illustrate many of the points raised above, and the price of getting things wrong for consumers, for organisations, and for the industry.

Where risks are being transferred to consumers, regulators are likely to seek assurance that the consumer protection lens has adequately assessed the risks and ensured that sufficient protection against consumer detriment is in place.

Endowment mortgages offer a lesson in how organisations can fail to truly think through the potential risks associated with their products and services and the protections required. In doing so, they face impacts such as reputation damage, remediation, and redress to put things right, along with potential fines.

Endowment mortgages and the redress that followed provide some useful points of reflection. Here, we only superficially touch on the issues given the scale of the problem, but the points raised serve some food for thought on how the outcome of a product needs ongoing monitoring and calibration where outcomes are variable and their duration long.

Endowment mortgages generally involved both a debt on one side, and an investment vehicle on the other, which was put in place to satisfy the debt at some later date. Often, customer expectations were that the investment would outweigh the debt and result in both the debt being satisfied and a lump sum being available at the end of the term. Such forecasts were based on assessments of likely growth rates on the investment and costs of the debt. As reality began to diverge from the assumptions underpinning forecasts used with consumers, the scene was set for a problem.

As interest rates fell, consumers saw their monthly mortgage payment fall. However, on the investment side, the returns being earned also fell. For the consumer, the link between those two factors and the implications this had for the repayment of their mortgage was often a connection that was not made. Consumers continued in the expectation their mortgage would be paid off, however, the long-run impact of the shifts in interest rates meant that for many this was not the case. Whatever communications were put in place to raise the risks to consumers and set in place corrective actions were not effective where they existed, and as such the industry found itself in a redress and remediation situation. This represented for the consumer a rather complex product, with inherent risk and variable drivers of performance, which was established for a long-run solution. The need for ongoing management and review of the risks, performance, and suitability was clear. The asymmetry of understanding between customers and organisations made the transfer of the management of this risk to consumers inappropriate and as such the regulator took further action.

FIGURE 1.9   Lessons from Endowment Mortgages

KEEPING CONSUMERS INFORMED OF RISKS TO INFORM CHOICES   Ensuring organisations are keeping the consumer informed so they can make appropriate choices, particularly of risks or issues that may impact them, is also at times a significant challenge for regulators. How regulators ensure organisations keep their customers informed and provide insight in terms of how matters are dealt with and communicated can sometimes pose interesting dilemmas. One fascinating example (see Figure 1.10) of the role of the regulator taking a lead in ensuring there is a balance in how new and emerging technologies are used and how their risks are communicated, is provided by the U.S. F.D.A.'s Center for Devices and Radiological Health (C.D.R.H.). The C.D.R.H. through its Patient Engagement Advisory Committee faced the challenge of how to communicate cybersecurity safety risks and threats to patients.

The U.S. Food and Drug Administration (F.D.A.) alerted patients, healthcare providers, and manufacturers to a family of 12 cybersecurity vulnerabilities known as "SweynTooth". The vulnerabilities risk allowing unauthorised users to access the device (e.g., pacemakers) and affect how it performs (e.g., stop it working or access its functions). The F.D.A. provided both additional information and recommendations to address the risks. (F.D.A. 2020, Brennan 2020)

FIGURE 1.10   F.D.A. Informs Patients, Providers, and Manufacturers about Potential Cybersecurity Vulnerabilities in Certain Medical Devices with Bluetooth Low Energy

The challenge of course is how to help articulate such risks up front so that patients could make informed choices. So, for example, if you were a patient with an implanted cardiac device, you would have such cybersecurity risks related to that device discussed beforehand. The challenge such a situation poses is well articulated by the C.D.R.H. (Brennan 2019) in the quote in Figure 1.11 and provides an intriguing example of how the views of a key stakeholder (the patient/consumer) needs to be carefully considered by the industry and the regulator in terms of how they may influence the future direction of regulatory scrutiny and oversight whilst balancing what is right for the patient.

"Unlike other safety messages, cybersecurity concerns pose the unique challenge of communicating potential risks for which the probability and/or likelihood of occurrence of a successful exploit is not known … currently, there is no suitable model or mathematical formulation that would enable risk quantification of a medical device cybersecurity vulnerability extrapolating to risk of potential patient harm. The absence of such a construct impedes informed decision making between patients and providers in determining whether the benefits of a patient receiving device updates for cybersecurity concerns outweighs the potential risks of undergoing the updates". (Brennan 2019)

FIGURE 1.11   To Communicate or not to Communicate …

If consumers are to influence the direction, particularly regarding risk acceptance, consideration is needed regarding how risks should be communicated, and, more importantly, how we know they are truly understood where we expect consumers to bear them. This poses an interesting challenge for organisations where there is inherent information asymmetry between the organisation and its consumers.

INFORMATION ASYMMETRY   Information asymmetry, or the lack of equality or equivalence between parties in the information held, is an important consideration for organisations when it comes to considering how the consumers of their products and services make informed choices.

Figure 1.11 demonstrates some of the potential challenges information asymmetry can cause. However, regardless of the difficulty in risk quantification, the fact remains that the risk exists, and in this respect, whether the transfer of that risk is to a patient or consumer, regulators will seek to ensure there is an appropriate path to supporting those who bear the risk in developing their understanding to facilitate an informed choice.

Where organisations are delivering products and services that are widely understood, such as in the food, drink, travel and, despite their modern-day complexities, even mobile phone and telecommunications industries, consumers may have a good chance of understanding the inherent risks and issues. However, in industries where the inherent complexities of the product or service are high, such as medical and financial services, the potential for a consumer to have a much lower understanding of risks and issues significantly increases. In such industries, there can be an imbalance of information and, therefore, power to influence decision making. Here, regulators will recognise the potential dangers of such an imbalance and will seek to ensure through their regulatory relationships that industries and organisations within them do not exploit it.

HOW CONSUMERS INFLUENCE   How consumers influence the regulatory relationship is an interesting question. Of course, the customer can always vote with their feet. However, inertia, inconvenience, and barriers to exit can all challenge the true impact of such a right. As a result, regulators will often use data, information, and insight to gather a *house view* on how customers are being treated, with effective consumer engagement now recognised as being an essential part of the regulatory process (U.K.R.N. 2017). In addition to data provided by organisations, industry complaints data, social media postings, consumer group insight, ombudsmen services, and feedback from a range of consumer support organisations can all help build that picture. Regulators will increasingly investigate potential areas of unfair treatment through specific requests for information or market studies, or require organisations to proactively engage with consumers to get them more integral to decision making processes. Useful case studies on the engagement of consumers in this way are provided by the U.K. Regulators Network (2017). Here, examples from regulators across different industries demonstrates progress from the likes of the Legal Services Board (L.S.B.), the Office of Communications (Ofcom), the F.C.A., the C.A.A., the Office of Gas and Electricity Markets (Ofgem), the Water Services Regulation Authority (Ofwat), the Office of Rail and Road (O.R.R.), the Northern Ireland Authority for Utility Regulation (N.I.A.U.R.), and the Water Industry Commission for Scotland (W.I.C.S.).

These sources provide regulators with a powerful body of evidence upon which to act. Such actions gather up the implications of organisational activity to allow regulators to form judgements on whether the activities of an organisation are meeting the interests of consumers in a fair and proportionate way. Consumers therefore influence through expressing their dissatisfaction in ways that allow their voice to be captured. Let's not also forget that it doesn't have to be dissatisfaction. The stampede of consumers toward a particular product or organisation whose offering is just too good to miss, or the take up being suspiciously high, may also be fertile ground for checking that the outcomes for consumers are going to be appropriate. The lessons of the Payment Protection Insurance (P.P.I.) mis-selling scandal within U.K. financial services is an example that organisations can learn many lessons from in this regard.

RELATIVE POWER AND INFLUENCE IS IN FLUX   As a final note, it is worth considering how the power of consumers is shifting. For regulators and organisations, this potentially poses a significant challenge and one that many are struggling to address. The emergence and rapid expansion of social media is disintermediating traditional ways for the consumer to get their voice heard. For those that embrace this channel of communication it can be a powerful way to build a body of opinion and quickly escalate issues to the consumer's chosen audience (e.g., media, politicians, regulators, competitors). Consumers have new ways with which to influence and these new ways can reach audiences quickly, which were only achievable historically through traditional media interfaces. As this capability unfolds, organisations will need to adapt to be able to better respond to all who may be interested in what is being raised. For regulators, this provides a whole new source of direct insight through which to view the activities of the organisations and industries they regulate.

The relative power of consumers is in a state of flux. Whilst the burden of risk is increasingly transferring to them (see Figure 1.13), they are being enabled by technology and increasingly protected by regulation. This tension between taking accountability and responsibility for their actions, whilst being sufficiently protected, is an area that will continue to play out and remain a focal point for regulatory relationship discussions.

Organisation (Including Their Extended Value Chain)

The term organisation can seem rather abstract. For our purposes, let's refer to everyone from the Board to the newest recruit, and all those relationships a business relies upon to deliver to the customer (suppliers, infrastructure providers, advisors, etc.). The rationale for this broad definition is that the sum of what their combined efforts produce is what the customer experiences and what the regulator will see in terms of how organisations are set up, operate, and are driven. As well as the outcomes organisations deliver to consumers, regulators are increasingly interested in how organisations get there, how resilient they are, how they are driven, how that assures fairness and value for consumers, and how sustainable their approach is. For example, if the salesforce is inappropriately targeted and incentivised, which results in poor sales practices, the organisation may appear to be financially strong and performing well. Organisationally it may feel progressive, dynamic, and record high morale as achievement flourishes; however, if sales are potentially problematic, then that entire foundation evaporates and an entirely different picture reveals itself, along with the harm caused to stakeholders and the organisation.

For the organisation, what it does, how it does it, why that is justified and the results it produces, are all part of the picture that needs to form in the ebb and flow of the regulatory relationship. Not only that, but those results that are produced need to be appropriate to the customer's needs, be resilient, have longevity, and be sustainable and dependable. In short, the right outcomes, for the right customers, delivered in the right way. Organisations more and more will need to *walk in their customer's shoes* over the short, medium, and long term and keep a close eye on the outcomes they produce for them and the risks their actions entail.

Those same standards and expectations also apply to *connected* organisations, who perform critical services on behalf of the organisation as it delivers to its customers.

Regardless of the service or product being supplied by the regulated organisation, most will rely on the services, expertise, and undertakings of others in the delivery to the end consumer. These relationships can be fundamental to the performance of an organisation, and as such, the way in which those relationships are managed, governed, and controlled will be of great interest to regulators. For example, an airline manufacturer's reliance on an external supplier of avionics or a major banking institution's outsourcing of its core technology platforms bring different considerations in terms of demonstrating how the extended chain of delivery is governed to protect the end consumer (see also Chapter 2). Should these supplier organisations themselves suffer issues with their products and services, the potential knock-on effects for the organisation and its customers are obvious. As such, where organisations rely on networks of key suppliers whose failure could cause harm or detriment, organisations need to ensure their core capabilities and controls around such structures are sufficient to protect consumers.

For the organisation, as a key counterparty to the regulatory relationship, their challenge is significant. It is about building a relationship with its regulator that has a foundation of trust and confidence resulting from a full understanding of how the organisation delivers on its objectives. From what it sets out to achieve, how it sets itself up for success, how it drives the organisation for results, and how it ensures those results are appropriate for its customers, both now and throughout the relationship. Fundamentally the road to a relationship built on trust and confidence involves ensuring items that can undermine it (across the relationship ecosystem) are appropriately addressed. This, by definition, implies a sound knowledge and thorough assessment of the risk organisations pose to their various stakeholder expectations.

Regulator

The regulator is one of many of a regulated organisation's key stakeholders that can influence the direction of an organisation and the relationship using any number of powers they may have been granted.

The powers regulators hold can range, but often they are able to determine whether an organisation is authorised to undertake its business at all through their licencing and authorisation powers. In addition to overseeing the organisation as an entity, regulators often also authorise individuals operating in the industry to establish clear thresholds of competency and training.

In determining items such as licencing, authorisation, or competency standards, regulators will deploy regulatory rules, principles, and standards that are aligned to deliver their regulatory objectives, and *prevention of harm*. Setting clear objectives regulators are striving to achieve, determining rules and standards in support of achieving those objectives, and establishing frameworks through which regulators engage with industry to ensure standards are being met are all part of the systems that regulators deploy to influence industry behaviour and allow them to *follow the harm and correct it* where things aren't operating as they should.

The regulator's powers of influence are therefore usually significant. How they influence can be done across various mechanisms at their disposal, and whilst their rules and frameworks may be the cornerstone, they also share their concerns directly through interventions, signal concerns to the industry through their business plans and engagements with industry, and, of course, through direct intervention, direction, and sanction.

Regulatory powers can be applied at speed and can be impactful on your organisation (examples of which we will see in the coming chapters). Organisations, as they assess their regulatory strategies, will need to keep such powers in mind and assess the risks their strategies run vis-à-vis the organisation's risk appetite.

Politicians

Politicians, as democratically elected members, exist to represent the will of the public. As a result, they will hear broad and diverse views across a whole range of subjects and from a wide array of individuals and organisations.

In executing these duties, politicians will regularly engage in matters that are of public interest, have caught the attention of the media, or are part of their agenda in executing their committed manifesto. Through these activities, they exercise their ability to influence the progression of political thinking, legislative development, and wider organisational development. In this respect, the governing political party of the day holds (directly and indirectly) a great deal of power over the future operation of industries and organisations alike. History has provided many examples of political power being used either in favour or to the detriment of industries that felt the will of the political party of the day on their environment.

Dame Deirdre Hutton (2015) provides good advice regarding the influence of politicians and their interaction with regulators:

> *"The C.A.A. is not a government department. It is a public corporation funded by industry and neither I, nor the staff, are civil servants. That does not mean a divorce from government but rather a relationship that needs to be constantly worked at… Sometimes, straightforwardly, politics will intervene, and government will require that it take control of an issue over which it feels strongly… As a regulator, I am clear that if you don't take government with you, you are likely to fail. So, work out what really matters to you and, if you do want to have a fight with government, make sure you have picked your fight carefully and that you are having the fight on a proper, legally, and factually valid, basis".*

When things do go wrong and the government seeks answers, the implications of investigations can be significant for industries, organisations, and their regulators[2].

Just as regulators hold organisations and individuals to account, so your regulator is also under scrutiny. Governments around the world from America to Australia also focus on ensuring public bodies are held to account by ensuring the systems of regulation are working effectively. In the U.K., for example, the National Audit Office (N.A.O. 2019) in their role to scrutinise government departments, agencies, and other public bodies shines a light on the effectiveness of regulatory bodies and their ability to demonstrate they were effectively protecting consumers. In the United States, the Government Accountability Office (G.A.O.) provides an equivalent independent, nonpartisan agency that works for Congress. The G.A.O. examines how taxpayer dollars are spent (including regulatory bodies) and provides Congress and federal agencies with objective, reliable information to help the government save money and work more efficiently. In Australia, this role falls to the Australian National Audit Office.

The examples could continue for countries around the world however, the key point is that politics plays a central role for both organisations and their regulators, both of whom come under scrutiny. Should a loss of trust arise, or a shift in power occur, the implications for organisations, regulators, and industries of political intervention can be swift, direct, and far reaching. In short, political stakeholders matter.

Ombudsman Services/Consumer, Pressure, Trade, and Industry Groups

An organisation's performance and impact are often subject to assessment by a wider group of interested parties. Whether they are ombudsmen attempting to reconcile the disputes of organisations and their customers, consumer or pressure groups trying to surface unfair practices, or trade and industry groups trying to lift the standards of their members.

All such groups have an ability to bring a degree of attention to the operations of organisations, be they positive or negative, and as such, all warrant consideration in terms of how the functioning of your organisation affects the views held within the walls of such institutions. Their influence is often through surfacing concerns and raising attention to matters that they deem need correction. This can at times be done through the media, but often is through more formal routes such as raising challenges to the attention of key stakeholders such as regulators, politicians, or government organisations. Understanding the views of such organisations can therefore help organisations calibrate their response and consider any regulatory attention it may drive.

Society

Whilst we can classify certain groups as we have previously, it is worth noting that these are simply representative segments of society at large; interested parties with common perspectives, if you like. The public at large will also have a view on the acceptable level of risk they are willing to take. Where organisations and regulators mis-judge and expose the public to more risk than is acceptable, a tide of change momentum begins to build, which results in governments being forced to act as the elected representatives. The Global Financial Crisis (Figure 1.12) is an example of the shift in power away from an industry given the risk it exposed the public to, and a prudent flag for why business and industry should scrutinise their work with regard to how it contributes to society and the risks it may pose.

Financial Services is one industry where the public will likely be able to quickly recall the catastrophe that unfolded over a decade ago and the terrible consequences this had for societies across the globe. The human cost and broader consequences of this event have been truly devastating. The issues of the industry, its organisations, and individuals within them have been dominating headlines for the best part of a decade and still to this day we see consequences unfolding. The Global Financial Crisis opened a whole new chapter for banking. Banks saw their whole way of working challenged, from the fundamentals of their business models, their approach to leadership and culture, their governance and approach to risk management and control, through to the fairness, transparency, and value of their offering to the market. There were few areas of the banking model that did not come under challenge. In other words, a wholesale re-think.

From a U.K. perspective, a brief search of the Prudential Regulation Authority (P.R.A.) and Financial Conduct Authority (F.C.A.) websites provides many examples of the issues faced by organisations and reveals one aspect of the costs faced by organisations who were found wanting in the face of regulatory scrutiny. For their year ending 2018, fines issued by the F.C.A. alone totalled over £60 million (F.C.A. 2018a). Eye watering this may be, but it is a far cry from the £1.5 billion peak in 2014 (F.C.A. 2014a). The list of failings is extensive, however, underpinning those issues are more fundamental challenges that should be reflected upon. Matters of trust in the relationships and how that will have shifted as events arose, along with questions of openness, transparency, and proactivity in surfacing risks before the issues transpire. Fines, therefore, are just one part of the story. As the Global Financial Crisis progressed, the relationships between stakeholder groups began to fracture. Financial service organisations, politicians, and regulators quickly saw relationships breakdown as the events unfolded. Trust evaporated and a decade of issues emerged, which beset the industry. Furthermore, as a global phenomenon, issues were seen across the globe and their implications often felt far and wide with significant ramifications for the organisations concerned. A review of examples of regulatory sanctions since the financial crisis really highlights how extensive and far reaching those issues have been.

FIGURE 1.12   Financial Services U.K. – An Industry That Hit the Rocks[4]

Similarly, in a more recent example, the social media industry felt the scrutiny of society and the commencement of political and social discourse on whether greater protection should be in place given the challenges the industry has faced in recent years[3].

Having considered how organisations approach defining their regulatory relationship strategy, reviewed the purpose and importance of the relationship and considered how relationships can operate in different ways, and the role stakeholders often play in regulatory relationships, it brings us to a natural junction. So far, we have considered relationships in terms of how they are currently thought about and operate. However, we opened this book with reflections on how rapidly things around us are changing. Therefore, this is a good point to pause and consider how regulatory relationships are changing through the lens of the drivers of change, which in turn will help us begin to consider in subsequent chapters how regulatory strategies driving such relationships may change in the future.

WHAT ARE THE DRIVERS OF CHANGE?

The world around us is both exciting and challenging. At the start of this book, we reflected on some of the incredible changes we have experienced in recent years and the questions they pose for industries and regulators in how to navigate them whilst ensuring appropriate safeguards continue to prevent detriment. Here, we explore some of those drivers of change a little further and demonstrate how the picture is changing and how that influences what we need to consider in terms of its potential impact on our regulatory relationships. Figure 1.13 lists each of the drivers we will explore in turn.

The drivers represent key areas where we have started to see their implications unfold already, and where there remains a steady march in terms of the direction of travel.

1. Democratisation of risk
2. Failure to protect
3. Resilience
4. Complexity and connectivity
5. Technological change and adoption
6. Growing demand for consumer protection
7. Rapid improvement in regulatory capability and insight
8. Environmental, social, and governance

FIGURE 1.13   Drivers of Change in Regulatory Relationships

Democratisation of Risk

Risk is everyone's business and manifests itself in many forms in our daily lives. Some we are aware of, others we are not. Some risks we consciously choose to accept, some we do not.

Every day, in all walks of our lives, we engage in activities with an element of risk. In doing so, we consider our activity, consider its risks, and choose whether to engage in it. However, not all risk is of our choosing, and some risks we find it hard to avoid even if we would like to. It is in these circumstances where our choices over the risks we accept are constrained, where we see the challenges of the democratisation of risk in their clearest forms. It is also in these areas that regulators will be increasingly interested in considering the activities of organisations and the protections that may help mitigate such risks.

If we take matters of financial security as a brief example, it may be that we consider the risks we endure through a number of lenses, such as our financial product choices as individuals (and the transparency of the risks involved, e.g., asymmetry of information between the organisation and consumers), at a policy level, such as changes in pension and healthcare provision, or at a national level such as the implications and devastation of financial crises. At each of these levels, the risks around our financial security are not always entirely within our control. If we take financial crises, which have taken many forms and have littered history, each tends to have implications that ripple far and wide. Whether its impact is that governments step in to save institutions with the *public purse*, those that have invested in their own homes, businesses, or investments see their value fall, or economic shocks that impact people's jobs, incomes, or well-being. The risk that was inherent can become a shared issue...democratised to those that were unable to see it coming and avoid its impact.

Given the impact and implications of democratised risk, governments, legislators, and regulators are increasingly looking to improve consumer protection and ensure accountability is held by those driving such risks. This has seen significant interventions, with regulators becoming increasingly proactive in understanding the drivers of risk and the mitigants and controls that need to be improved by the organisations concerned. In terms of regulatory relationships, their scope, scrutiny, and intensity have in some industries experienced a step change and rather than reaching a plateau in terms of approach, continues to see progressive expansion of the areas regulators seek to understand, be involved in, and challenge. Regulatory relationships increasingly accommodate a far more dynamic, forward-looking relationship that delves into every aspect of how organisations progress and perform, such as assessments of the business objective, model and strategy, the leadership and culture, and the outcomes they achieve. In addition to these more internally focussed areas of scrutiny, there are also the more externally focused influences on regulatory judgement, such as the regulator's direct engagement with consumers, consumer bodies and their reading on the organisation's environment.

Where there is the potential for risks to be democratised, particularly to those less able to mitigate or avoid such risk, we are likely to see greater regulatory scrutiny, greater protection, and an increased expectation on organisations to demonstrate how they are protecting their stakeholders.

Failure to Protect

At a fundamental level, many of the drivers for regulation and increased protection for consumers arise from a failure (perceived or otherwise) to sufficiently protect the interests of individuals by organisations, or a consideration that the level of protection is insufficient.

This failure to protect can happen on many levels. For example, it could arise from the failure and closure of an organisation, the failure of its products that do not live up to the expectations set, the failure of services that are relied upon by users, or at times related matters such as the failure to appropriately conduct their operations with sufficient care and attention leading to environmental impact. One common implication, regardless of the nature of the failure, will be an assessment of whether the protection for individuals was sufficient.

As organisations become increasingly complex, change and develop their products and services with accelerating pace, and reach, engage, and serve consumers with greater velocity and across more channels, the challenge to deliver consistently, reliably, and with acceptable levels of risk is constantly present[5].

Regulators against this backdrop will increasingly seek to understand how organisations identify their key risks, how protection is designed in to mitigate those risks, and how controls are designed and tested to ensure that protection continues to operate effectively. Whether it is understanding the financial resilience of the organisation through different business cycles, understanding how consumer protection is designed into every stage of the product and service life cycle, or understanding the related environmental, social and governance dynamics, and performance of the business, regulators are increasingly *looking through the cycles* of business operation to understand how organisations are set up and driven to achieve the right outcomes, with the right control and protection for those that engage with them[6].

Resilience

Whereas with failure to protect above, we are concerned with the absence or omission of actions that could form to sufficiently protect consumers. With resilience, our focus is more on the ability to withstand impacts on an organisation and recover the situation.

Over the years, we have seen countless challenges face organisations and witnessed their ability to withstand or deal with the implications. Some of those challenges have been external in source and some self-inflicted from internal actions, such as an organisation's own change programme. As organisations constantly adapt and change to sustain their competitiveness and keep pace or indeed set the pace with the march of technology, so their focus on assuring resilience in their organisations becomes a constant theme. In addition, as new and exciting ways develop in delivering products and services across different industries, so new challenges will arise in terms of resilience, an example of which has been the increase in criminals looking to exploit vulnerabilities in systems to obtain valuable customer data, disrupt services, or extort value. Whether the challenges are external in origin or self-inflicted by internal change and development, their impact can be significant[7].

For organisations, example issues such as resilience, change control, single points of failure, the insights regulators can impart through raising their concerns, and the reliance on outsourced partners and their impact on your consumers and business become points of focus. As failures arise, so we see the fuel being added to our drivers of change. As no organisation sets out to get such things wrong, great lessons can be taken from such events, like the insight regulators can bring as they engage with organisations during such difficult times.

Complexity and Connectivity

The path of organisational development has seen a huge change in how organisations are configured and operate. Today's organisations increasingly rely on complex technologies, are increasingly interconnected with the services and products of other organisations, and more and more deliver their products and service across multiple platforms, including digital interaction with end consumers. It is a world where the interdependence and reliance on systems of interaction raises the stakes for all involved, where missteps can impact far beyond organisational walls, and where the costs can be significant[8].

A world where the rigour and robustness of lifecycle events such as planning, development, testing, change control, implementation, maintenance, back up, contingency plans, business continuity and disaster recovery (the list could continue…) are all critical capabilities. And a world where our desire to get to market first, execute quicker, reduce cost

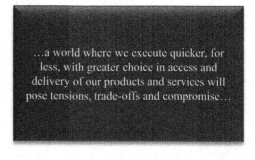

…a world where we execute quicker, for less, with greater choice in access and delivery of our products and services will pose tensions, trade-offs and compromise…

to serve, be more agile, and provide greater choice in access and delivery of our products and services poses tensions, trade-offs, and compromise.

With growing interdependence and complexity comes new risks. Risks that regulators will increasingly wish to understand, be assured organisations understand them and be convinced that sufficient control and protection is in place to avoid detriment and harm. As the pace quickens in development to deployment, regulators will need to engage earlier and be taken on the journey so that organisations can demonstrate how such protections are *designed in* and assured throughout.

Technological Change and Adoption

Much of what we have covered so far in this section has focused on the institutional side of the equation: what organisations must consider and as a result, what regulators will seek to assure. However, there is clearly a consumer dimension to consider.

As technological developments progress with accelerating velocity, we are increasingly faced with an exciting and enticing range of technological solutions. Our adoption of technological change has been staggering as the work of Comin and Hobijn (2004) and others, demonstrates. In their study of technology adoption, we can see interesting trends emerge (see Figure 1.14). Here, we focus on the United States and show three charts. The first is the overall list of technologies and their pace of adoption. The second and third charts split out the list of technologies into older technologies and more recent ones. This allows us to see the pace of adoption accelerating more clearly, noting particularly the short periods and steep adoption lines of newer technologies such as computers, social media, and tablets. In fact, with the onset of the Covid-19 pandemic, we have seen examples of the pace of adoption making even the recent history on those charts look sluggish. For example, organisations and individuals, who more and more were asked to work and stay at home, reached for the latest technologies aimed at video conferencing to enable them to stay in touch with work, friends, and family. Taking one example, the Zoom platform saw their maximum daily usage grow at a staggering pace, from 10 million users in December 2019, to 200 million users in March 2020 (Yuan 2020).

With such adoption, however, comes personal responsibility and accountability as we engage with these new technologies. Consider for a moment the

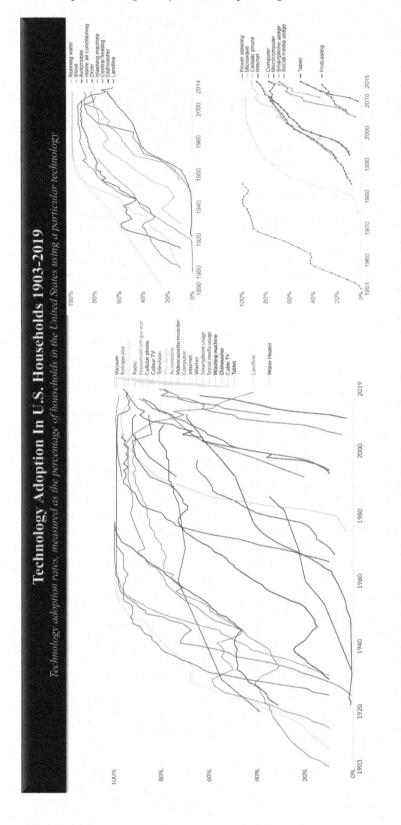

FIGURE 1.14 Technology Adoption in U.S. Households 1903–2019

implications (see Figure 1.15) of some of these developments that we can observe across our own network of family, friends, and colleagues for example:

Platform adoption – e.g., Proliferation of relationships, passwords, payment methods as we engage with technologies
    Propensity to share – e.g., Lives are increasingly lived online. More is disclosed as our familiarity grows
    Processing power – e.g., Automation, connectivity, and greater application of technologies as capability advances
    Data storage – e.g., Personal data in more places we do not govern, as storage costs fall and availability increases
    Activity tracked – e.g., More of what we do and where is known and tracked by services and organisations we engage
    Acceleration of cybercrime – e.g., Opacity of digital counterparts enables criminals, whilst security awareness develops
    Familiarity and contempt – e.g., De-sensitised to risks involved in digital interaction as reliance and familiarity grows.

FIGURE 1.15   Technological Change and Adoption Example Implications

Here we begin to see how our engagement with the progressing world around us starts to pose challenges for how we keep control of everything we now engage with and ensure we engage appropriately and securely. Whilst at a one-on-one relationship level with an organisation, this may be manageable, as our adoption of technologies increases, our relationships broaden, and our world as individuals in this technological age becomes more complex, regulators are becoming increasingly aware of the dangers and issues consumers can face, for example, that the risks may not be as clear to consumers as they are to the organisations they deal with. In such times, the level of protection needed (and who provides it) is likely to be a debate of increasing interest across stakeholders, not least regulators and regulated organisations during their regulatory relationships.

Growing Demand for Consumer Protection

As the drivers of change have taken shape, there has been an appreciation that with every new development, opportunity, and change comes new challenges and risk. From a consumer point of view, the previous example developments have also been accompanied by broader changes that also raise the stakes. For example, the shift in employment behaviour and security around our working lives has meant our expectations of *jobs for life* have eroded with a shifting momentum toward working lives typified by multiple employers over time, self-employment, and the *gig economy*. This combination of broader changes in the protection we enjoy, combined with drivers of change, is likely to continue to weigh on the balance of protection governments and regulators consider appropriate.

In an increasingly complex, uncertain, and rapidly changing world, the balance of protections afforded to consumers are on an upward trajectory which appears unlikely to change for some time.

Rapid Improvement in Regulatory Capability and Insight

Across many industries, we have seen the role, objectives, and powers of regulators steadily expand as we heed the lessons of history and try to adapt our regulatory frameworks to modern challenges.

Just as organisations are taking advantage of new capabilities and new technologies, so our regulators are also adapting and leveraging these advances, which is likely to be a key driver of change in the approach to regulatory relationships. Whether it is the growth in data we capture, the deployment of enormous processing capabilities to turn that data into information and insight, or the advances in machine learning and artificial intelligence to help use these new and significant resources to greater effect, regulators are also tapping into the new opportunities that arise.

With these new capabilities, regulators increasingly have greater sources of information and insight from right around an organisation's ecosystem, both direct and faster access to information, and improved capability to assimilate and understand that information. In addition, the regulator is building this picture right across the industry and as such, has a view an organisation cannot easily replicate. This view can highlight both good and poor practice, and quickly understand where organisations sit vis-à-vis any particular concern or opportunity. The regulator's *looking glass* is becoming far more powerful and effective.

For organisations, this poses both opportunities and challenges when considering their regulatory relationship. On the one hand, their regulator will have access to information and insight an organisation cannot see, which can make organisations feel like they are on the back foot; on the other hand, where organisations broaden their own understanding of their organisation's impact and performance across its entire ecosystem, regulators can take comfort that appropriate attempts to understand the impact, implications, and outcomes are undertaken. At the very least, as the regulatory view improves, organisations will want to be across as much as possible what the regulator is seeing in order that they can be prepared and proactive in engaging on items of interest.

For organisations that are driven to pursue good regulatory relationships, regulatory views can also supplement the organisations view and help inform on items organisations may not see (e.g., the lessons of others in the industry). In this respect, taking a wider and more inclusive view of organisational impact can benefit relationships. It demonstrates a desire to understand your organisational impact, to learn from it, calibrate, change as a result, and constantly seek to improve outcomes, which is in the interest of all stakeholders.

Environmental, Social, and Governance

Environmental, social, and governance considerations have experienced a progressive rise in importance and priority in the activities of both organisations and their regulators. Indeed, across an organisation's stakeholder map, there are often groups interested from a whole array of perspectives. For example, environmental groups interested in an organisation's impact and environmental credentials, local communities or employees considering the impact of the organisation's activities in light of social changes, or investment groups considering the effective governance and risk management of an organisation in considering their investment and the likely performance of an organisation over time. Furthermore, such scrutiny and interest show no signs of abating and increasingly see these credentials as part of the assessment of how sustainable an organisation's activities may be given the outcomes they are generating and the way in which they are operating.

For organisations, it has therefore become increasingly common for these considerations to feature as part of their articulation of their strategic intent and their approach to achieving it, whilst their regulators can often be seen to encapsulate such considerations in their regulatory objectives and planned work.

In short, environmental, social, and governance considerations are having a greater influence and potential impact upon the operations and performance of organisations and represent a significant driver of change, as organisations increasingly feel the lens of scrutiny passing over these areas. That scrutiny is also likely to result in real implications, whether that be greater legislative or regulatory standards to achieve higher expectations and standards from investors, or more selective and discerning consumers voting with their feet and taking their business to those organisations they feel represent their values. Across stakeholder groups, these areas represent a significant potential impact and driver of change and, therefore, will be of greater interest to regulators who seek to understand what risks organisations may pose to their regulatory objectives.

THE CHANGING ECOSYSTEM AND WHAT IT MEANS FOR REGULATORY RELATIONSHIP STRATEGIES

At the start of this chapter, we considered how organisational approaches to establishing regulatory relationship strategies can vary significantly (including not having a strategy at all). Reflecting on how strategies and relationships may come about, we noted that organisations can often point at their regulator's requirements, the minimum standard expected, as a basis upon which to build their approach. However, we noted that organisations clearly have the option to go well beyond that minimum standard, and that such a narrow approach may only provide organisations with a partial view of what is happening in terms of how their regulator may be forming its judgements. Whilst accepting that the regulatory relationship is the key conduit to a regulator, we also considered that ensuring organisations fall on the right side of the regulator's objectives will involve the regulator looking much broader and considering the impact of the organisation across the breadth of its activities. Regulators, as we discovered, will operate in different *modes* and will consider the impact the organisation has on its stakeholders and its environment, all of which can become a catalyst and driver of the need for change. In short, regulators are increasingly looking across a regulatory ecosystem of insight and forming their opinions and judgements based on a growing field of insight. Against this backdrop, having a strategy for your regulatory relationship and understanding that relationship in terms of what informs it becomes increasingly important.

Regulatory relationships against this backdrop are likely to constantly need to adapt, be flexible, dynamic, and able to facilitate a growing agenda of subjects to consider from a broader range of sources that can arrive quicker, impact harder, and disrupt both organisational and regulatory objectives more profoundly.

For this reason, the traditional approach to regulatory strategy and the relationship approach needs to take a new perspective. That perspective needs to be more holistic, more forward facing, more dynamic, responsive, open, and transparent. It needs to truly integrate into the regulatory ecosystem around the organisation.

In this chapter, we considered how organisations traditionally approach defining their regulatory relationship, reviewed the purpose and importance of the relationship, considered how relationships can operate in different ways (*modes*), what role stakeholders often play in regulatory relationships, and some of the drivers for change that surround, shape and influence regulatory relationships. In the next chapter, we start to explore what this new perspective can entail and describe how changes in the way we think about regulatory relationships can help in building more effective relationships for the future.

NOTES

1. C.f. Financial Conduct Authority (2021a) consultation on a new Consumer Duty as an example of the consultation process and engagement with organisations on regulatory proposals. Following the consultation process for the Consumer Duty allows you to see how industry contributed and the process to final rules in 2022.
2. For an example, see the aftermath of the Global Financial Crisis and comments captured in the findings of the Parliamentary Committee on Banking Standards (2013).
3. See also recent developments as governments move to put in place greater powers to intervene, for example, Clayton (2022) reporting for the B.B.C. "UK government sets out plans to rein in Big Tech".
4. C.f. The following example references are provided for significant published historic sanctions and prosecutions as a useful introduction and insight into the issues faced historically in financial services. These examples provide further reading across a variety of issues and organisations that operate across a range of geographies. A review of sanction registers across regulators and industries as well as prosecution notices can provide a window into the outcomes generated at times and the implications and consequences that can unfold for organisations, which in these examples run to billions of dollars (selection only for illustration and not comprehensive nor representative of all issues). Federal Reserve (2012a), "Federal Reserve Board issues consent cease and desist order, and assesses civil money penalty against Standard Chartered PLC and Standard Chartered Bank"; Federal Reserve (2012b), "Federal Reserve Board issues consent cease and desist order, and assesses civil money penalty against HSBC Holdings PLC and HSBC North America Holdings, Inc."; D.O.J. (2013), "Justice Department, Federal and State Partners Secure Record $13 Billion Global Settlement with JPMorgan for Misleading Investors About Securities Containing Toxic Mortgages"; Federal Reserve (2013), "JP Morgan Chase & Co. to pay $200 million for oversight,

management, and controls deficiencies"; F.C.A. (2013b), Final Notice, "JPMorgan Chase Bank N.A."; F.C.A. (2013a), "Final Notice - Coöperatieve Centrale Raiffeisen–Boerenleenbank B.A. ('Rabobank')"; F.C.A. (2014c), "Final Notice – HSBC Bank plc"; D.O.J. (2014a), "Bank of America to Pay $16.65 Billion in Historic Justice Department Settlement for Financial Fraud Leading up to and During the Financial Crisis"; F.C.A. (2014g), "Final Notice – UBS AG"; D.O.J. (2014b), "BNP Paribas Agrees to Plead Guilty and to Pay $8.9 Billion for Illegally Processing Financial Transactions for Countries Subject to U.S. Economic Sanctions"; F.C.A. (2014f), "Final Notice – The Royal Bank of Scotland plc"; F.C.A. (2014d), Final Notice, "JPMorgan Chase Bank N.A."; F.C.A. (2014b), "Final Notice – Citibank N.A."; F.C.A. (2015a), "Final Notice - Barclays Bank PLC"; F.C.A. (2015b), "Final Notice – Deutsche Bank AG"; F.C.A. (2015c), "Final Notice – Lloyds Bank plc, Bank of Scotland plc and Black Horse Limited (together Lloyds Banking Group 'LBG')"; D.O.J. (2015), "Five Major Banks Agree to Parent-Level Guilty Pleas"; F.C.A. (2015d), "Final Notice – The Bank of New York Mellon London Branch ('BNYMLB'), The Bank of New York Mellon International Limited ('BNYMIL')"; D.O.J. (2016), "Goldman Sachs Agrees to Pay More than $5 Billion in Connection with its Sale of Residential Mortgage Backed Securities"; F.C.A. (2017), "Final Notice – Deutsche Bank AG"; Federal Reserve (2018), "Federal Reserve Board fines Goldman Sachs Group, Inc., $54.75 million for unsafe and unsound practices in firm's foreign exchange (FX) trading business"; D.O.J. (2018), "Royal Bank of Scotland Agrees to Pay $4.9 Billion for Financial Crisis-Era Misconduct"; F.C.A. (2019), "Decision Notice – Standard Chartered Bank"; F.C.A. (2020), "Final Notice – Goldman Sachs International"; Bank of England – P.R.A. (2020), "Final Notice – Goldman Sachs International (Firm Reference Number: 142888)".

5. C.f. The following example references demonstrate a number of challenges Facebook experienced as an organisation that by historic standards achieved a rapid growth and development, and could be seen as an example of a number of the items being discussed in this area, O'Sullivan (2018), "Facebook reveals bug exposed 6.8 million users' photos"; B.B.C. News Report (2019a), "Facebook to be fined $5bn over Cambridge Analytica scandal"; Federal Trade Commission (2019), "FTC Imposes $5 Billion Penalty and Sweeping New Privacy Restrictions on Facebook"; McCallum (2022), "Meta settles Cambridge Analytica scandal case for $725m".

6. C.f. The following reference provides background reading in areas related to this subject. Geyelin (1998), "Group of 46 States Agree to Accept $206 Billion Tobacco Settlement".

7. C.f. The following references provide background reading in areas related to this subject. B.B.C. (2019b), "British Airways faces record £183m fine for data breach" and the related ICO fine that was applied, ICO (2020), 'ICO Fines British Airways £20m For Data Breach Affecting More Than 400,000 Customers'; B.B.C. (2014), "RBS fined £56m over 'unacceptable' computer failure"; F.C.A. (2014f), "Final Notice – Royal Bank of Scotland Plc"; P.R.A. (2014a), "Final Notice – Royal Bank of Scotland Plc (FRN 121882), National Westminster Bank Plc (FRN 121878), Ulster Bank Ltd (FRN 122315)"; P.R.A. (2014b), "PRA fines Royal Bank of Scotland, NatWest Bank and Ulster Bank 14 million for IT failures"; Financial Conduct Authority (2014e), "Final Notice – Royal Bank of Scotland Plc, National Westminster Bank Plc, Ulster Bank Ltd"; T.S.B. (2019), "TSB Board publishes independent review of 2018 IT Migration"; B.B.C. (2019c), "TSB lacked common sense before IT meltdown, says report"; F.C.A. (2022), "Final Notice – TSB Bank plc"; P.R.A. (2022), "Final Notice - TSB Bank plc (FRN 191240)".

8. C.f. The following reference provides background reading in areas related to this subject. Ahmed (2017), "Five Corporate IT Failures That Caused Huge Disruption"; Masters, B., Moore, E. and Pickark, J. (2012), "The upgrade that downed Royal Bank of Scotland".

REFERENCES

Ahmed, M. (2017), 'Five corporate IT failures that caused huge disruption', [online], Financial Times, 28 May 2017, available: www.ft.com/content/270563ee-43b9-11e7-8d27-59b4dd6296b8

Australian Prudential Regulation Authority (2022), 'What does APRA do?', [online], accessed 16 May 2022, available: https://www.apra.gov.au/what-does-apra-do

B.B.C. News Report (2014), 'RBS fined £56m over 'unacceptable' computer failure', [online], 20 November 2014, available: https://www.bbc.co.uk/news/business-30125728

B.B.C. News Report (2019b), 'British Airways faces record £183m fine for data breach', [Online], 8 July 2019, available: https://www.bbc.co.uk/news/business-48905907

B.B.C. News Report (2019a), 'Facebook to be fined $5bn over Cambridge Analytica scandal', [Online], 13 July 2019, available: www.bbc.co.UK./news/world-us-canada-48972327

B.B.C. News Report (2019c), 'TSB lacked common sense before IT meltdown, says report', [online], 19 November 2019, available: https://www.bbc.co.uk/news/business-50471919

Bank of England, Prudential Regulation Authority (P.R.A.) (2014a), 'Final Notice – Royal Bank of Scotland Plc (FRN 121882), National Westminster Bank Plc (FRN 121878), Ulster Bank Ltd (FRN 122315)', [online], 19 November 2014, available: https://www.bankofengland.co.uk/-/media/boe/files/prudential-regulation/enforcement-notice/en201114.pdf?la=en&hash=7483F66E5533498680F8C2CD9F34CE9C10FD5EA8

Bank of England, Prudential Regulation Authority (P.R.A.) (2014b), 'PRA fines Royal Bank of Scotland, NatWest Bank and Ulster Bank 14 million for IT failures', [online], 20 November 2014, available: https://www.bankofengland.co.uk/news/2014/november/pra-fines-rbs-natwest-and-ulster-bank

Bank of England, Prudential Regulation Authority (P.R.A.) (2020), 'Final Notice – Goldman Sachs International (Firm Reference Number: 142888)', [online], 21 October 2020, available: https://www.bankofengland.co.uk/-/media/boe/files/prudential-regulation/regulatory-action/final-notice-to-goldman-sachs-international.pdf?la=en&hash=0905E04952BFE7C4B05B7AFBB11467F21A069E3F

Bank of England, Prudential Regulation Authority (P.R.A.) (2022), 'Final Notice – TSB Bank plc (FRN: 191240)', [online], 20 December 2022, available: https://www.bankofengland.co.uk/-/media/boe/files/prudential-regulation/regulatory-action/final-notice-from-pra-to-tsb-bank.pdf

Brennan, Z. (2019), 'CDRH Committee Discusses Challenges in Communicating Cyber-security Concerns', [online], Regulatory Affairs Professionals Society, Regulatory Focus, 10 September 2019, available: www.raps.org/news-and-articles/news-articles/2019/9/cdrh-committee-discusses-challenges-in-communicati?utm_source=MagnetMail&utm_medium=Email%20&utm_campaign=RF%20Today%20%7C%2010%20September%202019

Brennan, Z. (2020), 'FDA Warns of Cybersecurity Vulnerabilities in Pacemakers, Blood Glucose Monitors', [online], Regulatory Affairs Professionals Society, Regulatory Focus, 3 March 2020, available: www.raps.org/news-and-articles/news-articles/2020/3/fda-warns-of-cybersecurity-vulnerabilities-in-pace?utm_source=MagnetMail&utm_medium=Email%20&utm_campaign=RF%20Today%20%7C%203%20March%202020

Civil Aviation Authority (C.A.A.) (2017c), 'CAP 1508: Getting the most out of the Accountable Manager Meeting', [online], 12 January 2017, available: https://publicapps.caa.co.uk/modalapplication.aspx?appid=11&mode=detail&id=7724

Civil Aviation Authority (C.A.A.) (2022a), 'Our Role', [online], available: https://www.caa.co.uk/our-work/about-us/our-role/

Civil Aviation Authority (C.A.A.) (2022d), 'Performance Based Regulation', [online], available: https://www.caa.co.uk/safety-initiatives-and-resources/how-we-regulate/performance-based-regulation/

Civil Aviation Authority (C.A.A.) (2022b), 'General Aviation Policy Framework', [online], available: https://www.caa.co.uk/general-aviation/working-with-you/general-aviation-policy-framework/

Clayton, J. (2022), 'UK government sets out plans to rein in Big Tech', [online], B.B.C. News, 6 May 2022, available: https://www.bbc.co.uk/news/technology-61342576

Comin, B. and Hobijn, B. (2004), 'Cross-Country Technology Adoption: Making the Theories Face the facts', Journal of Monetary Economics, Vol. 51, No. 1, pp.39–83

Federal Reserve (2012a), 'Federal Reserve Board issues consent cease and desist order, and assesses civil money penalty against Standard Chartered PLC and Standard Chartered Bank', [online], 10 December 2012, available: https://www.federalreserve.gov/newsevents/pressreleases/enforcement20121210a.htm

Federal Reserve (2012b), 'Federal Reserve Board issues consent cease and desist order, and assesses civil money penalty against HSBC Holdings PLC and HSBC North America Holdings, Inc.', [online], 11 December 2012, available: https://www.federalreserve.gov/newsevents/pressreleases/enforcement20121211b.htm

Federal Reserve (2013), 'JP Morgan Chase & Co. to pay $200 million for oversight, management, and controls deficiencies', [online], 19 September 2013, available: https://www.federalreserve.gov/newsevents/pressreleases/enforcement20130919a.htm

Federal Reserve (2018), 'Federal Reserve Board fines Goldman Sachs Group, Inc., $54.75 million for unsafe and unsound practices in firm's foreign exchange (FX) trading business', [online], 1 May 2018, available: https://www.federalreserve.gov/newsevents/pressreleases/enforcement20180501b.htm

Federal Trade Commission (2019), 'FTC Imposes $5 Billion Penalty and Sweeping New Privacy Restrictions on Facebook', [online], 24 July 2019, available: https://www.ftc.gov/news-events/press-releases/2019/07/ftc-imposes-5-billion-penalty-sweeping-new-privacy-restrictions

Financial Conduct Authority (F.C.A.) (2021a), 'CP21/13: A New Consumer Duty', [online], 20 December 2021, available: https://www.fca.org.uk/publications/consultation-papers/cp21-13-new-consumer-duty

Financial Conduct Authority (F.C.A.) (2021b), 'Supervisory Principles', [online], available: (https://www.handbook.fca.org.U.K./handbook/SUP/1A/3.html)

Financial Conduct Authority (F.C.A.) (2013a), 'Final Notice – Coöperatieve Centrale Raiffeisen–Boerenleenbank B.A. ('Rabobank')', [online], 29 October 2013, available: https://www.fca.org.uk/publication/final-notices/rabobank.pdf

Financial Conduct Authority (F.C.A.) (2013b), 'Final Notice – JPMorgan Chase Bank, N.A.', [online], 18 September 2013, available: https://www.fca.org.uk/publication/final-notices/jpmorgan-chase-bank.pdf

Financial Conduct Authority (F.C.A.) (2014a), '2014 Fines', [online], 31 August 2016, available: https://www.fca.org.uk/news/news-stories/2014-fines

Financial Conduct Authority (F.C.A.) (2014b), 'Final Notice – Citibank N.A.', [online], 11 November 2014, available: https://www.fca.org.uk/publication/final-notices/final-notice-citi-bank.pdf

Financial Conduct Authority (F.C.A.) (2014c), 'Final Notice – HSBC Bank plc', [online], 11 November 2014, available: https://www.fca.org.uk/publication/final-notices/final-notice-hsbc.pdf

Financial Conduct Authority (F.C.A.) (2014d), 'Final Notice – JPMorgan Chase Bank N.A.', [online], 11 November 2014, available: https://www.fca.org.uk/publication/final-notices/final-notice-jpm.pdf

Financial Conduct Authority (F.C.A.) (2014e), 'Final Notice – Royal Bank of Scotland Plc, National Westminster Bank Plc, Ulster Bank Ltd', [online], 19 November 2014, available: https://www.fca.org.uk/publication/final-notices/rbs-natwest-ulster-final-notice.pdf

Financial Conduct Authority (F.C.A.) (2014f), 'Final Notice – The Royal Bank of Scotland plc', [online], 11 November 2014, available: https://www.fca.org.uk/publication/final-notices/final-notice-rbs.pdf

Financial Conduct Authority (F.C.A.) (2014g), 'Final Notice – UBS AG', [online], 11 November 2014, available: https://www.fca.org.uk/publication/final-notices/final-notice-ubs.pdf

Financial Conduct Authority (F.C.A.) (2015a), 'Final Notice – Barclays Bank PLC', [online], 20 May 2015, available: https://www.fca.org.uk/publication/final-notices/barclays-bank-plc-may-15.pdf

Financial Conduct Authority (F.C.A.) (2015b), 'Final Notice – Deutsche Bank AG', [online], 23 April 2015, available: https://www.fca.org.uk/publication/final-notices/deutsche-bank-ag-2015.pdf

Financial Conduct Authority (F.C.A.) (2015c), 'Final Notice – Lloyds Bank plc, Bank of Scotland plc and Black Horse Limited (together Lloyds Banking Group 'LBG')', [online], 4 June 2015, available: https://www.fca.org.uk/publication/final-notices/lloyds-banking-group-2015.pdf

Financial Conduct Authority (F.C.A.) (2015d), 'Final Notice – The Bank of New York Mellon London Branch ('BNYMLB'), The Bank of New York Mellon International Limited ('BNYMIL')', [online], 14 April 2015, available: https://www.fca.org.uk/publication/final-notices/bank-of-new-york-mellon-london-international.pdf

Financial Conduct Authority (F.C.A.) (2017), 'Final Notice – Deutsche Bank AG', [online], 30 January 2017, available: https://www.fca.org.uk/publication/final-notices/deutsche-bank-2017.pdf

Financial Conduct Authority (F.C.A.) (2018a), '2018 Fines', [online], 15 January 2019, available: https://www.fca.org.uk/news/news-stories/2018-fines

Financial Conduct Authority (F.C.A.) (2018b), 'Principles For Businesses', [online], available: https://www.handbook.fca.org.uk/handbook/PRIN/2/?view=chapter

Financial Conduct Authority (F.C.A.) (2019), 'Decision Notice – Standard Chartered Bank', [online], 5 February 2019, available: https://www.fca.org.uk/publication/decision-notices/standard-chartered-bank-2019.pdf

Financial Conduct Authority (F.C.A.) (2020), 'Final Notice – Goldman Sachs International', [online], 21 October 2020, available: https://www.fca.org.uk/publication/final-notices/gsi-2020.pdf

Financial Conduct Authority (F.C.A.) (2022), 'About the FCA', [online], last updated 19 July 2022, available: https://www.fca.org.uk/about/the-fca

Financial Conduct Authority (F.C.A.) (2022), 'Final Notice – TSB Bank plc', [online], 20 December 2022, available: https://www.fca.org.uk/publication/final-notices/tsb-bank-plc-2022.pdf

Gaffney, A. (2015), 'Meeting with FDA? Here's what Regulators do (and don't) want from drug companies', [online], Regulatory Affairs Professionals Society, Regulatory Focus, 10 March 2015, available: https://www.raps.org/regulatory-focus™/news-articles/2015/3/meeting-with-fda-here-s-what-regulators-do-(and-don-t)-want-from-drug-companies

Geyelin, M. (1998), 'Group of 46 States Agree to Accept $206 Billion Tobacco Settlement', The Wall Street Journal, 23rd November 1998, [online], available: https://www.wsj.com/articles/SB911777383137557500

Hutton, Dame Deirdre. (2015), 'The Role of Stakeholder Relationships in Regulatory Excellence', [online], The Regulatory Review, 27 July 2015, available: https://www.theregreview.org/2015/07/27/hutton-regulatory-excellence/

Information Commissioner's Office (ICO) (2020), 'ICO Fines British Airways £20m For Data Breach Affecting More Than 400,000 Customers', [online], available: https://ico.org.uk/about-the-ico/news-and-events/news-and-blogs/2020/10/ico-fines-british-airways-20m-for-data-breach-affecting-more-than-400-000-customers/

Masters, B., Moore, E. and Pickark, J. (2012), 'The upgrade that downed Royal Bank of Scotland', [online], Financial Times, 25 June 2012, available: https://www.ft.com/content/4ecdb67c-beb9-11e1-b24b-00144feabdc0

McCallum, S. (2022), 'Meta settles Cambridge Analytica scandal case for $725m', [online], B.B.C. News, 23 December 2022, available: https://www.bbc.co.uk/news/technology-64075067

National Audit Office (N.A.O.) (2019), 'Regulating to protect consumers in utilities, communications and financial services markets', [online], 20 March 2019, available: https://www.nao.org.uk/report/regulating-to-protect-consumers-utilities-communications-and-financial-services-markets/

O'Sullivan, D. (2018), 'Facebook reveals bug exposed 6.8 million users' photos', CNN News Report, [online], 14 December 2018, available https://edition.cnn.com/2018/12/14/tech/facebook-private-photos-exposed-bug/index.html

Parliamentary Commission on Banking Standards (2013), 'Changing Banking for Good', Vol. 1, London, The Stationery Office, pp.8, 57

T.S.B. (2019), 'TSB Board publishes independent review of 2018 IT Migration', [online], 19 November 2019, available: https://www.tsb.co.uk/news-releases/slaughter-and-may/

U.K. Regulators Network (U.K.R.N.) (2017), 'Consumer Engagement in Regulatory Decisions – A Guide to How U.K. Regulators Involve Consumers, Hear Their Views and Take Their Interests into Account', [online], April 2017, pp.5, 7, 11, [online], available: https://www.ukrn.org.uk/publications/consumer-engagement-in-regulatory-decisions-april-2017/

U.S. Department of Justice (D.O.J.) (2013), 'Justice Department, Federal and State Partners Secure Record $13 Billion Global Settlement with JPMorgan for Misleading Investors About Securities Containing Toxic Mortgages', [online], 19 November 2013, available: https://www.justice.gov/opa/pr/justice-department-federal-and-state-partners-secure-record-13-billion-global-settlement

U.S. Department of Justice (D.O.J.) (2014a), 'Bank of America to Pay $16.65 Billion in Historic Justice Department Settlement for Financial Fraud Leading up to and During the Financial Crisis', [online], 21 August 2014, available: www.justice.gov/opa/pr/bank-america-pay-1665-billion-historic-justice-department-settlement-financial-fraud-leading

U.S. Department of Justice (D.O.J.) (2014b), 'BNP Paribas Agrees to Plead Guilty and to Pay $8.9 Billion for Illegally Processing Financial Transactions for Countries Subject to U.S. Economic Sanctions', [online], 30 June 2014, available: https://www.justice.gov/opa/pr/bnp-paribas-agrees-plead-guilty-and-pay-89-billion-illegally-processing-financial

U.S. Department of Justice (D.O.J.) (2015), 'Five Major Banks Agree to Parent-Level Guilty Pleas', [online], 20 May 2015, available: https://www.justice.gov/opa/pr/five-major-banks-agree-parent-level-guilty-pleas

U.S. Department of Justice (D.O.J.) (2016), 'Goldman Sachs Agrees to Pay More than $5 Billion in Connection with its Sale of Residential Mortgage Backed Securities', [online], 11 April 2016, available: https://www.justice.gov/opa/pr/goldman-sachs-agrees-pay-more-5-billion-connection-its-sale-residential-mortgage-backed

U.S. Department of Justice (D.O.J.) (2018), 'Royal Bank of Scotland Agrees to Pay $4.9 Billion for Financial Crisis-Era Misconduct', [online], 14 August 2018, available: https://www.justice.gov/opa/pr/royal-bank-scotland-agrees-pay-49-billion-financial-crisis-era-misconduct

U.S. Food & Drug Administration (FDA) (2020), 'FDA Informs Patients, Providers and Manufacturers About Potential Cybersecurity Vulnerabilities in Certain Medical Devices with Bluetooth Low Energy', [online], 3 March 2020, available: https://www.fda.gov/news-events/press-announcements/fda-informs-patients-providers-and-manufacturers-about-potential-cybersecurity-vulnerabilities-0

Yuan, E. (2020), 'A Message to Our Users', Zoom Blog, [online], 1 April 2020, https://blog.zoom.us/a-message-to-our-users/

CHAPTER 2

A Framework for Building More Effective Relationships

CHAPTER SUMMARY

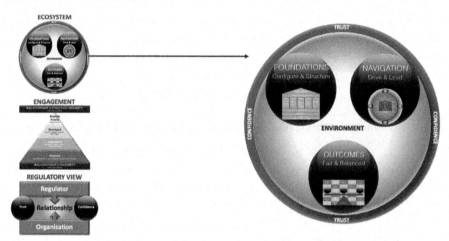

In this chapter, we explore the opportunity for organisations to take a new perspective on their regulatory relationship strategy. That opportunity includes taking a more strategic view of their relationship whilst broadening their insights in a way that can better inform their activities, actions, and interactions with regulators.

To enable organisations to build that strategic view, we introduce the concept of the *regulatory ecosystem,* and discuss how this can help organisations understand how the sum of their activities and the impact these have influence and impact their relationships. We cover how this understanding can assist organisations and allow them to calibrate their approach, build better relations with their regulators, and how it can be helpful to think about the boundaries of their regulatory relationship in terms of the boundaries of the regulatory ecosystem they impact. In having this broader understanding

DOI: 10.4324/9781003297963-2

and thinking about their relationship in these terms, we explore how this can help organisations keep regulators better informed, provide appropriate and timely context, and support them as they form their opinions and judgements.

Finally, we recap on some of the drivers of change (including considering emergent relationships) and consider the case for why taking this new perspective is important. Here, we look at how theory supports relationship development and conclude by introducing the framework we will follow throughout the rest of the book that will facilitate your thinking on how to build your regulatory relationship strategy.

THE REGULATORY ECOSYSTEM – TAKE A NEW PERSPECTIVE

Organisations often establish their regulatory relationship strategy (overall objective, scope, planning and directing of activities, resources dedicated, approach) to consist of that which is prescribed by the regulator of a particular industry, at times supplemented by areas the organisation feels it can control and measure. Similarly, they often view what a relationship entails in narrow terms, which tends to result in an interpretation lacking a more strategic perspective and risks organisations falling out of step with regulatory developments, their regulator's view of their organisation, and the direction of travel.

In this section, it's suggested that organisations have an opportunity to re-think their approach to regulatory relationship strategy, and as a result, take *a new perspective* on how they think about and drive their regulatory relationships. That approach should be more holistic, should *stand in* the regulator's shoes, and should feedback and inform the organisation's activities and actions.

With their regulatory relationship being the core conduit to help the regulator better understand the organisation, taking such an all-inclusive perspective – *a regulatory ecosystem perspective* – can help organisations consider how the sum of their actions and activities influence and impact the regulatory relationship. This in turn can help them consider how they might adjust and calibrate to build better relations with the regulator.

> **Regulatory Relationship Ecosystem**
>
> The sum of information and insight used by a regulator to form its judgements and opinions

Thinking about the regulatory relationship in terms of a regulatory ecosystem of interaction also provides a useful analogy to what it entails. The interaction of an organisation within its environment is akin to the natural world of organisms interacting with and adapting to their environment. When we think about the regulatory relationship in these terms, we start to appreciate that the regulatory relationship can be influenced by any aspect of an organisation's impact upon its environment and stakeholders. To this end, the boundaries of the regulatory relationship can be thought of as the boundaries of the ecosystem you influence, i.e., all that informs the regulator's opinion and judgement, organisations can think of as being part of their regulatory relationship.

To demonstrate how this perspective can shape the strategy and relationship, a framework is provided that can support organisations in systematically thinking through their strategy and the key areas to consider when it comes to regulatory engagement. Here we don't set out to provide a fixed prescription for your strategy and relationship approach as there is no *one best way*. Instead, we lay out an approach for what should be considered as you formulate your strategy. In doing this, organisations can tailor their approach given this broader understanding of what the relationship with your regulators can entail. It provides a new perspective of the breadth of opportunity to support regulators in forming their view of an organisation, and how organisations can think differently about how the regulatory relationship is approached.

A New Perspective Can Help You Better Inform Your Regulator's Opinion

As the judgements and opinions regulators build of your organisation are a function of all they see that influences their position, and as the sources and breadth of information regulators engage with increases, organisations risk becoming blindsided to the insight regulators enjoy if they fail to step back and see their organisation and its impact from a broader perspective.

Some of the insight regulators now enjoy will be specific to your organisation, some may be industry wide, some of it you will directly influence, and some of it will be out of your control. However, this system of insight and influence, has a bearing on the regulatory relationship you enjoy. It feeds your regulator and helps them assess how your organisation is functioning, how they should engage with you, and what areas they should explore. Reading and interpreting your broader regulatory ecosystem it is suggested, should be central to how organisations inform their strategy and understand and manage their regulatory relationships.

> The judgements and opinions regulators build of your organisation are a function of all they see that influences their position. As the sources and breadth of information increase, organisations risk becoming out of step with insights regulators enjoy

Thinking about the relationship in this broader context of a regulatory ecosystem provides an opportunity for organisations to engage more proactively, ensure there are no surprises and keep your regulator well informed. In addition, it helps deliver a richer level of insight with which to help regulators build their opinions, inform their view, and form their judgements.

REGULATORY RELATIONSHIPS – THE KEY CONDUIT

To facilitate this more holistic and productive approach to engagement requires a keen focus on developing the regulatory relationship you enjoy. That regulatory relationship an organisation has with its regulator can be thought of as having two distinct elements.

The primary element is that which the organisation directly drives, engages with, and informs. The secondary element is the data, information, and insight that the regulator acquires through other means, but which helps them form judgements and opinions of the organisation. Thinking about the regulatory relationship

> **Regulatory Relationship**
> The conduit through which the regulator and the regulatee seek to understand each other's position vis-à-vis their respective objectives. This includes considering the ecosystem of insight and information that flows. Some will be formal, some informal, some direct, and some consequential, all of which builds a picture of the organisation

in terms of these primary and secondary elements is helpful, as it reminds us of the importance of stepping back and considering how regulators form their judgements and opinions, which are driven by much more than may seem at first apparent. It also underscores the importance of organisations themselves reading their broader ecosystem, anticipating the messages it may be sending, and placing the whole picture in context in order that it can be discussed and explained. Being able to help regulators by building such a picture and ensuring there are no surprises in what it sees is crucial in building positive and proactive relationships that engender trust and confidence.

The regulatory relationship therefore is the key conduit through which to consider the ecosystem of insight and information flows, some of which will be formal, some informal, some direct, and some consequential, each of which builds a picture of the organisation.

Theory Underscores the Importance of Relationships

Theory provides useful supporting insights on the role and importance of relationships and how important the choices are that organisations take in terms of their success.

Klijn, Edelenbos, Kort and van Twist (2008) emphasised that the higher the value-add of a relationship, the more collaborative such a relationship needed to be. This notion of linking the scale of impact of relationships to the degree of collaboration and attention given to it may seem an obvious linkage, however, it is not always the case that such connections are made and many still conduct regulatory relationships in line minimum standards. Indeed, many have no regulatory relationship strategy at all (see Figure 5.2). Balasubramanian and Tewary (2005) offer the view that collaboration and involvement in relationships should be considered on a case-by-case basis, which offers an approach that can provide a very efficient focus to relationships based on their importance...for which most readers it is suspected, would rank regulatory relationships right up the list. Similarly, from a regulator's perspective, it may be that it chooses how to prioritise the oversight and engagement it has with regulated organisations based on a variety of factors, such as their potential impact, scale, or complexity. Schaeffer and Loveridge (2002) argue that the relationship needs to develop according to organisational needs, again a nod to the importance of organisations considering carefully how they choose to invest in their relationships. Finally, Schaeffer and Loveridge (2002) and Balasubramanian and Tewary (2005) all point to there being no one optimal model to be followed as a blueprint for success, again pointing to the need for organisations to tailor their approach given their unique circumstances. However, as Usher (2004, p.357) points out as a cautionary reminder (something we explore later), there is also one significant variable in the mix when considering how relationships will develop and how successful they may be, and that is that success relies on people and they can be unpredictable.

Emergent Regulatory Relationships are Important Too

Comments so far have assumed that there is some aspect of formal regulatory relationship in place, however, for those organisations that currently operate in unchartered regulatory territory, there is also the worthwhile consideration of what can be thought of as the *emergent relationship*. This relationship covers organisations whose operations to-date aren't governed by a formal regulator for their core operations (although they may be regulated in other more generic areas, such as data protection). As we shall see, these organisations still need to consider their actions in a wider context in order that they can sustain that largely unregulated position, or proactively build positive foundations in preparation for when more formal regulatory oversight may be put in place.

One of the best recent examples of this can be seen in the field of social media in recent years. As some technology companies have launched ever more sophisticated applications offering extensive content sharing with significant market growth achieved in short timescales, some have attracted attention around the world for items such as their alleged lack of sufficient control or social responsibility. This attention has centred on the emergence of scandals, misuse, and poor consumer protection. For example, in the U.K., the Office of Communications (OFCOM), the U.K. telecoms regulator, has outlined potential approaches for social media regulation. This is a direct result of growing unease around the operations of organisations catching the attention of regulators in ways that raise questions about protections that need to be in place. In addition, in the U.S., the Department of Justice (2020) announced its intentions for new legislation that would remove liability protection online platforms currently enjoy under S.230 of the Communications Decency Act, with the department stating:

> The Act had left these organisations *"Immune for a wide array of illicit activity on their services and free to moderate content with little transparency or accountability. Taken together, these reforms will ensure that Section 230 immunity incentivises online platforms to be responsible actors."*

In recognition of this changing landscape for social media and technology companies, even the largest of organisations were recognising the change in relationship now beginning to take shape, including the CEO of Apple, Tim

Cook (Kuchler 2018) who commented on the shortfalls of self-regulation in aspects of the Technology industry:

> *"I'm a big believer in the free market. But we have to admit when the free market is not working, and it hasn't been here. I think it's inevitable that there will be some level of regulation…I think Congress and the Administration at some point will pass something".*
>
> ————————————
>
> Source: Kuchler, H. (2018).

Two years on from his quote and we found Tim Cook (Apple), Jeff Bezos (Amazon), Mark Zuckerberg (Facebook), and Sundar Pichai (Alphabet) all facing scrutiny as part of the U.S. House of Representatives enquiry into competition in the technology industry.

The regulatory relationship therefore can be emergent, where moves are afoot to progress toward a more robust regulatory framework, including regulatory oversight.

Again, even in the context of an emergent regulatory relationship, how organisations approach such developments can be undertaken in a minimalist narrow way aimed at meeting the most basic expectations, or it can be more progressive and broad ranging, setting out with a strategic intent to work closely with regulators for the common good of improved outcomes.

EMERGENT REGULATORY RELATIONSHIPS HAVE IMPLICATIONS   Where potential emergent regulatory relationships are forming, perhaps as regulations are progressing and powers are in the process of being established for regulators through legislative processes, organisations have decisions to make and time to prepare. Not only does new regulatory oversight necessitate that those organisations think about their regulatory strategy and how they will conduct their relationships (see Figure 1.4), oversight will also have implications across many facets of the organisation in terms of how it is configured, led, and driven.

Organisations facing into a new regulatory environment, by way of a few examples, may need to consider:

Participation – At the most fundamental level, an organisation will need to consider whether it intends to continue to participate in the activities and markets concerned. For example, an organisation may focus on key areas it feels it has greatest competence and exit from others. It may expand into new areas where it sees regulatory oversight bringing new opportunities and encouraging a better competitive environment or breaking down protective practices. Or it may choose to exit where it sees the standards are beyond that to which it feels it can attain or sustain its operations. An emergent regulatory environment therefore drives fundamental strategic considerations.

Fees/levies – Regulatory oversight must be paid for, and for many industries this is covered by the fair allocation of the costs of regulatory oversight across industry participants. As emergent regulatory frameworks develop, organisations need to consider the financial costs of regulatory oversight carefully and prepare for its arrival.

Capability – As organisations head toward a new system of regulatory oversight, it is prudent to consider what new capabilities will be required and what investment will be needed. Depending on their starting point, this could necessitate change and investment across a whole host of areas. For example, considering whether existing risk and compliance processes and skills are adequate for a new regulated environment; assessing systems and control capabilities; ensuring governance is appropriate; reviewing the availability, quality, and cadence of organisational reporting; and thinking about some of the more fundamental drivers of business activity and behaviour, such as culture, incentivisation, and the objectives and targets that flow through an organisation. In short, there is a cost of compliance from a capability point of view that needs considering.

Emergent regulatory relationships are important. They allow the organisation to begin a dialogue, begin to form relationships, and begin to understand what a new regulatory environment may entail to allow them to adequately prepare. Even at this early stage, the way an organisation engages and prepares for a new era of regulation and regulatory oversight will provide an interesting perspective from which regulators will begin to form their opinions. Emergent relationships are still relationships after all, and as such, will be subject to all the same considerations we cover in the chapters ahead.

Intermediated Regulatory Relationships

As organisations build their capability over time, it can often be the case that they conclude that aspects of that capability are best served by external third parties. This can be for many reasons, such as seeking to access superior skills, knowledge, and expertise in their industry than the organisation is able to develop internally, or taking advantage of technologies and developments in other fields that it sees as supplementing its capability and improving its product and service offering. For example, it may be that a water utility company relies on external expertise to provide leakage detection, as they seek to improve their performance using the new and emergent technologies of specialist organisations to locate and fix issues. It may be that medical device manufacturing companies rely on the expertise of those who specialise in developing perimeter defences in the protection of their devices from cybercrime, or it may be financial services organisations seeking the services of specialists supplying compliance interpretation, guidance services, and technology infrastructure to support their business operations.

Such a modular approach to building organisational capability can have implications that organisations need to consider carefully. As these organisations often intermediate the relationship with one of your regulators and may well themselves be regulated by the very same regulator, it can be tempting to see them as accountable for your obligations to that regulator's requirements. It is here where it is important to remember that, whilst there may be an intermediated regulatory relationship, the accountabilities for the outcomes for your organisation, including the outcomes of those you trust and incorporate into your organisational build (e.g., external suppliers), will remain with you.

ACCOUNTABILITIES AND RESPONSIBILITIES – IMPORTANT CHOICES   As a regulated organisation, you have the choices on the foundations you build and how you navigate your organisation. The choices you make in terms of what capability you build internally versus those you seek to access externally through suppliers are important ones.

When it comes to your regulator (see Chapters 4, 5, and 6), they will be interested both in the foundations of how you build and run your organisation, and how you exercise a good degree of control over those activities to ensure the right outcomes are achieved (e.g., how you know they are themselves compliant). Where you rely on external parties for critical elements that drive those outcomes for your customers, regulators will be keen to ensure you can demonstrate sufficient levels of expertise and control in those areas to enable you to appropriately manage the activities and supply of all such services in an appropriate and compliant way. In this regard, organisations may delegate (e.g., outsource) responsibility for elements of their organisational capability (e.g., a process or knowledge and expertise supply), however, they may not abdicate their accountability for the results and outcomes of that activity.

INTERMEDIATED REGULATORY RELATIONSHIPS AND YOUR STRATEGY   As organisations consider their broader relationships with their suppliers, it is important that they do this in the context of their regulatory relationship strategy (see Figure 1.4). As they consider their own strategy, they can consider how their relationships (existing or potential) with their suppliers fits in and aligns with that strategy. This is an important step in ensuring that the right partners are selected. For example, does the organisation share or have the same directional approach toward the regulator (indeed do they have a strategy at all?)? Do their objectives toward the regulator align to your own? Does their history provide any indications as to their focus on compliance? Is their posture toward the regulator one that aligns to your strategy? Is it clear what emphasis and investment they make in their regulatory relationship? As you are trusting an organisation to effectively become part of your story to the regulator and part of that ecosystem of the regulatory relationship, are you comfortable that you have the right partner, with the right capability, the right approach, that you can appropriately integrate, manage, and control in a way that protects your brand, reputation, and relationships?

Being clear on your own regulatory relationship strategy and those of your suppliers is an important consideration in an intermediated relationship structure.

THE CASE FOR THIS NEW PERSPECTIVE & THE DRIVERS OF CHANGE

We have covered how regulatory relationships offer a window through which a regulator can assess an organisation against the priorities the regulator has laid out in order to meet its own objectives. Whilst, historically, the picture the regulator saw through this window was dominated by what organisa-tions themselves supplied, this has now changed, given regulators have expanded their sources of insight. Similarly, where regulators may have his-torically been focused on outcomes such as rule adherence, increasingly they are taking a full spectrum view of organisations and the drivers of perfor-mance as well as the outcomes. In doing this, they may consider everything from how organisations structure and govern themselves, to how they drive their business and the culture, leadership, and conduct they foster to assure the right outcomes are generated (points we cover in Chapters 4 and 5).

By way of example, in the financial services industries across many coun-tries, we may all remember the headlines regarding scandals and failures sur-rounding issues ranging from leadership and culture, through to poor conduct and the devastating outcomes these drove. As issue after issue unfolded, so the appetite of stakeholders intensified to ensure the industry was well regulated, with strong regulatory oversight, but most importantly rigorously challenged to fundamentally re-think how they establish and drive their businesses to achieve better outcomes. With such rigorous challenges came an interest in a far broader array of organisational activity that would become part of the fab-ric of relationship expectations and oversight. In other words, the landscape of what the regulator would scrutinise and what became part of the regulatory relationship agenda developed and expanded.

Whilst the example may be financial services, the drivers of change in regulatory relationships cut across many industries, and the implications this has for how regulators now approach their supervision of organisations means organisations have an opportunity to re-think how they consider their strategy and relationship. These drivers raise questions for organisations to consider in terms of how regulators will need to be engaged, informed, and assured in order that they feel comfortable that how the organisation approaches such developments is appropriate, controlled, and rigorous in its execution. Similarly, where failures arise in one industry or organisation, regulators increasingly read across and seek assurances that those under their regula-tory framework do not have the same weaknesses. In this respect, the regula-tory ecosystem that surrounds our relationships has become more diverse and dynamic. Regulators may increasingly probe (or seek the powers to probe) any aspect of an organisation where it feels it could undermine its objectives. Such an approach by regulators takes them right into the fabric of how organ-isations are set up and driven.

This framework provides a new perspective upon which to drive your strategy and relationship, which better prepares organisations for building more effective relationships. In understanding an organisation's regulatory ecosystem, the organisation can consider how each aspect positively or nega-tively impacts the views and opinions held by regulators, and in doing so can calibrate their actions and activities in order to build and proactively engage in the relationship with their regulator.

In today's age of interconnectivity, relationships are more pervasive, more diverse, and more dynamic, making relationship management as much about scanning what is around and ahead of us (both inside and outside our organisations), as it is about interacting in the moment of a supervisory meet-ing. How that full picture comes together is very important in terms of the opinions and judgements of those involved in the relationship...if it is part of the picture, by definition, it should be considered part of the relationship. As one CEO succinctly framed it:

> *"...and the thing I think is very important, is that each organisation needs to think very carefully about how they appear to their regulator".*

That picture the organisation paints in turn can alter the tone and intensity of the relationship, which acts as a catalyst for progressive or regressive interaction.

How we continue to paint the picture our regulator sees will be increasingly important. In the next section, we introduce the framework that will help us explore, consider, and contextualise the ecosystem of our organisation so that we can use this to better inform and shape our strategy and relationships we build.

BUILDING YOUR REGULATORY RELATIONSHIP STRATEGY – ECOSYSTEM FRAMEWORK

What are the components of the *regulatory ecosystem* that can be considered and should inform your strategy and how we engage with regulators? Figure 2.1 provides a view of the core elements of the framework we will use to explore the regulatory ecosystem of an organisation.

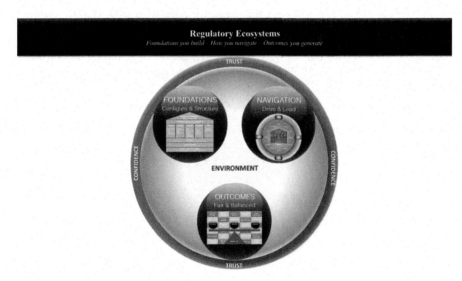

FIGURE 2.1   Regulatory Ecosystems

This will form our core structure of the next few chapters, as it takes a step-by-step look at how an organisation can build trust and confidence with their regulator, through exploring each core element in turn. For each element, in the chapters that follow, we will then drill down into greater detail.

The elements cover the *foundations* an organisation establishes and the way it's configured, how the organisation is *navigated*, driven, and led to achieve its objectives, and the *outcomes* it achieves.

For each building block of the ecosystem framework, we will investigate and consider how it can help us build the picture the regulator sees and help us shape our regulatory relationship strategy. From these building blocks, we develop the strategic story of our organisation for the regulator and feed the regulatory relationship from the organisation's perspective.

As we consider how organisations configure and structure the organisation (lay their foundations), how it is driven and led (navigated), and how it balances that which it produces and generates as a result (outcomes), we also take a look at how the environment in which the organisation operates can dramatically change the course of progress in both positive and negative ways.

Finally, we consider the impact of every element of the regulatory ecosystem on that most important of ingredients, and the basis around which all relationships exist, *trust*. In fact, the importance of trust in regulatory relationships is so important that we start our exploration of the regulatory ecosystem by first considering the role of trust in the next chapter.

REFERENCES

Balasubramanian and Tewary, A. K. (2005), 'Design of Supply Chains: Unrealistic Expectations on Collaboration', Sadhana, Vol. 30, No. 2–3, pp.463–473, 463

Klijn, E. H., Edelenbos, J., Kort, M. and van Twist, M. (2008), 'Facing Management Choices: An Analysis of Managerial Choices in 18 Complex Environmental Public-Private Partnership Projects', International Review of Administrative Sciences, Vol. 74, No. 2, pp.251–282, 251

Kuchler, H. (2018), 'Apple boss says tech industry regulation is inevitable', [online], Financial Times, 19 November 2018, available: https://www.ft.com/content/b8bc0108-eb51-11e8-89c8-d36339d835c0

Schaeffer, P. and Loveridge, S. (2002), 'Toward an Understanding of Types of Public-Private Cooperation', Public Performance and Management Review, Vol. 26, No. 2, pp.169–189, 169

U.S. Department of Justice (2020), 'Justice Department Issues Recommendations For Section 230 Reform', [online], 17 June 2020, available: https://www.justice.gov/opa/pr/justice-department-issues-recommendations-section-230-reform

Usher, N. (2004), 'Outsource or In-house Facilities Management: The Pros and Cons', Journal of Facilities Management, Vol. 2, No. 4, pp.351–9, 351

CHAPTER 3

The Role of Trust in Regulatory Relationship Strategies

CHAPTER SUMMARY

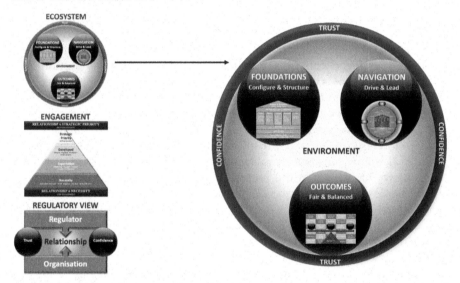

As this section forms the start of our exploration of the *regulatory ecosystem*, we introduce a subject in our framework that encircles all we will discuss in the chapters ahead and is the lifeblood of relationships: trust.

The discussion explores the importance and role of trust as the bedrock of regulatory relationships and considers how research underpins that importance and demonstrates the need for relationships to be fostered and based on mutual trust. Furthermore, we look at what we mean by trust, what we expect when we trust, how it relates to our relationships and how, for organisations, it is a strategic choice with significant consequences where it is lost.

We consider how trust can facilitate or hinder us by making our interactions simpler, our oversight lighter, and our transactions faster where trust exists, whilst having the opposite effect when lost. We demonstrate such

DOI: 10.4324/9781003297963-3

outcomes with real examples taken from across a range of industries that cover the implications that have unfolded where trust has diminished. Here, we see how a loss of trust can take years to rebuild, how confidence is undermined, and how the implications can be much broader than the immediate initial impact. In particular, we consider how organisations need to think carefully not only about *what* they do in pursuit of their organisational objectives, but *how* and *why* taking that path is the correct course in fostering trust, no matter through which stakeholder lens you peer.

Finally, we consider how trust involves judgement and balance, how ethics and morality are interwoven with trustworthiness, and how trust matters across a whole array of interactions and relationships. We discuss how trust develops and builds based on a body of evidence, and how words are not enough, without the support of evidence to underpin and justify trust is warranted.

Trust is introduced right at the outset purposefully, as it threads through everything we consider.

TRUST: THE BEDROCK OF REGULATORY RELATIONSHIPS

Across our daily lives, trust is woven into every aspect of our being on many different levels and in different ways. Where it exists, our daily activities are made considerably simpler, our transactions and use of services are faster and simplicity and speed conspire to help keep costs and process friction low. Therefore, trust enables us. Consider for a moment a couple of examples of just how much we rely on things that surround us every day that are fundamentally underpinned by trust. At the level of our most basic of needs, consider the trust we place in the system of food production and supply that allows us to enjoy our food free of fear of harm and ensures all we need is within easy reach. Consider also how tensions rise when a disruption to that system of supply arrives as we have seen in the recent Covid-19 outbreak. Who would have thought panic buying, food queues that stretch for miles, quotas on what can be purchased, and limits and restrictions on shopping would hit these times? Then consider the trust we place in areas such as the engineering standards of construction, which allow our homes, our daily travel, and our places of work to be safe environments.

Our reliance on systems of trust across a whole variety of relationships is extensive, and where trust fails, the consequences can be significant[1]. Indeed, such is our reliance on systems of trust that our inherent default state of being generally trusting of the world around us can often be used against us. Consider for example the rise in financial crime and the

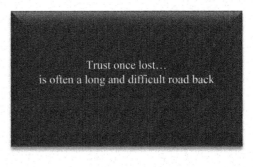

Trust once lost…
is often a long and difficult road back

rise of the *modus operandi* to socially engineer victims into giving away crucial information that fraudsters then use to defraud…trusting the untrustworthy can have consequences. As a result, trust, when lost, is often a long and difficult road back.

Research Highlights the Importance of Trust in Relationships

Research has highlighted the importance of trust. For example, in the field of regulatory relations (Braithwaite and Makkai 1994; Murphy 2004), we see theories discussing the relative merits of approaches to such relationships and their effect on trust. Similarly, the importance of trust has been highlighted in studies by the Dutch National Bank (2015), which recognises that establishing a reasonable sense of openness does not always come naturally for institutions that are engaged during their inspections of behaviour and culture. It reflects that its inspections require the sharing of sensitive information and, in this respect, the Dutch National Bank (2015, p.72) acknowledges that it seeks:

> *"...a middle position between distrust and blind trust". Whilst noting that: "Trust, though complex, is established through relationships. Every interaction is an opportunity to build trust".*

Trust has been argued to be essential for successful cooperation and effectiveness between organisations (e.g., Ring and Van de Ven 1994; Sydow 1998). Mary Parker Follet (1940) also added a useful dimension as she investigated how relationships needed to be fostered, rather than dominated. Follet goes on to discuss the concept of *integration*, a point of finding a third way in which neither side loses, instead including what both *A* wishes and *B* wishes.

These are interesting concepts, as organisations and regulators seek to understand the best ways to work together through the good times and challenges. Indeed, the more aligned organisations and regulators can be on key areas or objectives (e.g., appropriate consumer outcomes), the greater the opportunity for Follet's third way to arise. Regardless of which point of view appeals, such research serves to underline the importance and centrality of trust in relationships, which we will explore a little further next.

What Is Trust and How Does It Relate to Our Relationships?

There are many definitions of trust (for examples, see Rousseau, Sitkin, Burt and Camerer 1998, p.395; Hosmer 1995, pp.379–403), all of which describe those critical aspects that make trust what it is, i.e., the act of relying upon the actions or behaviours of others to do those things we need and expect.

Just as trust is crucial to a whole host of activities in our everyday lives, it is also fundamental to our personal and professional relationships. The way trust relates to our relationships is the same. For example, it can enable and facilitate them or hinder and restrict them. In a professional sense, with our regulators for example, the benefits could be that high levels of trust can provide the positive outcome of regulatory credit, can help reduce the regulatory burden, and can increase the speed of execution, and, as such, it can support the reduction of the cost of regulation overall. However, the stakes are high, and the converse is certainly true that a loss of trust can lead to severe implications for both organisations and industries. Wicks, Berman and Jones (1999, pp.99–100) noted for example, the importance of trust as a strategic choice in stakeholder relationships and its potential to impact on firm performance. Slovic (1993, p.677) also provides an important lesson of history for the development of trust, reflecting on how fragile trust can be: it takes time to build but can be lost very quickly. This is a point we will go onto demonstrate with examples of the disastrous implications that can unfold when trust is lost:

EXAMPLE 1 – THE IMPLOSIVE EFFECT OF LOSING TRUST

Few examples can demonstrate the destruction of trust across an industry like the Global Financial Crisis (G.F.C.), and for this reason, we use this as our core example given the extensive lessons it provides.

What started as a financial crisis broadened into a crisis that engulfed an entire industry and its practices. The result was more than a decade of interventions that left few stones unturned and will be a case study for many years on how to destroy trust and how its path of recovery is a difficult journey to tread.

Those interventions needed to immediately respond to the crises were significant in breadth and scale, as were the interventions aimed at resolving the issues and preventing such a crisis in the future. Next are examples that hopefully bring to life the scale of impact that can result from a loss of trust.

The First Casualty of Confidence...Trust

As the crisis unfolded, financial markets became the first casualty as confidence evaporated, trust plummeted, and markets began to stall. As stories, information, data, and rumour circulated, their impact on confidence reached epidemic proportions, a phenomenon well described by Akerlof and Shiller (2009):

> *"We might model the spread of a story in terms of an epidemic. Stories are like viruses. Their spread by word of mouth involves a sort of contagion. Epidemiologists have developed mathematical models of epidemics, which can be applied to the spread of stories and confidence as well...Just as diseases spread through contagion, so does confidence, or lack of confidence".*

Interventions aimed at restoring trust in the operation of markets across the globe began to emerge to build confidence. In the days and weeks that followed, we saw numerous interventions, two of the largest of which involved the Bank of England lowering the Base Rate to the lowest level in its 300-year history and the commencement of an economic experiment with the introduction of Quantitative Easing to the tune of £375 billion. Whilst interventions were colossal, the impact of this crisis would still result in devastating impacts in nations across the globe. As confidence exited stage left, trust followed, and the void created was filled by consequences all wished to avoid.

Losing Trust Paralyses Commitment with Much Wider Consequences

As confidence fell, the daily transactions and commitments that had fuelled markets, business, and commerce before the crisis suddenly became subject to a rapid reassessment. Governments stepped in, as noted, to support financial markets and keep liquidity flowing, businesses reassessed their investments, and individuals reassessed their spending. As the crisis turned into recession, the combined impact on the real economy quickly began to emerge, which according to King (2016, p.38) saw impacts on productivity and employment and the loss of 10 million jobs across the United States and Europe.

Despite the magnitude of response, the loss of trust had real and significant consequences on economies across the globe, but the consequences did not stop there, they would be felt much wider than in just our economic lives.

A Loss of Trust Has a Ripple Effect...Its Reach Can Be Significant

For some, those tragic consequences involved the loss of their jobs, businesses, and livelihoods. For others, it was loss of their health, marriages, and in the extreme cases, loss of life. The toll was enormous and its reach extensive, as that toll impacted across geographies, generations, and industries. It would prove to be a toll no one would ever wish to see repeated and laid bare how organisations and financial systems can fail. Each of those early days of the crises provided challenges against which convention, experience, academia, business principles, and social responsibility would be tested. Norms became exceptions, improbabilities became likelihoods, historic limits were broken, conventional practices were rewritten, trust became distrust, sales practices became conduct issues, profit became loss, and the funding and liquidity of the financial markets, upon which the promise on every Bank of England note reminds us the importance of, "I promise to pay the bearer on demand....", started to fracture as institutions saw their financial stability break down. Looking back, who could forget the images of sufferance, riots, protests, generations caught in excessive unemployment, and the impact of austerity. This sentiment of the pre- and in-crisis years was captured well by King (2016, p.1), in the opening lines of his book *The End of Alchemy*, which starts with the lines from Charles Dickens' *A Tale of Two Cities*:

> *"It was the best of times, it was the worst of times, it was the age of wisdom, it was the age of foolishness, it was the epoch of "belief", it was the epoch of incredulity..."*

The ripple effects of this crisis were significant in both magnitude and reach.

Losing Trust Has Consequences

The consequences for financial services were extensive, from fundamental questions of protection for those impacted and accountability for those leading failing institutions, to a root-and-branch review of every aspect of how financial services organisations were configured, how they were led, and how they delivered outcomes for stakeholders.

Given the impact of the financial crisis, regulators globally were responding to demands from across stakeholder groups for greater consumer protection, and for tighter regulation to try and prevent such issues in the future. Internationally, the focus was on consumer protection, and at the G20 meeting in October 2011 (O.E.C.D. 2011), high-level principles on Financial Consumer Protection were endorsed by G20 finance ministers and central bank governors.

Such developments touched all aspects of the system, including the regulators where the regulatory relationship approach in the U.K. underwent significant change. The regulatory oversight approach changed in tone, depth of scrutiny, frequency, and focus – all of which aimed at improving the oversight system to reduce the risk of failure. No longer would regulation be a light touch; from here on, all aspects of organisational activity (from how the organisation is set up to how it is led) would be scrutinised where it could potentially lead to consumer detriment.

Whilst the interventions were far reaching and the change in regulatory oversight significant, it would take many years of continued scrutiny and driving of new standards to see the scandals and issues associated with the industry begin to fall. Trust was a slow march and a journey of many, many years.

McDermott (2015) in a speech delivered to the British Banking Association conference in her capacity as the Director of Supervision, Investment, Wholesale and Specialists at the Financial Conduct Authority (F.C.A.), noted the impact of some of the scandals that hit the industry.

> "…as the Governor of the Bank of England has said, [such events] undermines the license of institutions to operate. And if that was not enough – look at the impact on the bottom line. The fines paid by large global banks in the past 7 years top some $235bn. Compensation paid out in relation to IRHP [interest rate hedging product] mis-selling approaches £2bn. That in relation to PPI [payment protection insurance] is approaching £20bn. We need to get better at this".

When an event as significant as the above is considered, it is easy with hindsight to argue why regulation and close regulatory relationships are important. There may be calls to understand why issues in organisations were not surfaced through the relationship or calls for more frequent interactions, more intrusion, more scrutiny, or more sharing of data.

Whilst these may be valid and assist, they offer only a partial solution. At a more fundamental level, it is often the case that the regulatory framework exists to drive certain desirable outcomes. In this respect, whilst the regulatory relationship can facilitate mechanisms that shepherd or compel organisations to move in a certain direction, fundamentally, the accountability for achieving the right outcomes always rests with the organisation itself.

> Whilst the regulatory relationship can facilitate mechanisms that shepherd or compel organisations to move in a certain direction, fundamentally, the accountability for achieving the right outcomes always rests with the organisation itself

Being Trusted Is About What You Do, How You Do It, and the Outcomes That Result

For regulators, ensuring their regulatory objectives are achieved and organisations do not pose a risk to them increasingly means getting a deeper understanding of the organisations they regulate. That understanding can aid the development of trust and can build confidence where the regulator observes good practice in operation. However, the outcomes delivered for those your organisation seeks to serve are the function of a whole series of organisational activities, and whilst the regulatory relationship allows a canular into those activities, we can never expect that the relationship will allow the regulator from a distance to identify all the potential risks to its regulatory objectives for itself…the organisation needs to engage, to disclose, and be open and transparent if this system of regulatory oversight is to work and trust and confidence is to build.

Getting to the right outcomes (that align with regulatory objectives) will fundamentally rest on how organisations set out to achieve their own objectives, how they put in place the right culture, the right values, principles, ethical standards, controls, and governance…that is, the spirit and letter of how they practice in their chosen discipline. The financial crisis laid out a clear example of how a permissive light touch regulatory framework that isn't checked by high standards of organisational self-discipline can lead to poor outcomes. This was well articulated by Bailey (2018), CEO of the F.C.A., when reflecting on the financial crisis:

> *"Prior to the financial crisis, the culture towards the public interest and ethical custom were essentially permissive, to the point of anything goes. In financial services, it was evident in the advocacy of light touch regulation, the view that left to themselves firms would succeed; and to paraphrase, just as a rising tide lifts all boats, so the whole public interest would benefit. It didn't work out that way, and in the wake of the crisis we have had to change the approach to regulation in the public interest".*

As Bailey notes, such events demand a root-and-branch review of the approach to regulation, a part of which is how regulatory relationships are conducted and the expectations on organisations. As part of that overall framework, regulatory relationships have become increasingly important to ensuring issues are anticipated, mitigated, proactively surfaced, and addressed to the satisfaction of all. How these relationships are conducted, therefore, also has the potential to improve matters for an organisation, as parties proactively work together and avoid the potential of increased oversight, intervention, and enforcement.

Trust – The Road Back Is a Long One

In financial services in the U.K., this notion of trust building taking work, time, and in this case, some fundamental industry change was well summarised by the Chairman of the F.C.A., John Griffith Jones in a speech to the *Trust in Banking Conference* at the London Stock Exchange. Here, Jones (2015) raised a series of points that demonstrated that the road had been a long one to that point (more than 8 years) and that the opportunity was approaching to restore public trust as the environment had changed economically and politically.

For the first time, there was a nod toward the environmental factors of economic impact and, more notably, political readiness to accommodate a new direction. These were interesting comments and made clear reference to items we've covered, such as the importance of stakeholders, in this case the power and influence that political will has on the direction of travel in the regulatory world.

Jones made further interesting observations, not least a theme that is well worth holding great store in – that history and experience tell us that trust is fragile, it takes a great deal of effort to build, and is very easily lost. This view is also illustrated in the work previously noted by Slovic (1993), who highlighted how fragile trust can be, how it is created slowly, and easily lost.

Whatever way you describe or remember this important lesson, it serves to remind us that relationships are underpinned by trust and it is the lifeblood of regulatory relationships.

From his reading of the events, Jones went on to describe his priorities in the pursuit of restoration of trust. The first was the linkage of trust to business purpose. Second, he noted behaviour and conduct and, finally, he noted an adequate system of control to seek to prevent or at least detect when things are going wrong. In summing up he noted:

> *"It remains a priority for us to move in step with the industry…this is not in any way a sense of "pendulum" regulation…it is a recognition that IF the firms' behaviour changes for the better, that should allow us to change our regulatory response…synchronization is however key and that requires having a relationship of trust between regulator and regulatee".*

From the outset of the G.F.C., the importance of trust, the impact of its loss, and the imperative to bring about change to enable it to be rebuilt remained a constant theme. It also took many years to arrive at the comments of the F.C.A. Chairman, especially when you consider where we started, which the following quote from the Parliamentary Commission on Banking Standards (2013) in the first volume of its work entitled *Changing Banking for Good* brings to life:

> *"The U.K. banking sector's ability both to perform its crucial role in support of the real economy and to maintain international pre-eminence has been eroded by a profound loss of trust born of profound lapses in banking standards. The Commission makes proposals to enable trust to be restored in banking".*

Trust is therefore a fundamental foundation of a good regulatory relationship. For example, Wicks et al. (1999, pp.99–100) reflected on some of those benefits of high trust in their work, including how trust can facilitate the smooth operation of relationships.

As one industry leader very succinctly put it to me in discussions on the subject:

> *"An effective regulatory relationship is one which is built on mutual trust".*

It takes work and time, but having a foundation of trust from which to base your interactions with the regulator is the ideal starting point.

What the Crisis Taught Us

Financial services provide so many lessons on the importance and role of trust in our relationships.

Once trust leaves, our confidence in those relationships generally follows. Commitments we may have made based on trust get questioned and progress stalls. The ramifications of a loss of trust, are usually much wider than we might expect. Like a pebble in a pond, the first splash of the crisis, as painful as it was, led to many ripples of implications over a prolonged period. As layer after layer of closer inspection of the industry took place, regulators discovered that *what* some organisations had built was in places deficient, *how* some organisations were being navigated on occasions drove the wrong behaviours, and the *outcomes* that some were generating at times were unfair and detrimental. For trust to be restored, all such areas needed to be sound and the foundations upon which to stand needed to be firm – that involved having confidence in the organisation construct, how it is led and driven, and the outcomes it produces. As the years passed by, unfortunately many organisations fell short and billions of pounds in fines, redress, remediation, and a rethink unfolded. A period of *renovation* took hold of organisations, their navigators were replaced or refocused and outcomes were scrutinised. More than a decade and billions of dollars later, global financial institutions have learned that their regulator is a key part of their success or failure.

EXAMPLE 2 – TRUST, VALUE, AND REPUTATIONS

Whereas the above case study represents issues that cut across activities the length and breadth of the banking industry, next we switch industries and provide a short, more specific, example of how one issue that undermines trust in a fundamental way can devastate an organisation and raise questions of industry-wide practice.

Lost Trust – That Will Be £13 Billion

The admission by Volkswagen in September 2015 (Boston and Sloat 2015) regarding software that could allegedly defeat U.S. emission tests, sent shock waves through the industry and had a significant impact on the business. Headlines placed the magnitude of the admission into context[2] and, for the industry and the organisation, it became immediately visible. Shares in Volkswagen fell 20% between the 18th and 21st of September, wiping £13 billion off the market capitalisation of the company and placing the industry under suspicion, which resulted in a wider fall in carmaker shares. In addition to the immediate market impact on the company and having admitted to a potential 11 million cars being affected by this technology, Volkswagen was ordered to recall nearly half a million cars in the United States after it admitted to the U.S. regulator, the Environmental Protection Agency, that there had been *defeat devices* fitted to their cars in an attempt to bypass environmental standards. Furthermore, upon receiving the admission, the Environmental Protection Agency immediately started procuring vehicles from other manufacturers to assess whether this was isolated or an industry-wide practice. Trust in the company's products and assertions regarding performance of their vehicles plummeted.

Lost Trust – Potential Sanction, Fines, Warranty Costs, Prosecution, and Class Action

The story did not stop there for Volkswagen, having sustained a significant impact on its share price, the reality of the implications to come were stark. Potential regulatory fines, warranty costs, possible criminal prosecution of executives, class-action claims against the company, a German government investigation, and brand damage, all had yet to impact the business.

The implications were significant and so too was the fact that the Chief Executive proclaimed his deep sorrow that trust had been broken (Kretchmer 2015).

From a regulator's viewpoint, where significant issues arise, there will of course be the consideration of whether such an issue is specific to an organisation or is an industry-wide practice. As noted above, the move of the U.S. Environmental Protection Agency to procure vehicles after the Volkswagen issues is a good example of a regulator moving quickly to establish the extent of an issue.

EXAMPLE 3 – THE IMPACT ON TRUST ISN'T ALWAYS OF YOUR OWN MAKING

The impact on an industry or organisation of a loss of trust isn't always of their making. For example, the rise and impact of terrorism around the world has seen the airline industry having to rethink air travel protection and security. As trust in security protection systems and processes fell, new standards of security were implemented to rebuild trust, resulting in disruption for millions of travellers around the world.

Similarly, the recent Covid-19 pandemic, as we will see in Chapter 8, has reset the bar on trust across many aspects of our daily lives, from trust in our food supply chain, to trust in the level of protection for workers. Some of the most fundamental of our taken-for-granted and trusted processes and protections have warranted a reassessment of our trust in their ability to deliver for us.

Where our trust is given in areas that fundamentally affect our basic human needs, such as our health, safety, and wellbeing, so our sensitivity to items that undermine the basis of that trust are heightened and the implications can be significant for the organisations that fall short.

EXAMPLE 4 – OUR LEVEL OF TRUST IS SENSITIVE TO THE RISKS INVOLVED

The basic staples of food and water, where our health relies on a significant system of trust, occasionally see issues where organisations stray from the standards that should bind regulatory and commercial interests. Here, our trust in an organisation's standards that protect us is of such importance that our sensitivity to the implications of increased risks is heightened.

When trust breaks down, the commercial and regulatory implications can be significant, as Southern Water found when it was handed a record penalty of £126m by its U.K. regulator OFWAT (B.B.C. 2019). However, of more significance are the questions such events leave in terms of whether we can trust such organisations to meet our expectations in the future and whether oversight and controls are sufficient.

The case of Southern Water demonstrates the regulator's willingness to extend record penalties where organisations fall short of the required standards.

THE DIMENSIONS OF TRUST, ETHICS, AND MORALITY…A CHAIN REACTION

Trust does not simply arrive, it is generally built, earned, nurtured, and reinforced through actions and activities that form a foundation of evidence that the right outcomes will materialise. In this respect, trust is, therefore, not about an event, not transactional, but as you may expect given the book you are reading, it is about the relationship and the consistency of what flows from it in terms of outcomes.

Figure 3.1 demonstrates these points, with the example of how rebuilding trust can be undermined where inconsistency exists between what is said and the outcomes that materialise.

Every journey begins with a first step, and along the way there will always be signals to guide and inform as to whether the path you are treading is the right one for your destination. For financial services in the U.K., that journey to the rebuilding of trust with the regulator faced a significant complicating factor. The corrosiveness of trying to re-establish trust, whilst issues challenging trust continually surfaced and undermined its basis (e.g., P.P.I., L.I.B.O.R., F.O.R.E.X. scandals).

Against this backdrop, it can be very difficult for a regulator to trust that significant issues are behind the industry when there is example after example of that not being the case. One individual made this point well as they were attempting to demonstrate to the regulator that steps that had been taken laid much better foundations. Their reflection was as follows regarding the regulator reaction:

"I don't want to use the word mistrust…I think they (the regulator) felt, hmm, I have heard a lot of this stuff before".

In summary, the foundations for trust need to be sound to commence building!

FIGURE 3.1   Trust Building on a Corroding Base, First Fix the Foundations

To achieve the right outcomes from a balanced stakeholder perspective will likely involve judgements on what is appropriate, acceptable, moral, ethical (see Figure 3.2), proportionate, and balanced given any situation an individual or organisation faces.

> *"Business ethics is the application of ethical values to business behaviour. Business ethics is relevant both to the conduct of individuals and to the conduct of the organisation as a whole. It applies to any and all aspects of business conduct, from boardroom strategies and how companies treat their employees and suppliers to sales techniques and accounting practices".*
>
> *"Ethics goes beyond the legal requirements for a company and is, therefore, about discretionary decisions and behaviour guided by values".*

FIGURE 3.2   Institute of Business Ethics (2020)

In this respect, moral and ethical judgements are connected considerations in the development of trust. Trustworthiness is, therefore, also about a commitment to principles and values. It's about ensuring people, organisations, and institutions deliver the outcomes that are expected and understood by those who will rely on them.

For those organisations that place their ethical goals and objectives front and centre with their brand, great care is needed to ensure every part of the organisation, including outsourcing arrangements and supply chains, reflect the standards expected[3].

On the flip side, whilst trust generally doesn't just materialise, it is often quicker to lose than it is to build. Any number of the examples that have been highlighted provide a subtext of the wider implications of the loss of trust and the impact it has on the reputation of the organisation or individuals concerned.

For trust to be a strong bonding agent upon which we can rely, the morality of outcomes and an alignment of expected ethical behaviour need to connect. Whilst the overarching objectives of the parties may differ in how they get to an outcome, there needs to be a shared set of acceptable parameters within which the parties are expected to function. When that bond of trust is broken, the interaction may break down as one or both parties lose sight of what are the acceptable bounds of behaviour and outcomes.

Andrew Bailey (2018), Chief Executive of the F.C.A. positioned very well how trust has a moral and ethical dimension to it:

> *"Trustworthiness demands 2 things: knowledge and skill; and good intentions and honesty. One of these is more technical in nature, the other more moral and ethical. From time to time I receive quite passionate advocacy that, particularly for banking, we should turn back the clock to a golden age when the entry qualification was to pass banking exams. Up to some point of course knowledge and skill matter, but the distinction drawn with good intentions and honesty demonstrates that there is more to it to be trusted in financial services, or any walk of life".*

For financial services in the U.K., as with other countries, the loss of trust has been a hard road to tread as the industry has attempted to recover the consumer's faith in the industry. The regulator has been proactive in messaging the nuances of the fundamental drivers it expects to underpin the functioning of organisations, and trust has been high up on that agenda.

This long road and the significance of the challenges faced for financial services in the U.K. were summarised well by McDermott (2015) at the British Bankers Association Conference, as she reflected on the attempts to change culture and rebuild trust against a backdrop of issues in the industry that continued to emerge such as L.I.B.O.R. and Foreign Exchange[4].

Situations such as these also raise broader questions of openness, transparency, culture, and control. As many regulators rely to some degree on self-disclosure, that is, to compel firms within their principles of regulation to disclose matters that it would be reasonable to expect a regulator would wish to know (for example, in financial services in the U.K., the industry regulator the F.C.A. has Principle 11 [F.C.A. 2018] along with the Fundamental Rule 7 from the Prudential Regulation Authority, "Fundamental Rules and Principles For Business" 2016). The question naturally arises for the regulator as to why such matters had not been brought to their attention much earlier given the practices in play and the risks they posed. Those questions could be about the openness and transparency of disclosure, they could be about a lack of control that such issues were not discovered, and they could be about the culture and what behaviours it tolerates. For trust to exist, regulators need to know organisations navigate their way appropriately with an appropriate cultural compass in place that drives the right expectations and results in the right behaviours and outcomes.

TRUST MATTERS ACROSS MANY DIMENSIONS

When we pause and consider all the relationships we as individuals engage in that involve trust at some level, we soon accumulate a significant list. Organisations are no different and leaders must balance a variety of objectives and satisfy stakeholders whilst building trust in the organisation and what it achieves.

As well as at an individual and organisational level, our trust relationships operate at other levels too, such as our trust in government or our trust in the functioning of the economy. Trust relationships appear to be everywhere and their importance is consistently high on the list of priorities. From an economic standpoint, Angela Gurría (2009) described trust as the "spinal cord of economics" and Tonkiss (2009) noted its importance in promoting economic efficiency. From a government perspective King (2016, p.10) also placed trust central to economic operation, whilst also providing a useful historic context on the operation and primacy of the importance of trust in authorities (such as government).

Trust matters, and it appears to have a long lineage of importance. It filters through our personal relationships, our professional relationships, and throughout the teachings, rules, and regulations with which we engage. When trust breaks down, all which sits on the foundation of trust can be fragile, including the relationships with which we surround ourselves.

Trust, as we have seen, has high stakes. It is often tied to ethical and moral judgements and knits itself through the very fabric of organisational life. Where it fails, we have seen the consequences and how impactful they can be on organisations: the brand and reputation aspect, the punitive notion of fines, and the friction caused in every dynamic of operation where speed slows, and costs rise. Across all that organisations do, they are fundamentally moulding the foundation for trust with their stakeholders, including their regulator(s). What you do, how you do it, and the outcomes you produce, can be a tax in that ecosystem or a dividend when it comes to trust and the fundamental building of relationships. What it cannot be is ignored, as demonstrated by Champ (2015) when discussing the importance of building trust in relationships with your regulator, in this case the U.S. Securities and Exchange Commission (S.E.C.):

"When firms were not known to the SEC and they had an issue of some type that involved the SEC, it put the company in a difficult spot. Members of the Board and management of such firms would scramble to get control of the situation and convince SEC staff that compliance or other procedures were adequate, but they faced an uphill battle because they did not have a relationship with regulators".

Norm Champ, Author and Former S.E.C. Director of the Division of Investment Management. Published on the Harvard Law School Forum on Corporate Governance.

In addition, the importance of good conduct to building trust and the centrality of trust in well-functioning markets is captured well by McDermott (2015):

"...the lessons of the last few years illustrate clearly that firms need to take proactive steps to improve conduct. Without a firm foundation in identifying the conduct risks inherent in your businesses, it will be hard to manage conduct, let alone show us, and others that it is being managed...most firms now understand the benefit of good conduct in terms of building customer trust and analyst confidence...trust is, and always has been, at the heart of financial markets and we need to ensure that it is restored and renewed".

Trust demands balance across different stakeholder needs and business objectives, it demands to be protected at all costs, and it demands attention if it is to be developed. As we see next, trust arises because of evidence that informs it and is adjusted based upon the observations and experiences of those who wish to rely on it.

BUILDING THE TRUST PICTURE

Trust resides in a whole array of situations and interactions, across all facets of our organisational engagements and across stakeholders. Every interaction will have an influence on trust, either reinforcing or undermining its position. Trust, therefore, is not something that can be thought of as transactional, it is about relationships, about *joining the dots* of evidence, and about how *the sum of the parts* that come together to build a picture on whether an individual, an organisation, or, indeed, an industry can be trusted with any particular situation. Trust builds based on a body of evidence; it is tested, and it is adjusted based upon the observations of those seeking to engage in a trust relationship. As we consider our ecosystem, we can consider how the messages and information that flow from the vast array of sources influence the basis of trust. For example, it is entirely possible to have a good relationship with your regulator and get on well in your personal interactions as you fill them with confidence of how well you treat your customers and the good outcomes they benefit from. However, if your organisation's interactions with its customers do not live up to that picture you paint, it is very likely that evidence will challenge and test whether the trust afforded through those personal relationships is justified…i.e., are your words truly reflective of your actions? This effect can also happen on many levels, for example, should an industry try to convince its regulator the industry is in good shape or has turned its fortunes around to head off further regulation or regulatory intervention, such efforts are likely to fail if, as time passes, continued industry-wide issues plague the organisations. Indeed, it is likely that such a situation would only exacerbate regulatory concerns through demonstrating that senior leaders in the industry appear not to have a good understanding of the situation the organisations face given the problems that continue to arise. Where relationships are strained and trust is in short supply, the tensions and work such a situation can create was captured well by one Director:

> *"I have witnessed what I would call a strained relationship between a firm and the regulator, where neither party trusted each other; as in all relationships where this attitude exists, it creates tension and additional work for both parties".*

In short, words are not enough. Demonstrating and evidencing that you have set your organisation up well and engrained a sound strategy and culture (firm foundations) and that it is driven by skilled and capable leadership that are doing the right things, the right way, (appropriate navigation) and for the right outcomes for consumers and broader stakeholders (balanced outcomes), are the fundamental starting points. As we shall see in later chapters, the sources of insight that allow a regulator a window into an industry and its participants are expanding. For organisations that set themselves up well and operate in the flow of the spirit and letter of regulatory compliance, the foundations for trust building begin to form.

Given the events of the past across industries, regulators are using these broader sources of insight to look right across an organisation's environment, including, to a far greater degree, the individuals operating within it. Laws, rules, best practice, and principles are good foundations, however, those same foundations still rely on the character and integrity of those who use them, as captured by former Chair of the U.S. Federal Reserve Alan Greenspan (2005):

> *"The Corporate scandals of recent years have clearly shown that the plethora of laws of the past century have not eliminated the less savoury side of human behaviour…. Rules cannot substitute for character".*

This chapter explored the importance and role of trust as the bedrock of regulatory relationships and how, for organisations, it is a strategic choice with significant consequences and a long road back where it is lost. Upcoming chapters build on this and explore the importance of each element of the ecosystem and its impact on regulatory relationship trust. We will look at the importance of ensuring your regulator understands and can feel confident in *what* you have built, *how* you use what you have built appropriately (navigate, drive, and lead), and *why* resulting outcomes (outcomes and how you progress and develop) are appropriate and balanced across organisational stakeholder objectives. We also consider how ensuring the regulator is well informed is fundamental to demonstrating that their trust and confidence in the organisation and its leadership is both warranted and continues to flourish.

NOTES

1. C.f. The following regulatory findings provide background reading on published historic sanctions and prosecutions in areas related to this subject. D.O.J. (2017), "Volkswagen AG Agrees to Plead Guilty and Pay $4.3 Billion in Criminal and Civil Penalties; Six Volkswagen Executives and Employees are Indicted in Connection with Conspiracy to Cheat U.S. Emissions Tests"; Ofwat (2019), "PN 12/19 Southern Water to pay £126m following Ofwat investigation"; F.C.A. (2013), "Final Notice 'AXA Wealth Services Ltd".
2. C.f. Sharman (2015) & Kretchmer (2015), for examples of how reporting captured the challenges faced.
3. C.f. The following references provide background reading in areas related to this subject. Financial Reporting Council (2020), "Decision Notice – Grant Thornton & Conviviality – July 2020"; Janiaud (2020), "Boohoo Shares Plunge On 'Unacceptable' Worker Revelations"; O'Connor (2018), "Dark Factories: Labour Exploitation In Britain's Garment Industry"; Jackson, P. (2020), "Time Critical – Boohoo Is Caught In An Ethical Crossfire".
4. See note 4 of Chapter 1, which includes a series of examples around this subject, including example references relating to the issues of L.I.B.O.R. and Foreign Exchange.

REFERENCES

Akerlof, G.A. and Shiller, R.J. (2009), 'Animal Spirits – How Human Psychology Drives The Economy, and Why it Matters for Global Capitalism', Oxford: Princeton, p.56

B.B.C. News Report (2019), 'Southern Water punished over 'shocking wastewater spills', [online], 25 June 2019, available: https://www.bbc.co.uk/news/business-48755329

Bailey, A. (2018), 'Trust and ethics – a regulator's perspective', [online], Financial Conduct Authority,16 October 2018, available: https://www.fca.org.U.K./news/speeches/andrew-bailey-trust-ethics-regulators-perspective

Bank of England, Prudential Regulation Authority (2016), 'Fundamental Rules and Principles For Business', [online], January 2016, available: https://www.bankofengland.co.uk/-/media/boe/files/prudential-regulation/new-bank/fundamentalruleprinciples

Boston, W. and Sloat, S. (2015), 'Volkswagen Emissions Scandal Relates to 11 Million Cars', [online], Wall Street Journal, 22 September 2015, available: https://www.wsj.com/articles/volkswagen-emissions-scandal-relates-to-11-million-cars-1442916906

Braithwaite, J. and Makkai, T. (1994), 'Trust and Compliance', Policy and Society, Vol. 4, pp.1–12

Champ, N. (2015), 'Building effective relationships with regulators', [online], Harvard Law School, 22 October 2015, available: https://corpgov.law.harvard.edu/2015/10/22/building-effective-relationships-with-regulators/

Dutch National Bank (2015), 'Supervision of behaviour and culture', [online], available: https://www.dnb.nl/media/1gmkp1vk/supervision-of-behaviour-and-culture_tcm46-380398-1.pdf

Financial Conduct Authority (F.C.A.) (2013), 'Final Notice – AXA Wealth Services Ltd ("AXA")', [online], 12 September 2013, available: https://www.fca.org.uk/publication/final-notices/axa-wealth-services-ltd.pdf

Financial Conduct Authority (F.C.A.) (2018), 'Principles For Businesses', [online], available: https://www.handbook.fca.org.uk/handbook/PRIN/2/?view=chapter

Financial Reporting Council (2020), 'Decision Notice – Grant Thornton & Conviviality – Jul 2020', [online], available: https://www.frc.org.uk/search?searchtext=grant+thornton+sanction&searchmode=anyword&page=2

Follet, M.P. Metcalf H.C. and Urwick, L. (eds.) (1940), 'Dynamic Administration', Harper and Row, New York

Greenspan, A. (2005), 'Remarks by Chairman Alan Greenspan', [online], Wharton School, University of Pennsylvania, 15 May 2005, available: https://www.federal-reserve.gov/boarddocs/speeches/2005/20050515/default.htm

Gurría, A. (2009), 'Responding to the Global Economic Crisis – OECD's Role in Promoting Open Markets and Job Creation', [Online], 21 May 2009, available: http://www.oecd.org/tad/benefitlib/respondingtotheglobaleconomiccrisisoecdsrolein-promotingopenmarketsandjobcreation.htm

Hosmer, L. T. (1995), 'Trust: The Connecting Link Between Organisational Theory and Philosophical Ethics', The Academy of Management Review, Vol. 20, No. 2, pp.379–403

Institute of Business Ethics (2020), 'What is Business Ethics', [online], available: https://www.ibe.org.U.K./knowledge-hub/what-is-business-ethics.html

Jackson, P. (2020), 'Time Critical – Boohoo is Caught in an Ethical Crossfire', Investors Chronicle, 31 July–6 Aug, pp.20–21

Janiaud, A. (2020), 'Boohoo Shares Plunge on 'Unacceptable' Worker Revelations', Investors Chronicle, 10 July–16 July, p.6

Jones, J. G. (2015), 'Chairman's Speech to the Trust in Banking Conference', [online], Financial Conduct Authority, 22 October 2015, available: https://www.fca.org.uk/news/speeches/chairmans-speech-trust-banking-conference

King, Sir M. (2016), 'The End of Alchemy – Money, Banking and the Future of the Global Economy', Little, Brown, London, p.1, p.10

Kretchmer, H. (2015), 'The man who discovered the Volkswagen emissions scandal', [online], B.B.C., 13 October 2015, available: https://www.bbc.co.uk/news/business-34519184

McDermott, T. (2015), 'Wholesale Markets and Risk: FEMR and Beyond', British Bankers Association Conference, [online], Financial Conduct Authority, 24 July 2015, available: https://www.fca.org.uk/news/speeches/wholesale-conduct-risk

Murphy, K. (2004), 'The Role of Trust in Nurturing Compliance: A Study of Accused Tax Avoiders', Law and Human Behaviour, Vol. 28, pp.187–209

O'Connor, S. (2018), 'Dark Factories: Labour Exploitation in Britain's Garment Industry', [online], Financial Times, 17 May 2018, available: https://www.ft.com/content/e427327e-5892-11e8-b8b2-d6ceb45fa9d0

Ofwat (2019), 'PN 12/19 Southern water to pay £126m following Ofwat investigation', [online], available: https://www.ofwat.gov.uk/pn-12-19-southern-water-to-pay-126m-following-ofwat-investigation/

Organisation for Economic Co-operation and Development (O.E.C.D.) (2011), 'G20 High-Level Principles on Financial Consumer Protection', [online], October 2011, available: https://www.oecd.org/daf/fin/financial-markets/48892010.pdf

Parliamentary Commission on Banking Standards (2013), 'Changing Banking for Good', Vol. 1, London, The Stationery Office, p.8, 57

Ring, P. S. and Van de Ven, A. H. (1994), 'Developmental Processes of Cooperative Interorganisational Relationships', Academy of Management Review, Vol. 19, No. 1, pp.90–118

Rousseau, D. M., Sitkin, S. B., Burt, R. S. and Camerer, C. (1998), 'Not so Different After All: A Cross Discipline View of Trust', Academy of Management Review, Vol. 23, No. 3, p.395

Sharman, A. (2015), 'Volkswagen Emission Test Cheating Rocks Europe's Car Manufacturers', Financial Times, 22 September 2015, p.1, 19

Slovic, P. (1993), 'Perceived Risk, Trust and Democracy', Risk Analysis, Vol. 13, No. 6, p.677

Sydow, J. (1998), 'Understanding the Constitution of Interorganisational Trust' in C. Lane and R. Bachmann (eds.), Trust Within and Between Organisations, Conceptual Issues and Empirical Applications. Oxford: Oxford University Press

Tonkiss, F. (2009), 'Trust, Confidence and Economic Crisis', Intereconomics, Vol. 44, No. 4, pp.196–202

U.S. Department of Justice (D.O.J.) (2017), 'Volkswagen AG Agrees to Plead Guilty and Pay $4.3 Billion in Criminal and Civil Penalties; Six Volkswagen Executives and Employees are Indicted in Connection with Conspiracy to Cheat U.S. Emissions Tests', [online], 11 January 2017, available: https://www.justice.gov/opa/pr/volkswagen-ag-agrees-plead-guilty-and-pay-43-billion-criminal-and-civil-penalties-six

Wicks, A., Berman, S. and Jones, T. (1999), 'The Structure of Optimal Trust: Moral and Strategic Implications', The Academy of Management Review, Vol. 24, No. 1, pp.99–100, 108

CHAPTER **4**

Foundations
Establishing Trust in What You Build

CHAPTER SUMMARY

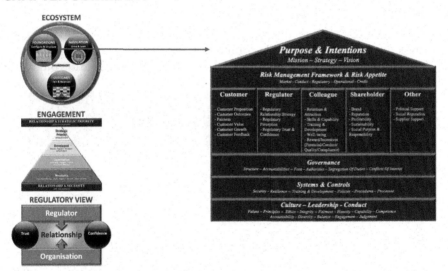

In this chapter, we briefly introduce and explore the foundations section of our framework. Here we see how the fundamental foundations an organisation establishes can have a significant impact on the outcomes it achieves for stakeholders and the environment in which it operates. We argue that ensuring regulators understand your organisation's foundations is central to building trust and confidence and will be an area of increasing scrutiny by regulators keen to understand the internal as well as external risks facing organisations that could impact their regulatory objectives.

We consider how an organisation's purpose and objectives, its attitude toward and appetite for risk, its approach to stakeholders, governance systems and controls, or the culture, leadership, and conduct it fosters, are increasingly scrutinised by regulators that see the significant risks inherent in organisations that are *wired up* inappropriately. Given the potential impact, we consider how regulators challenge how organisations are configured, driven, and led, and

DOI: 10.4324/9781003297963-4

the implications that has in terms of how organisations need to think about their strategy and relationship.

Whilst we briefly explore each element of the organisational foundations and setup here, we also in the next chapter delve deeper into those aspects of the organisation that fundamentally drive its direction and how it is navigated. Areas such as strategy, culture, and leadership whilst introduced here, are given greater consideration in the chapter that follows due to the way they permeate and influence all aspects of organisational performance.

Our starting point is the organisational foundation you lay, and how it sets the stage for how we approach our strategy and relationship with regulators. This is a good place to begin our journey around the organisational ecosystem, as foundations can provide the platform for stability to all you build upon them, including your regulatory relationship. Set things up correctly, and you have the foundations for a good start and a basis for trust and confidence to build – lay them inappropriately, and before long, all you build upon them will begin to expose cracks that can undermine your progress.

FOUNDATIONS – A TOUR OF WHAT YOU HAVE BUILT THROUGH A REGULATOR'S LENS

To help us navigate this section on the foundation organisations build for their business, we introduce a simple framework (Figure 4.1) to explain linkages and relationships across organisations – the organisational building blocks.

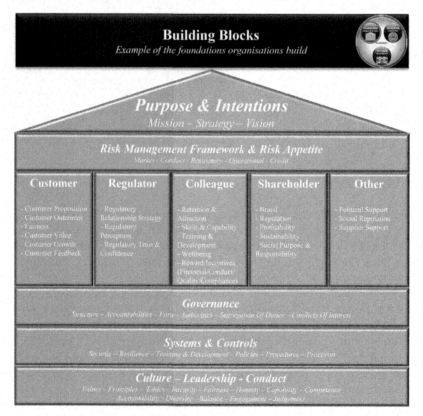

FIGURE 4.1   Organisational Building Blocks

Using this framework, we will briefly discuss examples (for illustration purposes) of the common elements that underpin organisations and consider *why* regulators may be interested in them and, therefore, *what* organisations should consider when thinking about their strategy and relationship approach. The organisational story around how it is *wired up* is important to regulators as, fundamentally, risks to regulatory objectives are inherently linked to the activities and actions of organisations. Ensuring organisations are heading in the right direction, and across the key facets of what fuels and assures appropriate outcomes, is therefore of increasing importance to them. If you want your regulator to have trust in your organisation, you need to ensure you have a firm basis upon which it can be built, and how you set your organisation up for success is that fundamental foundation stone you lay. Next, we look at each element of an organisational *build*, starting with its purpose and intentions (Figure 4.2) as the driving forces behind the organisation.

Purpose and Intentions

All organisations have a purpose and intention in their sights around which they organise their resources and efforts as they set out in pursuit of them.

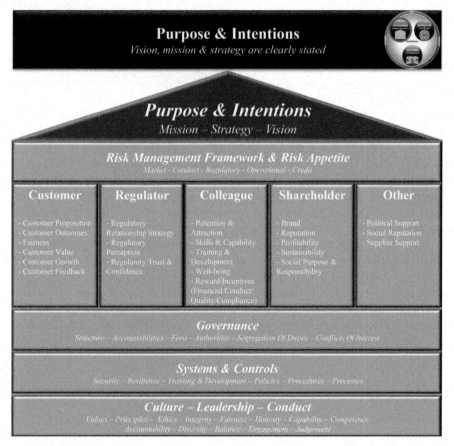

FIGURE 4.2   Purpose and Intentions

Organisations traditionally have laid such ambitions out in *mission statements, visions, and strategies*, whilst some articulate their purpose and intentions in other ways. Regardless of the articulation approach, the common thread remains that organisations take whatever resources they have and direct them at achieving something that has become their focus of attention in terms of what they wish to achieve…we will simply refer to that point of focus as their *purpose and intentions.*

What organisations seek to achieve is of interest to regulators. Not only does it give a clear indication of the organisation's focus, it also allows regulators to consider that focus in the context of their own regulatory objectives (alignment or otherwise) as well as consider how that focus may drive their actions and activities. For example, if an organisation were to appear skewed toward an aggressive market share and profit focus, regulators may wish to look more closely at how the organisation was seeking to achieve this and whether it risked being detrimental across other measures, such as, to consumers through aggressive sales practices, sacrificing safety standards through aggressive cost containment, or environmental impact through a lack of investment.

Given an organisation's purpose and intentions sets out the direction it intends to head, regulators will increasingly wish to understand that direction, understand how organisations intend to achieve those intentions, and consider the implications this may have. Organisations, therefore, have an opportunity to build into their  strategy how they intend to ensure their regulator is well informed of their organisation's purpose and intent and how they will be kept informed of progress. As the strategic path to realising your vision of the future is likely to have twists and turns along the way, keeping the regulator informed of progress, what has changed, how the road in front of you is changing, and what that means in terms of calibrating your strategy becomes key, as it provides contextualisation to the actions and activities regulators will see the organisation take.

As the organisation executes its strategy, it will do so with a clear picture of what its risk appetite is across a whole series of measures. We turn to this next (Figure 4.3), given that whatever your organisation's mission and vision of the future it wishes to create, and no matter how comprehensive your strategy to get you there, there will be risks to identify, to understand, to mitigate against, and control within acceptable boundaries. What appetite organisations have for risk and how they manage the risk they endure along their strategic journey will, therefore, be a key area regulators will wish to understand.

Risk Appetite

Risk is an integral part of our daily lives. On an individual level, we all have our own *attitude* toward and *appetite* for risk, and we develop our capability for *identifying, assessing,* and *monitoring* the risks around us and *adjusting* our *actions* to keep ourselves comfortable with the risks we run. Organisations are no different, and clearly articulate their risk appetite in the context of the strategy they are executing as well as establishing frameworks to manage them.

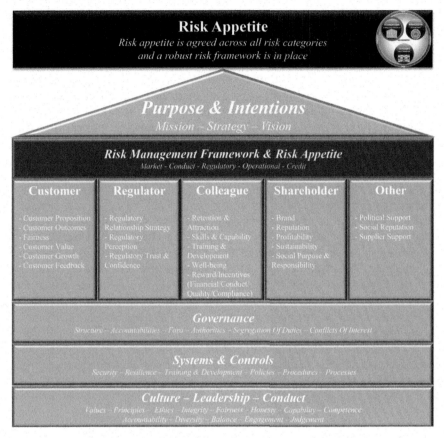

FIGURE 4.3   Risk Appetite

Being clear on their *attitude* toward risk and articulating that in terms of a statement of *appetite* provides clear markers against which to consider the risks they are prepared to endure as they progress. Combining this with robust *monitoring* and tolerance triggers that allow organisations to *adjust actions* to ensure the organisation remains within acceptable bounds of risk are key.

Across different industries and organisations, risk appetites can vary significantly, however, as you would expect, an organisation's attitude toward and appetite for risk will clearly be of interest to regulators. Here, the regulator's picture of the organisation is enriched, as it now places the organisation's strategy in the context of the risks it articulates in terms of its appetite.

This combined view of what the organisation's purpose & intentions are, along with its risk appetite in pursuit of it, provides key information on where the organisation is heading and what risk it is willing to take to get there

This can be a revealing picture, as not only can it see what risks the organisation is considering (comprehensive? realistic? aligned to risks the regulator sees?), but it also provides a view of the risk it is willing to endure (risk appetite expanding or contracting? realistic? balanced and reasonable?). This combined view of what the organisation's *purpose and intentions* are, along with its *risk appetite* in pursuit of them, provides key information on where the organisation is heading and what risk it is willing to take to get there. Already, our foundations are informing the regulator and allowing them to form their views on the reasonableness of the journey the organisation intends to take. The importance of keeping the regulator informed of the direction you intend to take, the risks you are willing to take in that endeavour, and how you are progressing as your journey unfolds was captured well by one industry leader:

"I put myself in the regulator's shoes and think about what they need to know before it happens…we must remove surprises and be on the ball. So that means sharing the strategy and the actions in pursuit of it. Being clear on the risk appetite that is inherent and demonstrating how you are measuring and tracking those things. That strategic view gives insight into how the company's mind is working as it scans the future, how it is challenging that the strategy is fit for purpose, what new risks it is identifying and how it seeks to manage that risk. In particular, keeping the regulator informed and in the debate is key, which means being ready to explain things that you didn't expect to happen, not pretending abnormal items are normal and being up front on the challenges such items pose and what you will do…and of course, how that will feed back into your strategy and risk appetite".

As a stakeholder, this view clearly puts the regulator front and centre in ensuring they are kept informed, considered in terms of their needs (anticipating what they need to know and standing in their shoes), and valued in terms of their views and input (keeping them in the debate and ready to explain things). In terms of strategy, organisations need to consider how they wish to build their relationships. Time spent proactively engaging so your regulator understands the course you are charting and how you are navigating the risks along the way can be time very well spent. Not only does it build a basis of understanding on which both parties to the relationship can build, but it can have other benefits, such as avoiding surprises and misunderstandings that lead to both organisations committing valuable resources to items that could have been avoided or intrusive interventions where misunderstandings fall in areas of significant concern and focus of your regulator[1].

Whilst we have focused on the regulator here as a key stakeholder, next, we widen our scope and consider stakeholders more broadly (Figure 4.4) and how their interests form part of the story the regulator will wish to understand.

Stakeholders

In Chapter 1, we took a look at the broad range of stakeholders that organisations may need to consider and how different stakeholders can influence the regulatory relationship.

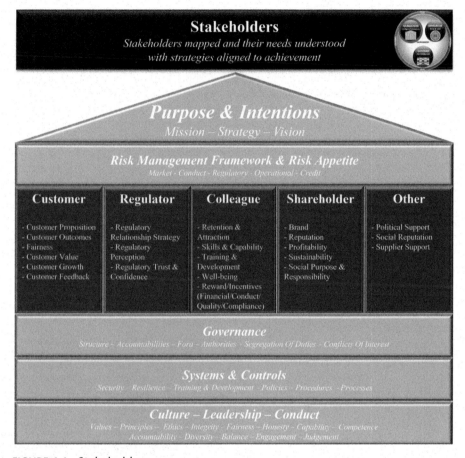

FIGURE 4.4   Stakeholders

We recognised that organisations are constantly delivering for a variety of stakeholder groups and that the outcomes they generate can have a significant impact on those groups. Based on those outcomes, the power, influence, and importance of stakeholders can shift as they adjust their position in response. For example, if outcomes cause consumer detriment or have environmental impact, a variety of stakeholders could become more actively involved with the organisation, (e.g., consumers, regulators, consumer groups, politicians, environmental action groups).

How organisations manage these different stakeholder groups is important given shifts in their respective power and influence can directly impact an organisation, sometimes in significant ways.

There are many examples that can demonstrate how the shift in a particular stakeholder group's opinion can significantly impact the direction of organisations. One example (Figure 4.5) that had an impact felt around the globe and offers a vivid illustration of the power of stakeholder shifts is the Global Financial Crisis. This example is chosen as it demonstrates how that shift in power can make an impact on every level, whether it affects the industry, the organisation, or the individual.

> With the commencement of the Global Financial Crisis, the financial services industries spanning many geographies experienced an immediate response in terms of regulatory, legislative, and political interventions focused on making the financial services sector a safer industry for the future.
>
> The loss of trust and confidence led to shifts in the power and influence of stakeholders and, in turn, wholesale change across the industry. As the demands of stakeholders gathered momentum, they led to investigations, interventions, and a drive for higher standards across most aspects of banking operations. Everything was challenged, from the strategies being pursued, the leadership and cultures being deployed, the risks being run, the governance, systems and controls being deployed, all the way down to the processes and procedures being followed.
>
> The scale of impact of the crisis was enormous, and so was the will of stakeholders to dramatically change the industry.

FIGURE 4.5 Stakeholder Shifts – Global Financial Crisis Example

Regulators, whilst a key stakeholder themselves, clearly have a keen interest in the organisation's broader impact across stakeholder groups, particularly as such impacts may also cover areas where their regulatory objectives operate.

> From a strategy and relationship perspective, it is therefore key that organisations are able to articulate how they are delivering to the interests of their stakeholder groups, and most importantly, how that represents an appropriate and reasonable balance to strike

From a strategy and relationship perspective, it is therefore key that organisations can articulate how they are delivering to the interests of their stakeholder groups and, most importantly, how that represents an appropriate and reasonable balance to strike. Too much focus on one stakeholder group to the detriment of others could lay the foundation for issues down the line. Having a good understanding of your organisation's *stakeholder map*, how you deliver to their respective needs, and how that represents a good balance is also useful in understanding the relative power, influence, and importance stakeholder groups hold at any one time, and how you navigate those shifts as an organisation. Being well informed in this respect also helps you keep your regulator informed as to how stakeholders may behave and whether there are any aspects of activities regulators need to be aware of or ready for.

Having considered the interest regulators have in understanding what organisations seek to achieve, their attitude and appetite for risk in achieving it, and the impact on stakeholders, we now move onto some of the fundamental workings of organisations, starting with the importance of governance, systems, and controls.

Governance, Systems, and Controls

Understanding the fundamentals of how governance, systems, and controls (Figures 4.6 and 4.7) function in your organisation are aspects that are increasingly of interest to regulators as they seek to establish how robust the underpinning of organisational functioning is.

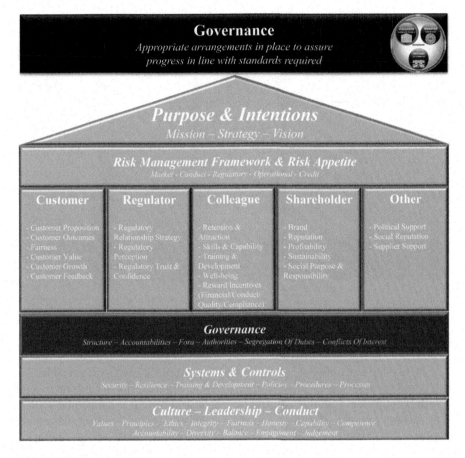

FIGURE 4.6   Governance

Organisations deploy a whole series of practices that seek to ensure the organisation can progress in an orderly fashion with the right checks and balances in place. Here, we provide examples of some of those practices.

From a governance point of view, areas such as the fora (meetings, committees, etc.), structure, accountabilities and responsibilities, levels of authorities, and approach to decision making, are all examples of components that form part of many organisations' governance arrangements. Such areas aim to provide a structured framework around which the organisation can arrange its activities, review performance, allocate ownership, facilitate decision making, and govern the prioritisation and escalation of the business of the organisation.

Similarly, the systems and controls an organisation deploys will be of equal interest and importance for regulators to understand.

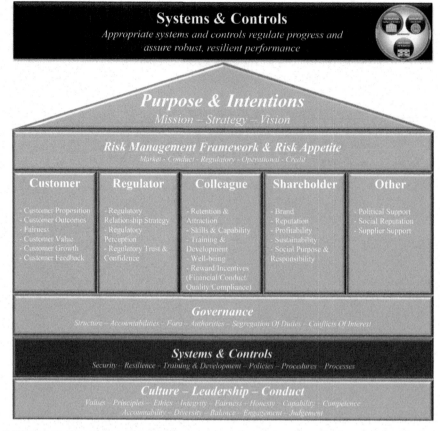

FIGURE 4.7   Systems and Controls

Whilst systems and controls can be thought of on many different levels, which will vary across industries and different organisations, understanding how the picture fits together, how it operates, and how it is calibrated will be of particular interest. Whether the organisation's overall risk management framework is being explained through to the fundamentals of the operation of systems and controls across the organisation, it is important regulators get comfort that the right practices are in place, they are being tested for efficacy, they are being calibrated where necessary, and remain robust.

Given the importance of such practices, regulators will be interested in understanding how the organisation is governed and how robust systems and controls are deemed to be. In obtaining this view, they will be interested and enquire as to how organisations know such practices operate effectively, and where organisations see their risks, both now and in the

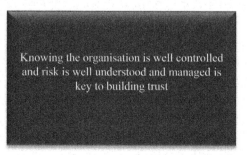

Knowing the organisation is well controlled and risk is well understood and managed is key to building trust

future. Organisations can help inform their regulator on such aspects, keeping them advised on how they are developing their capabilities in these areas, what programmes of work surround them, and how they continue to pressure test that their frameworks are effective. Constantly challenging the standards of how the organisation performs in these areas is a good discipline in which both organisations and regulators will increasingly have a vested interest. As organisations progress, as their environments change around them, and as new developments and technologies unfold, so the operating rhythm of organisations will need to adapt and change to accommodate them. Here, regulators will be interested in how well equipped the leadership is to facilitate such adaptation and how well placed and focused the culture is on risk.

Culture, Leadership, and Conduct

The final aspects we explore in our brief overview of the foundations upon which organisations are built (Figure 4.8) are arguably the most influential and important in terms of outcomes the organisation will drive and how it will achieve them.

FIGURE 4.8   Culture – Leadership – Conduct

They are also an area of significant interest for many regulatory bodies, given they concern how organisations are driven and led in the achievement of their objectives. As we cover these aspects in more detail in the next chapter, here, we only briefly introduce the discussion, highlight (as in previous sections) why they are of interest to regulators, and again consider the implications for the strategy and relationship approach organisations employ.

The culture, leadership, and conduct in evidence in an organisation drives many aspects of how the organisation operates. Together they encompass a wide range of drivers of behaviour throughout the organisation and frame what is taken as acceptable and what is not. From the values and principles of the organisation to its ethical considerations and approach to diversity, such items act like the DNA that permeates the organisation – and like many things can become a positive force or a negative one. Given how they permeate the organisation, they fundamentally influence how an organisation goes about everything it does. From our foundations viewpoint, they influence how the organisation will shape its purpose and intentions and its attitude and appetite for risk in achieving them (e.g., how ambitious, bullish, cautious), they influence how governance and systems and controls are established and valued, and, of course, how the interests of stakeholders are considered and advanced, including those of the regulator.

These areas as we can see are powerful forces in the foundation and operation of organisations and, as such, regulators are increasingly interested in how they are cultivated, how they operate, and their impact across organisations.

In terms of an organisation's regulatory relationship strategy, they are fundamental aspects that organisations should consider. Ensuring your regulator understands your culture, can see how the leadership of the organisation operates, and can observe the conduct that unfolds as a result, is a key aspect of their appreciation of how the organisation is *wired up*. Given the importance of these areas, the next chapter explores them in more detail as they form a key platform upon which the organisation can begin to build the trust and confidence of the regulator. Demonstrating a thriving healthy culture, with great leadership and conduct that is strictly challenged and channelled toward the right outcomes is a great platform on which to build.

NOTE

1. C.f. see Federal Reserve (2018), "Responding to widespread consumer abuses and compliance breakdowns by Wells Fargo, Federal Reserve restricts Wells' growth until firm improves governance and controls. Concurrent with Fed action, Wells to replace three directors by April, one by year end".

REFERENCE

Federal Reserve (2018), 'Responding to widespread consumer abuses and compliance breakdowns by Wells Fargo, Federal Reserve restricts Wells' growth until firm improves governance and controls. Concurrent with Fed action, Wells to replace three directors by April, one by year end', [online], 2 February 2018, available: https://www.federalreserve.gov/newsevents/pressreleases/enforcement20180202a.htm

CHAPTER 5

Navigation
Establishing Trust in Strategy, Culture, Leadership and Conduct

CHAPTER SUMMARY

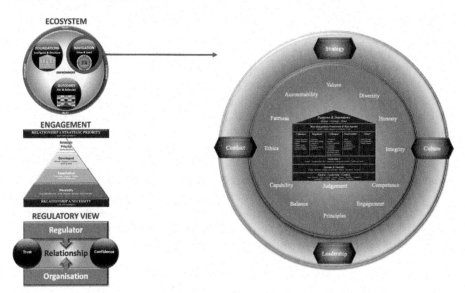

In this chapter, we look at how regulators are increasingly interested in the way organisations are being navigated by their Board and leadership teams. We cover this by examining how regulators consider the strategies, culture, and leadership of organisations as key barometers against which to consider the risk an organisation may pose to its objectives.

We start with the organisation's strategy and consider how the overall strategic approach cascades throughout the organisation and influences all lower-level strategies, including their regulatory strategy. Here, we note that organisations have an important strategic choice to make in terms of the level of engagement and commitment toward their regulatory strategy. A choice which will influence how the relationship will develop.

DOI: 10.4324/9781003297963-5

Having considered the importance of the strategic choices being made, we move onto consider how those choices cascade and influence throughout the organisation as colleagues become culturally tuned in to the expectations set by the strategy. Here, we explore the importance of culture from a regulator's perspective. We consider how culture is like the organisation's DNA and a useful early warning indicator for regulators to observe and seek to evidence.

Finally, we move on to briefly explore the areas of leadership and conduct, but given the vast landscape of leadership and conduct literature, we demonstrate the point of the importance of leadership and conduct by focusing in on exploring the more extreme leadership traits of hubris and narcissism and their implications by way of illustration. These are chosen to exaggerate the points regarding the *human factor*, both in terms of how these can influence organisational performance (in which regulators have a keen interest) and in terms of how they influence regulatory relationships.

STRATEGY – *HOW* WE EXECUTE IS IMPORTANT FOR TRUST BUILDING

Having created their mission and vision of where they see the organisation in future, the overall corporate strategy of how they intend to realise it needs to take shape (Johnson and Scholes 1999). A cascade of activity and action starts to permeate the organisation in pursuit of building and aligning the organisation's capability and resources to achieve its chosen direction (see Chapter 4).

That cascade and alignment of resources includes considering strategy across different levels and aspects of the organisation (e.g., this may be at a divisional, operation, product, and regulatory strategy level).

A key consideration will be the strategies to be followed for key stakeholder groups, one of which will be the regulatory relationship strategy. Figure 5.1 reminds us, using the organisational building framework from the previous chapter, of the importance of ensuring the regulatory relationship strategy is clearly articulated and aligns to the organisation's overall strategy.

Here, we highlight in our organisational building the strategy and stakeholder blocks and envelop them in an array of considerations that regulators will be keen to see drive good outcomes that align to their regulatory objectives.

Many organisations engaged in regulatory relationships can describe *what* is involved or expected of them in terms of engaging with regulators (even if that is a basic regurgitation of regulatory expectations from the regulator's website and materials), but *how* that engagement takes place is a matter of strategic

> The commitment an organisation puts into developing strong relationships with their regulators is a function of the strategy they wish to pursue with them

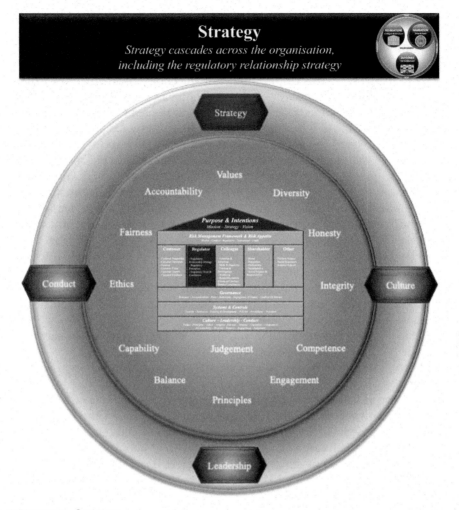

FIGURE 5.1   Strategy

choice at an organisational level. The commitment and investment an organ-isation may expend into developing strong relationships with their regulators is a function of the strategy they wish to pursue with them (see Figure 5.2). This is a key point, as many organisations do not consider what their strategy should be for such an important strategic relationship.

A survey of financial services firms by the Governance Institute of Australia found only 60% of respondents had a strategy and only 82% of those that had one thought it was fit for purpose in the environment they found themselves in (GIoA 2019).

FIGURE 5.2   Who Has a Regulatory Strategy?

Having a regulatory strategy for how you will build a relationship with your regulator is a good way of ensuring you're thinking through the respec-tive requirements of the stakeholders and how you intend to satisfy them.

As we saw in Chapter 1, that commitment to the relationship can be seen as a narrow and rule-driven adherence to the minimum standard right through to an all-encompassing holistic engagement that sees all an organisation does as having some interest and providing some information for a regulator to assess. In this respect, the strategic choice regarding how organisations engage with regulators is fundamental to everything else that we will see in terms of action taken and the organisational attitude toward regulatory engagement. As we focus in this chapter on how organisations navigate (drive and lead) toward their objectives and how that can influence the regulator, we will do so using the framework depicted in Figure 5.1. Here, we build on previous chapters and envelop *what* we have built in terms of the organisation with some of the key aspects of *how* it will function that regulators will be interested in understanding (strategy, culture, leadership, and conduct, together with their underpinnings such as values, ethics, and principles).

Having established how the organisation is set up, here, we get into how it operates and what regulators can glean from this. These represent those aspects that would be commonly considered, however, depending on the industry and organisation, this picture may differ and could be adjusted to accommodate their specific circumstances.

Once the regulatory relationship intent is set (regardless of the strategy, whether a proactive, passive, or confrontational approach), the cascade of influence throughout the organisation begins. Culturally, organisations become *tuned-in* to the expectations the strategy directs and, as a result, how the organisation behaves becomes a natural extension. This can result in a scale of responses toward regulators, from one which is very open and transparent through to a closed, challenging, and even confrontational relationship…and every variation in between.

The culture of an organisation will therefore naturally be an important aspect that many regulators will wish to understand given the influence it has on behaviour and decision making not only toward regulators but across the organisation's activities. Culture sets a tone of expectation that regulators can see as a positive or negative force in how an organisation drives its business. For example, should an organisation be driving its business culturally in a way that could be to the detriment of consumers, markets, society and/or their regulatory objectives, regulators may become increasingly interested in understanding that organisation in greater detail, potentially involving higher levels of scrutiny and more direct interaction. Culture can act like *the canary in the coal mine*, giving out early signals as to how the pursuit of strategic objectives comes to life in the day-to-day operation of a business. As one leading regulator put it:

"Absolutely culture has been the big thing, looking at how the senior people operate on a day-to-day basis and how the business strategy is articulated, is it just talking about profits, or is it talking about profit sustainability and putting the customer at the heart of that strategy".

CULTURE – A CLOSER LOOK

The culture of an organisation is a key ingredient from a regulatory relationship point of view as regulators become more and more interested in the drivers of performance. A demonstration of the importance of culture from a regulatory perspective is captured well in the opening preface of a discussion paper from the Financial Conduct Authority (F.C.A.) in the U.K. (2018, p.3(a)), "Transforming Culture in Financial Services". The foreword by Jonathan Davidson, Director of Supervision – Retail and Authorisations, starts with a reflection on the role of culture as a cause of major conduct failings and its importance as a priority for the F.C.A. (see also Davidson, J. [2018] (b) "Realising the benefits of purposeful leadership").

We all exist in spheres of culture that interact, overlap, and co-exist; some may be large and influential on our lives, others not so. However, the power of culture should not be underestimated as culture influences behaviour, and as covered in the quote mentioned previously, it can sometimes lead to a cumulatively devastating effect. Cultural influences may be driven from our background and upbringing, the groups we engage with and the organisations we work for. In this respect, we all approach the decisions in front of us with differing frames of reference, i.e., we are all part of cultures. Our influences, expectations, attitudes, biases, morals, values, and ethics, for example, will have been shaped as a product of our background and the influences around us. In an organisational context, given that culture influences behaviour, it is unsurprising that regulators will want to understand the organisation not only from the perspective of its performance and objective measures, but also from the perspective of its aspirations in terms of the culture, leadership and conduct it wishes to build, along with the values, principles, ethics, integrity, and behaviours is wishes to see. Figure 5.3 illustrates that *what* an organisation does may be important to a regulator (the mission and vision it sets out to achieve and the strategy deployed to get there), however, *how* an organisation does it, will be crucial to understand.

Figure 5.3 purposefully highlights in the *organisational building* that culture, leadership, and conduct, together with their underpinnings, act as its footings. They are crucial foundations and they influence everything else that is built upon them.

As organisational culture is just one of the influences on the individuals within the organisation, it is also important to remember culture is as much about the individual as it is the organisation they work for. The culture of the organisation will be one dynamic to understand, but just as important are the behaviours of individuals within an organisation, as it is individuals that make decisions and drive outcomes, not organisations. Later, we touch on this in a little more detail and think about leadership, but with a focus on the risk regulators may be more sensitive to, by covering aspects such as the challenges of dominant personalities and the impact this can have.

Culture, we have established, is important to the regulator, it is like our *autopilot* or organisational DNA that is shared – it can be what steers us toward one decision or another, it can influence what we choose to do, it can drive our natural response to a given situation regardless of whether times are easy or tough. Similarly, culture has tenure. It is something that builds and is cultivated rather than being switched on, off, or changed at will. When the cultural

FIGURE 5.3   Culture

influences converge and align toward a chosen organisational direction and the decisions we make conform to the right desired outcomes, culture may be working well. When what we espouse as a desired cultural state is not backed by what we do in the difficult decisions that arise from day to day, it could well be that *what* we set out to do is not evidenced in *how* we behave. The consequences of issues in this area can lead to significant problems and regulatory attention, as you might expect[1].

Culture, therefore, is about both *what* we talk about doing, about *how* we operate as individuals (all levels, all areas), and by the sum of our actions as an organisation.

In an organisational context, it is crucial that culture is cultivated. The foundation, once set by the Board, needs to be constantly tended and nurtured by the Chief Executive and Leadership Team to ensure there is a clear aspiration for the desired culture and behaviours that are understood throughout the organisation. Those behaviours drive actions and those actions have implications for all aspects of organisational performance, a key one being the outcomes for customers. Given its importance, culture – and its influence on behaviour – will remain a key area of regulatory scrutiny and an aspect that permeates the entire regulatory relationship, as signs of an organisation's culture are evident in every aspect of its being. Some regulators are already taking steps, for example, to understand in greater detail the behavioural risks of organisations as the reference to work by the Dutch National Bank (2015) demonstrates:

> The Dutch National Bank has undertaken behavioural reviews of their local banks in order that they can better understand the risk profile of organisations in their decision making. Their driver for such an understanding is that many of the problems impacting the performance and strength of organisations historically have had behaviour at their root. In assessing organisations in terms of potentially problematic behavioural traits, they seek to head off issues by taking a more forward-looking view of what aspects of an organisation's operating rhythm could cause issues further down the track. Where they see issues, they can compel organisations to take action through risk-mitigation plans to address them.
>
> Their approach involves supervisory teams and organisational psychologists working together to understand how the organisation makes its decisions, how it achieves its strategic objectives, how governance functions operate and the relative power influences at play (e.g., dominance of leadership/lack of challenge/flow of information and insight up, down, and across the organisation).

FIGURE 5.4   Dutch National Bank – Behavioural Reviews

Across many industries, regulators aspire for cultural influences to become far more proactive in actively flagging issues across the industry in order that the regulator can gain a better view of emerging risk, as this quote from Dame Deirdre Hutton (2015) regarding the aviation industry in the U.K. demonstrates:

> *"Finally, it is very helpful if there is a good reporting culture in the industry. Aviation has historically had an excellent record in reporting incidents. All the airline staff, whether cabin crew, engineers, or pilots, have access to reporting systems and use them. The challenge for the regulator is then to collate those disparate reports to pick up trends and identify what might be leading indicators of risk".*

Not only does culture influence how an organisation deals with the regulator, but it will also have a bearing on how the organisation is seen from the regulator's perspective.

Culture – There Isn't a Rule Book Big Enough

Why such a focus on culture from regulators? Apart from the example opening comments above from Davidson (2018) and Dame Deirdre Hutton (2015) noting what they see as a direct link between culture and outcomes, there is also the simple fact that a regulator cannot write a rulebook for every situation.

Not only would a rulebook that set out to achieve this be a significant tome for any industry, it would have to attempt to understand an unknowable future and the potential outcomes that may arise in that future that could potentially undermine their objectives or cause consumer detriment. Those issues are exactly why many regulators prefer to combine a mix of rules that send a clear boundary signal, with an underpinning of principles that provide guidance and intent. The letter and spirit are both of importance if an effective framework is to be in place. This sentiment was demonstrated well by Bailey (2018):

> *"In the traditional world of regulation, rules act as prescriptive statements that forbid, require or permit some action or outcome – thus forbidding, requiring or permitting must be present in a rule. That's a pretty fair description of rulemaking. And it follows – by assumption I would say – that if you can make enough rules, and of course the right ones, the culture will be good, and trust will be built and maintained. The problem is that in practice a set of rules tends to underdetermine what needs to be done – it is unlikely that a rulebook will be able to predict and determine every situation that a regulated party can face, and in any event we want to see a world in which regulated parties are encouraged and incentivised to exercise their own judgment reliably and regularly, drawing on their own competence and honesty. So, to the verbs of forbidding, requiring and permitting, I would add enabling, encouraging and incentivising as important tasks of the regulator".*

In dealing with regulators, demonstrating that the right culture is in place is not linear, it is not about simply knowing the rules, it is not about quoting rules back with evidence points of why you are inside that boundary (or asking your regulator where in the rules it says you cannot do something), and it is not about trumping the letter or spirit of regulation with a legislative argument to circumvent the issue. It is about context, perspective, judgement, balance, and the traits Bailey called out previously such as competence, honesty, and the reliability and regularity of doing the right thing given the situation faced. Anyone can follow a rule but end up at the wrong place and facilitate the wrong outcome, what is more important is the judgement, balance, and foresight to understand that just because you *can* follow that path and skirt the boundary to be inside the rules and principles technically, doesn't mean you *should* if on honest reflection that direction is not the most balanced and fair call that could be made given the situation or spirit of those rules and principles.

Culture is like a reputation, it takes hard yards to build and get it right, but it is so easily lost and undermined in the day-to-day decisions that fall in front of us. The regularity and reliability Bailey talked about previously are great guardrails for culture… which needs consistent and regular work to reinforce how an

> Those difficult decisions in difficult times become the organisation's stories and examples for the next round of difficult decisions. These can become a self-fulfilling framework for good or for poor outcomes as precedent is reflected upon in order to arrive at the next decision

organisation and its people are driven to do the right thing no matter what situation is faced. Those difficult decisions in difficult times become the organisation's stories and examples for the next round of difficult decisions. These can become a self-fulfilling framework for good or for poor outcomes as precedent is reflected upon to arrive at the next decision. Once they begin to drift in the wrong direction, it is amazing how quickly the norms and expectations of the organisation can shift as decisions become stories, stories become examples, and examples become frameworks for decisions for others to draw upon given similar situations they face.

Culture – It's Not Just a Statement

Getting a culture that is right for the organisation is clearly not just about the CEO announcement that cultural change needs to happen, is underway, or has been achieved. Seldom do the *re-wiring* activities required to bring culture to life happen quickly, spontaneously, or without the hard yards of more fundamental change and tough decisions, a point summarised very well by Fukuyama (1995, p.40), who noted that culture is a matter of ethical habit, which means it lags the ideas that drive a need for change.

Regulators, like other stakeholders, will look at the evidence that the right culture is in place regardless of the espoused position. They do this to understand the implications of culture, its benefits and value when healthy and vibrant, and its potential costs when navigating a troublesome course. This is captured well in the words of Steward (2015) of the F.C.A. in the U.K. who noted the dangers of culture being seen as simply a regulatory requirement, and pointed to the value in culture and the costs where culture fails.

For regulators, gathering evidence may again arise from a variety of touch points across an organisation's ecosystem. Of course, there are the assertions of the Board and Executive who set the tone and intent. However, there may also be more subtle observations. The behaviour and decisions of staff when issues arise, or difficult decisions arise, can sometimes be the junction where fractures in the cultural story can become evident. When the options in front of an organisation become difficult and challenge wider objectives, such as financial performance, it can be interesting to observe how steadfast the culture proves to be. Similarly, more subtle observations or challenges from regulators may feed their judgement on an organisation's cultural journey, for example: demonstrating how accountability for culture is owned; the extent to which diversity is valued and driven; how open an organisation is to challenge; and whether challenge is encouraged and acted upon. Such observations may provide useful insights into the organisational risks of issues like *group think* or *centralisation of decision making*, which can pose their own dangers if left unchecked (see Chesterfield and Smart 2018). Then there are indicators to watch for, such as the relative strength of functions (compliance, risk, legal, and audit) or how and where decision making is undertaken and the transparency of communication around them. Megan Butler (2018), Director of Supervision – Investment, Wholesale and Specialists at the F.C.A. provided a very clear steer on the importance to the regulator of the management of culture in financial services firms, noting that the regulator wished to see culture being treated as a leadership discipline.

Culture is a crucial element of an organisation that regulators will be keen to understand. In driving the right culture, the right leadership and conduct is fundamental to that journey (Figure 5.5), which is where we move next.

LEADERSHIP AND CONDUCT – BE AWARE OF DOMINANT TRAITS

Having considered the importance of organisational strategy and culture, we wrap up this chapter by turning in our framework to the subjects of leadership and conduct.

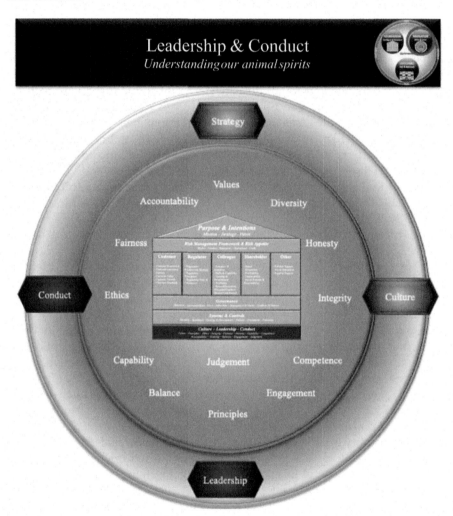

FIGURE 5.5   Leadership and Conduct

However, rather than an expansive discussion on these areas, we take it as accepted that good leadership and conduct is desirable. We also accept that there is plenty of literature on what *good* leadership might entail, so, here, we focus on those aspects that are likely to be of concern to regulators and examples of the more extreme traits that can impact organisations and their cultures. In providing this more focused view, we consider those aspects that are key for organisations, and in particular their Boards, to be alert to and focused on.

The Human Factor

Let's open by posing a question for our consideration:

> Are there aspects of our inner human traits that can drive the wrong behaviours and actions, make engagement more problematic, act as warning signs to wider stakeholders, or potentially undermine regulatory relationships and hinder an organisation's ability to build trust and confidence?

To answer this, we consider certain traits and offer these as illustrative examples of items we may need to consider more carefully in terms of how we understand them, monitor for them, and asses them in terms of their potential impact upon regulatory relationships.

Those examples for the purposes of these discussions are animal spirits, hubris, and narcissism. Such traits can heavily influence cultures, decision making, and behaviours and as such offer fertile ground for a consideration of how powerful and influential actors need to operate with care and balance.

ANIMAL SPIRITS AND BEHAVIOURAL ECONOMICS   We cannot expect that all decisions will be based on a rational and formulaic calculation of all possible outcomes, some will be based on *animal spirits*, but where powerful individuals make decisions that prove terminal for their organisation or impact industries, such matters rightly attract significant regulatory attention.

Economist John Maynard Keynes' observations on the influence of *animal spirits* in his 1936 book "The General Theory of Employment, Interest and Money", offers an interesting introduction to our exploration here with the following quote:

> *"Most, probably, of our decisions to do something positive, the full consequences of which will be drawn out over many days to come, can only be taken as a result of animal spirits – of a spontaneous urge to action rather than inaction and not as the outcome of a weighted average of quantitative benefits multiplied by quantitative probabilities".*

Keynes (1936, p.161–2) highlights that, animal spirits can also fuel significant benefit, so it appears balance is crucial. The extent to which the continuum between success and crisis is influenced by the behaviours and actions of people in positions of power, is something that warrants being understood.

> *"If the animal spirits are dimmed and the spontaneous optimism falters, leaving us to depend on nothing but a mathematical expectation, enterprise will fade and die".*

Just as Keynes described animal spirits in the 1930s, we hear in our modern day of the emerging field of behavioural economics and its explanation for how economic decisions are influenced and taken. Here, again, theory looks at how human behaviour really works and how such behaviour influences outcomes. Regardless of the theoretical position we take, how our understanding develops of such forces at work, what we look to observe that may highlight destructive behaviour, and how we assess when we are moving toward the wrong side of the fulcrum point in terms of balance, will be key to avoiding an insidious creep toward crisis.

HUBRIS   In the context of our upcoming exploration, we can think of hubris as a trait associated with an excessive sense of pride or self-confidence, usually accompanied by a high level of power.

Owen and Davidson (2009, p.1) in their study of U.S. Presidents and U.K. Prime Ministers over the last 100 years, investigated the area of hubris syndrome and put forward the idea that:

> *"Extreme hubristic behaviour is a syndrome, constituting a cluster of features (symptoms) evoked by a specific trigger (power), and usually remitting when power fades. "Hubris syndrome" is seen as an acquired condition, and therefore different from most personality disorders which are traditionally seen as persistent throughout adulthood. The key concept is that hubris syndrome is a disorder of the possession of power, particularly power which has been associated with overwhelming success, held for a period of years and with minimal constraint on the leader".*

As we saw with the Global Financial Crisis, characters were singled out and their behaviour scrutinised as stakeholders sought to explain how we had managed to arrive at the place we had. Criticism of powerful individuals for their dominant style led to items such as the cultures that grew around such individuals coming under the spotlight, as Owen and Davidson (2009, p.4) noted:

> *"The world has recently seen that in the financial collapse of 2008 some leading international bankers also displayed marked signs of hubris".*

In addition, the findings of reports such as Vickers (Independent Banking Commission 2011) and Turner (2009) laid out the shortcomings of the banks leading up to the crisis, with items such as poor culture, dominance of figureheads, and inappropriate incentivisation all being called into question and all being associated with the wrong type of leadership and tone from the top. Whilst poor culture and dominant figureheads proved problematic, the toxic mix of significant incentivisation added an accelerant to such behaviour. In terms of inappropriate incentivisation, the work of Six (2013) reflects on the area of Self Determination Theory, which may have some resonance with the issues these reports raised and regulatory concern with regards to reward culture. Those issues were the extent to which external incentivisation can lead to detrimental outcomes. Six (2013, p.170) describes how Self Determination Theory:

> *"…builds on earlier theories of intrinsic v extrinsic motivation…reflecting activities that people do naturally and spontaneously when they feel free to follow their inner interests".*

Six goes on to argue that when external rewards are introduced for these activities:

> *"People tend to feel controlled by the rewards, prompting a shift in the perceived locus of causality for the behaviour from internal to external".*

A poor culture, inappropriate incentivisation, and dominant leadership can be warning signs regulators will wish to investigate and understand.

Six (2013, p.172–3), also goes on to propose an interesting point about how the regulator-regulatee relationship may be better served by the approach taken by the parties:

> *"When the actors subjected to the formal controls (the "regulatees") internalize and integrate the values of the actors imposing the formal controls (the "regulators"), then the regulatees are more likely to comply with the regulation in a self-determined way, on their own volition. The quality of compliance will be higher. Self Determination Theory shows that value internalization is stimulated when the regulatees feel their needs for autonomy, competence and relatedness are supported by the regulators".*
>
> *"The more difficult it is to comply with regulation, because it requires more effort and competence, the more important it is that regulatees are motivated in a self-determined way".*

Six (2013) highlights that how the regulatory relationship unfolds appears to be important to assure a higher degree of engagement and compliance. Understanding the deeper operation of an organisation to identify its risk needs a very effective regulatory relationship to understand and unearth the deeper workings of the organisation and its culture. If the right things are going to be done the right way, the ideas put forward by Six (2013) appear to be useful insight into how stakeholders should consider their interactions.

How do such behavioural traits help us in understanding how we can improve regulatory relationships? Such factors run the risk of challenging the establishment of a balanced relationship and, in particular, the building of trust. Hubris tendencies can therefore offer a warning signal for stakeholders. However, the challenge is that successful leadership often depends on items such as charisma, grand aspirations, and self-confidence, so determining where a leader may be on the continuum between success and disaster may be more difficult to establish.

NARCISSISM   In the context of our considerations below, we can think of narcissism as the dangers of inflated self-views. Narcissism provides another human trait, which we can examine in the context of its possible effects on relationship building and trust. Chatterjee and Hambrick (2007, p.351) in their study of narcissistic chief executives describe narcissism in terms put forward by Campbell, Goodie and Foster (2004):

> *"Those who have very inflated self-views and who are preoccupied with having those self-views continuously reinforced".*

Chatterjee and Hambrick (2007, p.353, 378–9) point out that:

> *"Narcissistic CEOs are likely to favour strategic dynamism and grandiosity, as opposed to strategic incrementalism and stability. As a result, narcissistic CEOs tend to deliver extreme performance (big wins or big losses) and fluctuating performance for their organisations".*

Their findings established that CEO narcissism is related to:

> *"Extreme and irregular company performance" but that "there was no indication that CEO narcissism was related to the level of company performance generated....they do not generate systematically better or worse performance".*

Their studies provide insight into the workings of individuals and the influence of their behavioural traits on company performance.

Regulators, therefore, are increasingly looking at the leaders of organisations, the tone from the top, and the culture set throughout organisations for signs of appropriate leadership and positive cultures (including the echo from the bottom). Dominant traits that pose risks to regulatory objectives would attract little praise from regulators as they work to establish trust in the relationships. Indeed, the Dutch National Bank (2015), is an example of regulators monitoring for such risks. For many years, they have proactively assessed culture in banks via their management assessment process and focussed on aspects that would lead to concerns of dominance, such as the Board culture, how decisions are challenged, dominance of CEOs with a lack of countervailing power, and herd instincts.

A key point to stress here is that regulators (as should organisations) look for culture throughout the organisation…it needs to be shared and valued if it is to be an effective and consistent culture.

For the regulator, then, the strategy, culture, and nature of leadership all represent very real and powerful influences on an organisation that they will seek to understand. The right things (whatever they may be), done the right way (that does no harm), for the right reasons, in a balanced and fair way are threads that a regulator will wish to see demonstrated in outcomes for stakeholders, not least the customer.

Where a regulator can tap into an organisation and get a good sense this is the operating rhythm that is regularly and reliably at play, so the foundations for trust are more likely to be laid from which to build the regulatory relationship.

NOTE

1. C.f. See F.C.A. (2015), "Final Notice - Barclays Bank PLC".

REFERENCES

Bailey, A. (2018), 'The role of regulation in encouraging good culture', [online], Financial Conduct Authority, 6 November 2018, available: www.fca.org.U.K./news/speeches/role-regulation-encouraging-good-culture

Butler, M (2018), 'Women in finance, keeping up the pressure on progress', [online], Financial Conduct Authority, 22 March 2018, available: https://www.fca.org.uk/news/speeches/women-finance-keeping-pressure-progress

Campbell, W. K., Goodie, A. S. and Foster, J. D. (2004), 'Narcissism, Confidence, and Risk Attitude', Journal of Behavioural Decision Making, Vol. 17, p.297

Chatterjee, A. and Hambrick, D. C. (2007), 'It's All About Me: Narcissistic Chief Executive Officers and their Effects on Company Strategy and Performance', Administrative Science Quarterly, Vol. 52, p.351, 353, 358, 378–9

Chesterfield, A. and Smart, L. (2018), 'Psychological safety – the secret to effective teams', [online], Financial Conduct Authority, 8 May 2018, available: https://www.fca.org.U.K./insight/psychological-safety-secret-effective-teams

Davidson, J. (2018b), 'Realising the benefits of purposeful leadership', [online], 1 November 2018, Financial Conduct Authority, available: www.fca.org.U.K./news/speeches/realising-benefits-purposeful-leadership

Davidson, J. (2018a), 'Transforming Culture in Financial Services', [online], Financial Conduct Authority, available: https://www.fca.org.U.K./publication/discussion/dp18-02.pdf

Dutch National Bank (2015), 'Supervision of behaviour and culture', [online], available: https://www.dnb.nl/media/1gmkp1vk/supervision-of-behaviour-and-culture_tcm46-380398-1.pdf

Financial Conduct Authority (F.C.A.) (2015), 'Final Notice – Barclays Bank PLC', [online], 20 May 2015, available: https://www.fca.org.uk/publication/final-notices/barclays-bank-plc-may-15.pdf

Fukuyama, F. (1995), 'Trust: The Social Virtues and the Creation of Prosperity', London, Penguin, p.40, 41, 151, 153

Governance Institute of Australia (GIoA) (2019), 'Strategy for engaging with regulators', [online], available: https://www.governanceinstitute.com.au/resources/governance-directions/volume-71-number-7/strategy-for-engaging-with-regulators/

Hutton, Dame Deirdre. (2015), 'The Role of Stakeholder Relationships in Regulatory Excellence', [online], The Regulatory Review, 27 July 2015, available: https://www.theregreview.org/2015/07/27/hutton-regulatory-excellence/

Independent Banking Commission (Vickers) Report. (2011), 'Interim Report, Consultation on Reform Options, [online], available: http://bankingcommission.independent.gov.U.K., p.7

Johnson, G. and Scholes, K. (1999), 'Exploring Corporate Strategy', London: Prentice Hall Europe, p.10, 13

Keynes, J. M. (1936), 'The General Theory of Employment, Interest and Money', Palgrave Macmillan, New York, p.161–162

Lord Turner, A. (2009), 'The Turner Review – A Regulatory Response to the Global Banking Crisis', Financial Services Authority, p.5, 8, 11–49, 11, 22, 86, 91

Owen, D. and Davidson, J. (2009), 'Hubris Syndrome: An Acquired Personality Disorder? A Study of U.S. Presidents and U.K. Prime Ministers Over The Last 100 Years', Brain A Journal of Neurology, Oxford University Press, p.1, 2, 4, 7

Six, F. (2013), 'Trust in Regulatory Relations', [online], Public Management Review, Vol. 15, No. 2, pp.163–185, available: http://www.tandfonline.com/loi/rpxm20, publisher Taylor & Francis Ltd, http://www.tandfonline.com reprinted by permission of the publisher, p.164, 170, 172, 173

Steward, M. (2015), 'Culture and Governance', [online], Financial Conduct Authority, 24 November 2015, available: http://www.fca.org.U.K./news/firms/culture-and-governance

CHAPTER 6

Outcomes
The Ecosystem Informing Regulatory Opinion

CHAPTER SUMMARY

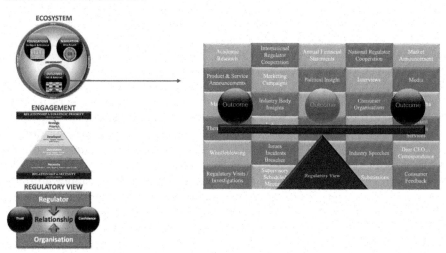

In this chapter, we consider all that informs your regulator's opinion. The availability of data, information, and insight have significantly expanded for regulators, and this poses challenges for organisations in terms of ensuring they understand how that information is informing their regulator.

We explore some of these sources of information, how regulators use such sources (including cross-regulator cooperation) and consider examples of how they may influence your regulator's view and help them form judgements on the picture building before them.

Finally, we explore how this *ecosystem* of information needs to be considered as a key part of the regulatory relationship and understood by the organisation so regulators can be kept fully informed, with context proactively placed around what they are seeing. This we do by considering a wide array of situations that arise for organisations in which regulatory interest may be experienced, from scheduled supervisory meetings to the day-to-day pricing

DOI: 10.4324/9781003297963-6

and product change or marketing campaign, we take a more practical look and use examples to demonstrate how insight and information builds for regulators.

OUTCOMES – WHAT INFORMS YOUR REGULATOR'S OPINION, ARGUABLY IS THE RELATIONSHIP

So far, we have considered how the organisation you build and how you navigate it should be considered in terms of how these aspects impact and inform your regulatory relationship and how they will be of interest to the regulator.

As organisations use these assembled resources and navigate their journey, they interact with and impact their environment, which forms an ecosystem of insight. This ecosystem is crucial to the organisation, forming, in many respects, symbiotic associations that help them deliver on their objectives. The organisational relationships in that ecosystem can take many forms, such as relationships with suppliers who are crucial in the delivery of products and services; an industry body who might assimilate insight from across the industry and share best practices or lobby for support that assists organisations along their journey; and clearly your customers and consumers for whom brand and values are becoming an increasingly important decision factor in choosing with whom they engage. The rich and varied relationships that exist between an organisation and its environment can be significant in number and scope, and all create outcomes. It could be that, for consumers, your organisation is a leading light in your industry, or alternatively, the latest organisation to suffer significant issues impacting consumer confidence. For your suppliers, it could be that you are their main customer and have a relationship that is held out as a gold standard in supply-chain effectiveness, or you could have a reputation of dominating suppliers and forcing unreasonable terms upon them. With the industry body, your organisation may be steering the thinking of the industry in new and exciting ways or it may be seen as a driver of resistance and lobbying against reforms seen as beneficial to broader stakeholders, such as your regulator. Whatever the nature of your impact on the ecosystem, those outcomes register a *footprint of the path you tread*. Your regulator can observe and assess that path, and as such, it can help them form their opinion on the operation and functioning of the organisation. The ecosystem, then, is a diverse and important source of information for regulators. How you have built your capability and how you deploy that capability will drive outcomes that will appear positive or negative when set against the objectives of your regulator. Regulators will use this expanding resource of insight to inform their judgement and help them form their opinion on the organisation, its leadership, and its progress. Arguably then, what informs your regulator's opinion can all be thought of as part of the relationship with them, given that whatever they observe they can make part of their agenda for how they engage and what they need to discuss with you.

REGULATORY INSIGHT – A RAPIDLY EXPANDING RESOURCE

Building on the last chapter, let's assume your organisation has a sound and well-thought-through strategy, one that you feel can provide the organisation with an advantage to win in your chosen markets and that provides value to your various stakeholders in a balanced, fair, and transparent way. The culture and leadership in the organisation are well tuned and calibrated to deliver consistent and sustainable performance. Your stakeholders both understand your strategy and view your organisation as having a healthy culture and strong leadership whilst delivering robust outcomes for customers. The culmination of the situation you face is a growing belief in *what* you are aiming to achieve and *how* you intend to get there, which is forming a strong basis for trust to flourish between you and your regulator. In other words, you have great foundations from which the regulatory relationship can continue to grow. However, all businesses face constant challenges as their environment is fast moving and constantly changing, and whilst we may have sound foundations, that regulatory relationship will continue to be informed and shaped by the events in which we are involved day to day. Throughout this book, we have considered the fascinating and challenging world in which we live. A world where the pace of change and development is increasing in velocity. Across many industries, these opportunities exist and arise at pace and across a breadth not experienced before. Such developments clearly pose challenges for regulators as they consider how they regulate for such dynamic times, how they tap into and use new sources of insight, and what appropriate responses are needed to continue to deliver on their objectives.

The Ability to Distil Key Insights Is Increasingly Important

In such a dynamic and fast-changing world, the ability to keep across the flow of data, information, and insight to allow an assessment of how an industry and its constituent businesses are operating becomes more challenging for regulators, particularly as the sheer volume, sources, and variety of information proliferate.

As regulators have a growing array of regulatory insight, for those who are regulated, it is key that they think more broadly about the ecosystem of information that is building around them and influencing the regulator's view. As your ecosystem grows, so does your regulator's view of how your organisation operates. Whilst you may have a sound strategy, strong culture, and a good foundation of trust between you and your regulator, how you manage your ecosystem and keep your regulator informed will be crucial to ensuring those firm foundations continue to be built upon in terms of keeping the regulator positive about the organisation and its contribution to the industry and regulatory objectives.

Of course, the ecosystem is a two-way information flow. Whilst you may have clear regulatory rules to refer to, the regulator may also provide further materials to bring those rules to life, illustrate them, and provide examples to highlight the spirit as well as the letter of the rules. Such context can allow you to *read between the lines* where necessary in terms of future areas of focus. There may also be policy updates, speeches, news reports on research undertaken, or comments on industry practices, all of which help you understand the regulator's *house view* on where they stand on any subject. For both parties, keeping the other well informed and distilling insights of progress and developments is key.

A good example of how events can quickly turn and become a matter of regulatory interest due to an ecosystem beginning to surface issues and concerns, can be observed in the explosion of social media and the scandals that followed, which resulted in calls for greater regulation and control of those new capabilities. These new and exciting technologies transformed communication pathways, and as such, were adopted at an incredible pace. The power of social media organisations grew along with the wealth of information they held on their users. As their use and application began to hit the headlines for the alleged risks they pose, so societies demanded greater regulatory control. The ecosystem around these organisations began to *light up*, and with that visibility came the scrutiny of assessing the risks and potential harm that could result from such technology and how that could be controlled. The organisations had clear business strategies, which they executed to great effect, their cultures were used as examples of a new dynamic and modern way of operating, and the trust placed in these organisations was high. However, as the concerns began to build, an ecosystem of insight revealed the more challenging aspects of these businesses and their services, and with it the tide began to turn in terms of the debate on whether and how the industry and organisations within it should be regulated.

Against a background of rapidly expanding insight flooding into their regulators, along with an increasing pace of change and increasingly complex relationships, organisations have an opportunity to enhance their approach and be more dynamic and proactive in their regulatory relationships. Organisations can be proactive and dynamic as to be aware and tuned into the signals their organisation and its environment emits and quickly place context around those signals to help make sense of such messages in respect of their organisation's strategy. After all, your strategy, by definition, will take you into an unknown future – some things will work out as expected, but some may not, and where these can pose significant challenges and new risks, organisations need to be able to demonstrate that they are considering its challenges and implications to enable them to protect their customers, their organisation, and in extreme instances, the wider system in which they operate. As we covered under Figure 4.3 in Chapter 4, one Director captured this sentiment well, and during those discussions expressed a keen interest in truly understanding the broader ecosystem of the organisation. Scanning the environment was seen as crucial, as was keeping the regulator informed of what they saw as the implications for the organisation or the broader market.

> Organisations have an opportunity to enhance capability and be more dynamic and adaptive in their approach to their regulatory relationships based upon what is happening in their ecosystem

Assuming the regulator has a view across that full ecosystem is a good starting point and one where organisations can ensure they are providing the context appropriate to what they may be seeing. In short, the regulatory relationship is changing across industries. With new enabling technologies, it is no longer, for example, just a quarterly or monthly meeting of counterparts circling a fixed pre-prepared agenda supplemented by periodic data submissions as it was for some in the past. It is a dynamic, real-time, 24-hour holistic *looking glass* that regulators now peer through. As such, the picture regulators see is constantly changing and, therefore, constantly building the view in the regulator's mind. For those managing regulatory relationships, being tuned into that same looking glass and anticipating the questions is key. Filling in the gaps and context the regulator may not see and ensuring that this picture aligns with the organisation's stated intent and objectives in terms of outcomes it is seeking to deliver will all help build a stronger relationship. Deltas between the perspectives of what is said and what is delivered by organisations are unlikely to instil confidence and build trust. The relationship therefore takes on a new dimension. In this digital and connected world, it's a real-time and constantly moving picture that needs appropriate interaction at key points, along with an ability to balance priorities and judge what is important in an ever-growing pool of information.

THROUGH THE LOOKING GLASS

So, what are the points of connection through which the regulator can build a view of your organisation, and as such, influence the direction and content of the regulatory relationship and engagement? Clearly, in previous chapters, we have already covered those that are about the configuration (organisational set up) and approach to navigation (how organisations are driven and led), so here we focus more on those items that are more attuned to outcomes. The following is by no means a definitive list, it is more a range of examples that, hopefully, demonstrates the point that your organisation's ecosystem is feeding a regulatory view in a constant flow of insight whether you control that flow or not. This picture, whilst having many areas of similarity, will likely vary across industries and of course organisations. As you consider your own industry, it is a useful exercise to consider all the different avenues of insight available to your regulator, supplement this list that follows, or re-write it specific to your own industry. It may surprise you how diverse it is.

How you engage with that ecosystem and the actions you take as an organisation are, therefore, important regarding how you engage with the regulator and the context they need to be given. Being mindful of how your organisation is operating will help in determining what information is needed and when. For example, if social media *lights up* due to the fact your core operations are down or some incident is occurring, your regulator may be very interested. Hopefully, social media will not have been how they found out about it, but in these days of instant communication methods, that may of course happen from time to time.

By way of examples, some of which are more traditional channels of interaction or insight and some of which are emergent, the following provides a snapshot of some of the *insight feeds*…the construct of the *looking glass* of regulatory insight if you will.

As a regulator takes a view of what it sees in relation to your organisation, this will inform what the regulator is interested in and what requests it makes of the organisation. This setting of the agenda and expectations by the regulator is a critical part of the context within which the organisation will need to operate. Being clear on the signals being sent, where necessary reading between the lines, and ensuring that the organisation is delivering and responding to such areas of focus is a cornerstone of how the relationship will need to progress. In this respect, as we will see throughout, there is no *one size fits all* approach to navigating

> There is no 'one size fits all' approach to navigating regulatory relationships, only proactive adaptation to the circumstances and situation that exists between a specific organisation and its regulator

The Looking Glass Of Insight – An Illustration				
Academic Research	International Regulator Cooperation	Annual Financial Statements	National Regulator Cooperation	Market Announcement
Product & Service Announcements	Marketing Campaigns	Political Insight	Interviews	Media
Market Studies	Industry Body Insights	Benchmarking	Consumer Organisations	Social Media
Thematic Reviews	Industry Consultations	Business Change	Suppliers	Complaint Resolution Services
Whistleblowing	Issues Incidents Breaches	Licencing / Applications	Industry Speeches	Dear CEO... Correspondence
Regulatory Visits / Investigations	Supervisory Scheduled Meetings	Company Officer Approvals	Data Submissions	Consumer Feedback

FIGURE 6.1   The Looking Glass of Insight – An Illustration

regulatory relationships, only proactive adaptation to the circumstances and situation that exists between a specific organisation and its regulator.

Similarly, as we have covered previously, organisations can choose to have a narrow approach to engagement, where the relationship is engaged with on a reactive, minimalist basis (across only a few of the *must do* items in Figure 6.1), through to a more proactive approach engaging on a wide array of items across the ecosystem. One point to note, regardless of the relationship strategy being followed, is that the priority of engagement on any of these subject areas can shift. As such, their relative position of importance an organisation assigns to areas of insight regulators may see across your ecosystem should be proactively kept under review. For example, in an industry that is subject to significant political scrutiny, as social media has been recently, the *political insight* area may well be placed front and centre in regulatory discussions whilst issues are worked through. Where an organisation actively monitors and understands its impact on their ecosystem, it can be more proactive in steering its direction, signalling its path, providing context where necessary, and explaining how what the regulator may be witnessing is being navigated by the organisation.

CHANGING APPROACHES TO REGULATORY INSIGHT

With the proliferation of information comes a further challenge for regulators. How do you as a regulator, orchestrate the flow, consumption, analysis, and insight that all these sources of information provide? As a regulator your data flow has expanded significantly and your *looking glass* is now full of disparate pieces of a puzzle you need to put together to drive insight and build a picture from which you can form views. This is a significant challenge in the world of regulatory relationships and another area where new technologies offer new possibilities.

As regulators grapple with an increasing array of service providers, products, services, and methods of delivery, they need to constantly develop and hone their ability to distil vast amounts of data. In a world of increased regulatory scrutiny, new and emergent technologies are being utilised to provide the tools required to facilitate that analysis, however, before you assume we are on a path to *programme regulatory oversight*, some good news is, to date, there is still plenty of value and need for human judgement as discussed by James Proudman (2018), Executive Director for U.K. Deposit Takers Supervision at the Bank of England. Proudman shared his expectation that we would see the development of cyborg supervision as machine learning and advanced analytics progress. His assertion being these technologies offer a wide range of opportunities for regulators as they grapple with huge amounts of data. Whilst Proudman sees the opportunities, he also asserts that algorithms and new technologies are still unable to fully replace human judgement[1].

Whilst progress is being made, the relationship looks set to stay in terms of regular interaction with regulators. What is interesting is that this new era of information transfer not only poses challenges for regulated organisations, but it is a challenge for the regulator, too. These new tools aim to provide the regulator with new opportunities, as they distil and draw insight on a level not achieved before. In doing this, they will be able to join the dots across information in new ways, indeed Figure 6.2 provides a recent example that

The regulators, having observed issues of resilience across financial services organisations, have moved in a coordinated way to place the subject of resilience high up their respective agendas, and ensure banks are prudent in their provisions for such matters. Consequently, we have the Financial Conduct Authority, The Bank of England, and the Prudential Regulation Authority moving in a coordinated way to lift the watermark across the industry in terms of their expectations and standards for their respective areas of responsibility. Their work involves making linkages across a broad range of information sources to provide the ability to get to the root of issues and respond accordingly. Information is taken from many sources and the implications worked through, for example:

- Incidents that arise along with their root cause and implications
- Changing consumer behaviour and their adoption and retirement of technologies, (e.g., the explosion of data sharing and capacity of data storage, move from branches, cash and ATMs to mobile banking, contactless payments, cashback solutions and the emergence of digital currency)
- Changing patterns of financial crime and the move from single-channel single-product fraud (e.g., cheque fraud to sophisticated scams involving both the social engineering of consumers and the use of data and online platforms)
- Changing operating methods and models (e.g., the integration of traditional batch banking platforms with around the clock digital solutions)
- The outlook in terms of technological advances (e.g., the rapid development of Fintech and new entrants to the banking and payments systems).

Regulators noted that resilience across various areas and the consequences of the loss of resilience in an increasingly digital world has the potential for significant disruption and harm for consumers.

As one example of this focus on resilience, Bailey (2018) highlighted key risks and the implications for the financial services industry and potential consequences of a lack of resilience in these changing times. Examples of those risks included areas such as cyber-risk and attempts of criminals to disrupt firms and their systems, risks arising from the increasing complexity of organisational platforms, and risks related to data, its use, and its security.

FIGURE 6.2   U.K. Financial Services – Regulators Focus on Resilience

this capability of distilling themes and making linkages is already providing opportunities across regulators to move in a united fashion as insights are used to identify and respond to industry trends or challenges.

In summary, the sources of insight for regulators have grown significantly and regulators are now tapping into a rich ecosystem of insight. At the same time, their ability to analyse rapidly growing volumes and sources of information is accelerating as they use new and emergent technologies to help distil insight. The combination of these growing capabilities is helping regulators to better identify risks (current and emergent) and understand their capacity to change over time as trends in consumer behaviour, products, services, and organisations develop. As one director noted:

> *"Even now there are times when submissions are provided to the regulator and context has not been appropriately articulated. Regulators, however, are often one step ahead in joining the dots".*

As a result of being better informed, regulators can focus their attention and prioritise key areas of concern, which can also benefit organisations that tune into their regulator's signals, as they can ensure they avoid risks that their regulator may see from their view across they industry, that the organisation may not fully appreciate.

REGULATORY APPROACH TO SUPERVISION – INTELLIGENCE LED AND DATA DRIVEN

Regulators, like any other organisation, generally have a clear set of constraints within which they try and achieve their objectives. This will include the scope of their activities in terms of what and who they regulate (their boundary of operation), what they seek to achieve in terms of objectives (sometimes also documented in legal requirements), and how they go about it (through their strategy, principles, and approach to regulating – see Chapter 1). It will also include the usual constraints most businesses face, such as funding, the resources they can deploy, and the legislative frameworks they operate within. In balancing these constraints, regulators will often formulate their approach to supervision, including how they will supervise firms of different scale and complexity, what principles they will follow in supervising firms, and how they will prioritise their activity.

Given these constraints, the data, information, and insight they tap into become valuable assets to leverage. Being intelligence led and data driven can help prioritise issues of greatest importance and facilitate a very efficient and effective use of resources to drive the maximum benefit. Data, information, and insight become the lifeblood feeding the operating

> Being intelligence led and data driven can help prioritise issues of greatest importance and facilitate a very efficient and effective use of resources to drive the maximum benefit

decisions day to day of a regulator, from insight they glean on industry practitioner business models, strategy, and culture discussed in earlier chapters, to the more operational and outcome-driven sources of insight we are discussing next[2]. To make best use of its resources, a regulator needs a constant flow of information from a variety of sources to enable it to focus in the right areas, prioritise the right issues, and shape its rules and principles in appropriate ways. As your ecosystem feeds that information to the regulator, it can be very useful if those flows build a coherent picture. It's even better if that is supported with appropriate context you provide that demonstrates progress is toward your stated strategic objective in a planned and controlled way that is aligned to the regulator's rules, principles, and objectives. That is, your words and your actions, as demonstrated by the signals your organisation and its environment are relaying, are well aligned.

EXPLORING THE ECOSYSTEM

So far, in this chapter, we have considered the fact that the regulator has and continues to enjoy an expanding source of insight. However, we also noted the challenges and changes being made by regulators as they seek to distil their regulatory insight from the vast array of data and information through the deployment of new technologies that can assist them. To demonstrate the point of how such insights can be used to join up the activities across regulators, we looked at an example of how differing regulatory bodies are now able to coordinate activities across significant industry challenges. We now look at the differing sources of data, information, and insight of the ecosystem (along with examples) and how they can inform the regulator on the activities being undertaken by an organisation. Whilst not an exhaustive view, it provides useful insights and ideas for how you may think about interactions with regulators and the messages and signals each part of the ecosystem is emitting. As we explore this array of touchpoints, it is worth reflecting on how you feel your organisation ensures there is an alignment between the strategy it pursues, the communications sent both internally and externally, and the signals the organisation's activities and outcomes relay to the regulator. 'Walk in the shoes" of the consumer and regulator as you consider each point or example and think about the messages and outcomes the organisation is producing.

As you consider the examples, think, as illustrated in Figure 6.3, if you would place such information on the positive or negative side of the opinion fulcrum when it comes to your regulator forming a view of your organisation.

Board, Supervisory, and Scheduled Meetings

This section is purposefully a broad category with which to get started. It considers all forms of face-to-face interaction (outside of dealing with issues and incidents that are covered below), whether part of a regular regulatory supervision cycle, in response to a specific request, or a need to discuss items further or in more detail. In short, they are the meetings you would expect to undertake in the execution of your day-to-day regulatory relationship.

These meetings are a great opportunity to build a thread of consistency in the story and evidence of organisational progress. They are an opportunity to review items that have – in the past –been areas of focus, to consider how

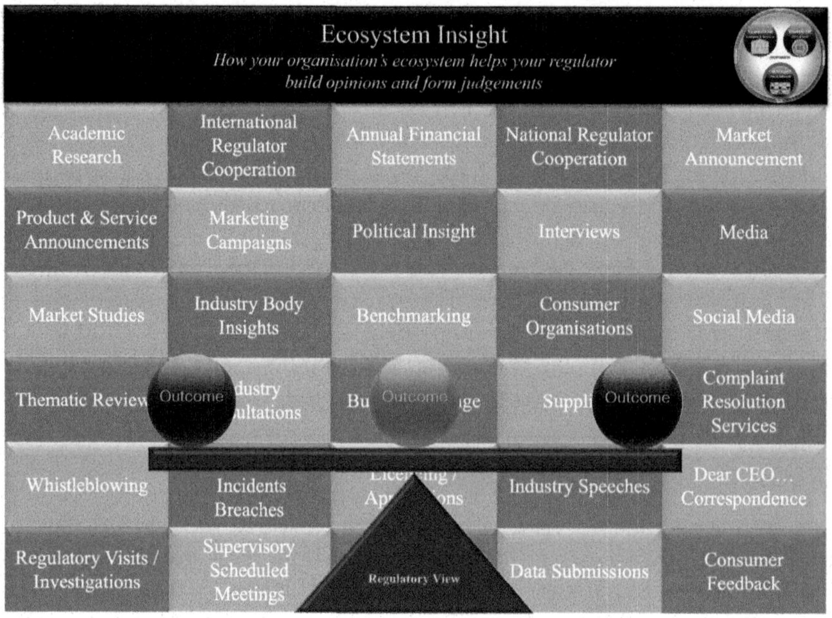

FIGURE 6.3   Ecosystem Insight

they have progressed, and to update on emerging items or risks the organisation sees ahead of it. In many respects, these meetings are the opportunity to check the *temperature* of the organisation, ensure there are no surprises, and, where necessary, delve deeper into areas of the organisation it would be helpful for the regulator to gain further insight.

In terms of the ecosystem of information flows, these meetings will often be a key opportunity to provide context, join up the story of conflicting or disparate points of evidence the regulator may be tuning into, and generally ensure that progress is understood. Remember, as we discussed earlier, all the information a regulator is seeing is set against a backdrop of what they understand to be your strategic direction. In that broader context, the dots need to join up, and these meetings are opportunities to develop the mutual understanding of progress and how that sits with the regulator against its objectives and priorities.

One point to remember, that will be discussed in more detail in the next chapter, is that all these discussions may be had across the breadth of the organisation (different levels of the hierarchy and across different areas or functions) and, as such, alignment is key. The regulator, for example, may be on cycles of interaction with different organisational leadership team members and, departments. There may be periodic discussions with the Chief Executive and the Board, to review how the strategy is progressing or any change in the organisational or environmental risk profile, whilst also having discussions with the risk department, technology department, operations, or broader divisions. Clearly, if there are significant disconnects in the messages being conveyed from these different areas regarding matters commonly discussed, this could lead to further enquiry into areas and concern around how organisational governance operates. It is, therefore, essential that the messages are aligned based on a common understanding and interpretation of a shared data and information base. Differing versions of the truth – the *telephone game* effect of layers and layers of committees and version amendment reporting up the governance line – can all lead to concerns building in the effectiveness of governance and control systems.

As will become apparent as you continue through the following paragraphs, the variety and breadth of information available to the regulator is copious. These meetings allow for connections to be made, summaries to be shared, and the organisational story to be presented.

Product and Service Announcements/Marketing Campaigns

The communication of new products and services, changes to existing products and services or the launch of marketing campaigns are a great resource and area of interest to the regulator. After all, products, prices, and service provision can be in regular flux depending on the industry and are the key point of interface with your customers. From a regulator's point of view, they provide a significant amount of information, especially when set against the strategy you have laid out. For example, in financial services over the years, changes in market conditions, bank operating models, and consumer behaviour have driven significant changes that have often been seen as warning flags or areas for further discussion due to the questions they raise. Whether it is the introduction, change, and ongoing resilience of technologies to support modern products and services (e.g., blockchain technology[8], mobile technology/security), the fragility of business models to major market shifts (e.g., capital and liquidity levels), or the migration of services to electronic channels, resulting in branch closures, experience has provided the regulator with insight into the impact and risks of such developments for the consumer. Next are just a few examples of some of the questions that may arise for a regulator as organisations make their day-to-day changes. They are provided as food for thought and to demonstrate the need to constantly walk in the regulator's shoes, as you will no doubt do with your customers. Taking a broader perspective of what feeds the regulatory picture can open thinking to the challenges and questions that may arise out of the actions you are taking…some of which may be expected…some may not.

PRICING EXAMPLE Changes in pricing can send signals to the regulator and spark further enquiry and action or, in some circumstances, could be overtly controlled, such as in the areas where monopoly situations exist[3]. In the utilities industries, for example, where the market is covered by a limited number of large providers, price increases, particularly as winter approaches or against the backdrop of stable wholesale prices, is often a signal for further regulatory scrutiny. In financial services, price increases on mortgage rates against the backdrop of stable official Central Bank and wholesale funding rates can have the same effect. Justifying why price rises are fair and reasonable is key to ensuring your customers and your regulator are comfortable with such a move. By contrast, aggressive savings rates taking an organisation to the top of the savings rate tables by some margin, may attract attention to your potential need for attracting funds at pace or re-balancing your forms of funding. Similarly, aggressive lending rates may signal a drive for growth or a shift in market conditions beginning to unfold that could challenge your profitability.

In short, pricing moves can and do trigger questions where they appear out of kilter with the market or out of character for the organisation given the strategy it has set out to follow.

TERMS AND CONDITIONS EXAMPLE   Onerous, complex, or unclear terms and conditions – whether changing or being launched with new services – can again signal to the regulator that the organisation may not be as open and transparent in their dealings with customers as the regulator would like to see. The basis of our contracts and the terms upon which we as consumers sign up to services is likely to receive an increasing degree of scrutiny, particularly given moves toward greater consumer protection. The world in which consumers now operate are increasingly digital. We share more of our lives digitally, whether it be through information sharing on social media, our migration to digital methods of transacting, or through the tracking of our behaviour and activities as we live our lives in the digital world more and more (e.g., web search and browser monitoring).

Against this increasingly complex set of relationships we hold, the need for an overhaul of how we contract may well be overdue and regulators are likely to become increasingly interested in how organisations can demonstrate their consumers truly understand the implications of the agreements they sign up to. The following questions organisations could ask hopefully illustrate the point regarding the difficulties faced here:

- How do you demonstrate agreements are understandable to your audience and are not overly onerous and legalistic?
- How do you monitor that consumers have read them rather than simply pushing "accept"?
- How do you demonstrate that the consumer's use of products and services demonstrates an understanding of their risks?

The basis of the law of contract is a significant enabler to business and commerce, but it needs to also operate in a way that delivers for consumers and is within the needs of the regulator's objectives, whilst facilitating fairness and transparency to not leave it open to challenge[4]. Contracts and terms are an important area for regulators as they provide a window into the way in which the organisation conducts its business and sets out the relationship with its customers in terms of the respective party's obligations. Where it sees unfair practices, regulators will step in, and whilst this is the realm of contract law, often the regulator has other powers it can bring to bear to convince or compel an organisation to take a different tack. Similarly, much as your terms may attract your regulator's attention, don't forget the consumer may also react vigorously. For example, we have seen backlashes from stakeholders, such as customers and suppliers, at attempts to change terms in ways that are seen as unfair. The following examples from social media to food delivery demonstrate this is not new, affects many different industries, and act as warnings that this area is one to tread with care from a regulatory and consumer perspective. Here, Facebook's updated privacy policy on Instagram and Uber Eats contract terms proved challenging for the respective organisations (see Hudson 2013 and Syamnath 2019).

MARKETING AND PROMOTION EXAMPLE   In a similar spirit to the terms and conditions example above, organisations can, at times, attract the attention of regulators in how they market their products and the claims, suggestions, or implied benefits they espouse. One example that illustrates this point arose whilst the world was in the early stages of responding to the Covid-19 virus (Mezher 2020). Here, the U.S. Food and Drug Administration (F.D.A.) and the Federal Trade Commission combined their efforts to issue warning letters to seven companies for making claims about their products with regard to Covid-19 that the regulators were unhappy with, noting:

"Fraudulent and unsupported claims about products" and their use in the treatment of Covid-19 infection.

F.D.A. commissioner Stephen Hahn went further to disclose how they monitored the activities of organisations, which provided a window into their processes for oversight and surveillance of the market:

"We have an aggressive surveillance program that routinely monitors online sources for health fraud products, especially during a significant public health issue such as this one".

Once again, this is a useful insight into the activities of regulators reading the environment around organisations to inform their opinion of regulatee activities.

SERVICE PROVISION EXAMPLE   Having considered price and the basis of contract and terms as fundamental trading examples, the final example to demonstrate how regulators can take an interest in changes organisations make will look at some of the more progressive changes to how services or products develop.

In Financial Services in the U.K., for example, let's consider for a moment the trends and shifts in behaviour for how banking is developing. As the online and digital world has expanded in the use and provision we enjoy, there are few areas of our lives that cannot be enabled by such capability. Of course, banking has also invested heavily in this digital world, and we can now see our entire banking relationships whilst on the move and transact whilst en-route. However, change in behaviour has implications for the economics of banking, and as such, we have seen the demise of the more traditional methods of delivery. As we tap and swipe electronic money around, our use of cash is falling and with it our use of the traditional branch and automated teller machines (ATMs). Whether you view this as a natural re-alignment of investment spend as banks plough money into the new technologies and reduce the costs of traditional lower-use services, or see this as a reduction in consumer choice, the fact is that organisational investment in new technologies to keep them relevant and competitive is enabling behavioural change for which we are seeing consequences unfold. From a regulator's point of view, there are implications to consider in all such change. These new technologies need to be introduced and run in a robust and controlled manner to avoid disruption to services consumers heavily rely upon. The technologies need to be safe, secure, and be resilient to the attempts of criminals to perpetuate financial crime. Why, you may ask, is this any different to any other time? Well, consider how behaviour and the provision of services has changed. In the past, we were less reliant on technologies and as such their disruption was less of an issue. Cash was more widely used and if the payments system or a store was *off-line*, we could revert to cash, cheque, or visit ATMs, bank branches, or post offices (some of which also had manual fall-back options). Generally, there were more options more immediately and conveniently available to us. Now, whilst we have some of the most convenient and advanced services at our fingertips, our reliance on them has grown and, as such, we feel their loss more keenly when they are not available. Ask your friends and family how many of them now do not carry cash. At one time it would have been unheard of, but now our card or phone is our new cash. Ask them how many of them have a cheque book (or know where it is) and how many of them carry it about with them or know if their bank card can guarantee a cheque. The next time you are in a store, look around and see if they even accept cheques anymore. Then consider where your nearest bank branch, post office, or ATM is. In simple terms, the regulator sees the change unfolding at an industry level and, in its capacity to look across the system, is recognising how that change poses challenges where reliability and resilience are undermined. Contingency, disaster recovery, fail over, crisis management, and back up and recovery planning are all terms the regulator will become increasingly interested in should your business model, and the products and services you deliver, lead to a place where reliability and resilience become increasingly important to your customers and the industry.

Media (Societal and Social)

The media is a 24-hour flow of insight and information to your regulator. It spans traditional formal media organisations such as print, television, and radio along with the whole array of online and digital delivery channels offered by media organisations.

Traditionally, these media channels and organisations were largely interacted with in an organised and ordered fashion, with announcements and stories released to the media to facilitate news stories associated with an organisation. As such, what was in the media could, to some degree, be coordinated and anticipated. However, over the years, what is understood as the media has advanced dramatically.

First, we have seen the role of media develop as the champion of the consumer, the guardian of value, the reflection and window on society, and the documenter of the consumer's day to day life. This has facilitated a whole host of consumer-focused programmes taking to task organisations who are seen to undermine the interests and fairness of dealings with the consumer. Investigating and surfacing such issues now sees numerous organisations having their day-to-day practices laid bare in front of the public and, of course, their regulator.

Second, we have seen the rise of a new form of media in terms of accessibility: social media. The disintermediation of traditional pathways to publicity has had a significant effect on the way organisations engage with their public. For example, platforms like Facebook, Twitter, and YouTube, provide a method for individuals to raise their concerns, build consensus, and generate reaction. Organisations are no longer in just a *one-to-one* relationship with their consumer base, they are in a *one-to-many* relationship, and that *many* can, of course, be counted to a number that not too long ago would have been unheard of. It can also include your regulator, which also has access to this new source of insight and information and can see how your public is responding to your organisation and its activities.

This age of likes, customer reviews, short messages, tweets, and posts across a variety of messaging platforms, allows opinion (whether accurate or not) to form quickly. Connections can build at unprecedented speed, as well as having an ability to *go viral* whilst measuring that progress in minutes and hours, rather than the months and years it may have historically taken to build such a consensus around an issue.

Media in the modern day is very different to its traditional form, and as such, the need to understand, engage with it, and manage it carefully is essential. When things go wrong, it may be that your customer who just suffered something negative is your first warning signal. In fact, when things go wrong, it is amazing how this connected world can now surface such issues that occur around the globe, at times occurring in remote places and with a pace that is measured in minutes. A brief review of the news or social media platforms each day reveals the power these technologies have provided in terms of sharing and distributing the events of the day, no matter where they may be taking place. Figure 6.4 illustrates the challenge and opportunity facing organisations today with such technology.

For organisations, social media provides both opportunity and challenge with its speed of impact and breadth of reach. Whether the news on social media is about the organisation, its products and services, or the implications of using them, big stories can quickly reach both the organisation and all its stakeholders often at the same time.

From devastating crises and accidents to products and services that fail, a camera in billions of pockets every day means these events are often captured, documented, and distributed with an immediacy history has not experienced.

When issues unfold, it is often that same channel that provides the opportunity for the organisation to gather images and information as quickly as possible so that it can start to build its own picture and respond. Those who have been involved in crisis situations where getting data, information, and images as quickly as possible to allow timely decisions to be made is crucial, have recounted the importance of social media in their efforts to build the picture quickly of what may have happened and what should be done next. Time for all stakeholders who may be impacted by difficult events often feels compressed by the speed at which data and information is moving. Of course, a whole array of stakeholders will also be using such information to build their own picture of the implications it may have for them and what actions, if any, they should take next. From consumers considering who they use for their future needs, regulators who gather information to allow them to understand the events, their drivers, and their implications, to shareholders and financiers who consider the potential impact on their investments, all information shared becomes part of the fabric of their understanding and decision-making process.

Social media, in this context, has become a very powerful and effective technology for the capture and escalation of events, including providing important evidence to build a picture from which we can understand and learn.

FIGURE 6.4   Building a Picture Through Social Media

Social media can be your quickest and best form of feedback. It is often near real-time, visible, and open to attracting the attention of traditional media organisations and your regulator. How organisations prepare and respond is key. The danger being that organisations can soon become overwhelmed should interest peak in areas you are not ready to deal with. As you can imagine, areas where your media is getting interested, and where the velocity and magnitude of impact can have implications for your business, will be areas of rapid enquiry and interest to any regulator.

Market and Thematic Reviews, Industry Consultations, Data Submissions, and Academic Research

In executing their duties, regulators will require a robust and regular stream of data, information, and insight. Different regulators will have different approaches, but, generally, these requirements will comprise a combination of standing data submissions that form the bedrock of their core supervisory and oversight requirements, supplemented by third-party information sources, market studies, thematic reviews, consultations with industry, and engagements with academia. In short, the information available to the regulator is both broad and comprehensive, and where there are gaps that emerge due to a particular change in behaviour or emergent risk, they can often compel the provision of supplementary data to ensure those situations can be fully understood and considered. As they assimilate this information, it provides insight to set your organisation in the context of your competitors, your industry, and the markets in which you operate.

Whilst there are different approaches captured under this section, a common theme is the desire to understand some element of how markets and organisations within markets are operating and performing. Whether a particular market or theme is being looked into for how it is functioning, or to review the current or emerging risks (e.g., motor finance, pension advice, social media data usage, vulnerability, utility pricing, price discrimination), or academic research is being used to understand certain elements of how individuals within markets or markets *per se* operate (e.g., behavioural economics, behavioural finance, the impact of social media on consumers), in all cases, the regulator is seeking to understand more. As such, it presents a great opportunity for regulators and regulatees to develop understanding collegiately.

Understanding the landscape of what research is underway and engaging positively in market studies and industry consultations can provide the opportunity to engage in a two-way information sharing exercise that can be a valuable backdrop to considering how your organisation sits in the environment in which you operate. Similarly, as regulators are often investigating matters at a macro level, the insights these pieces of research offer can provide valuable information for organisations across the industry. These engagements with industry don't always just involve one regulator or one regulatory jurisdiction either, which can provide even greater insight. A good example of regulators and industry coming together to look at opportunities to adapt in a rapidly changing environment is provided by the Innovative Medicines Initiative (2017). Here, more than 40 representatives of regulatory agencies came together to focus on common issues facing the industry, one of which was to share lessons and opportunities for enhanced and timely regulatory interactions as advances in medicine and medical devices increase in pace. Attendees represented a broad base, including the European Medicines Agency, U.S. Food and Drug Administration, EU Heads of Medicines Agency, the Pharmaceuticals and Medical Devices Agency, the European Federation of Pharmaceutical Industry and Association, the European Commission (Directorates General Research and Innovation and Health and Food Safety), and the IMI2 Scientific Committee. In fact, the subject of regulatory interactions thread throughout their report, such was the importance placed on effective regulatory engagements and relationships.

In supporting the regulator's work in these areas, the organisation also can demonstrate that it is proactive, open, and transparent in its dealings with the regulator, as well as supporting the progression of the industry and knowledge of how the market is functioning for the benefit of the consumer. This offers another opportunity to demonstrate how the regulatory agenda fits with your organisation's strategy and your organisational attitude toward your regulator, wherever you may have set that regulatory risk appetite dial.

Issues, Incident Management, and Dear CEO Communications

One of the situations no organisation wants to find itself in is responding to issues and incidents. Such issues could be industry wide, such as responding to a direct question regarding industry practice, which the regulator addresses directly to the CEO for their personal response (something you hope to be able to respond to positively given the regulator's clear concern), or an issue or incident specific to your organisation, which for the purposes of this section, we will cover next.

Issues and incidents specific to your organisation, given their impact, will clearly demand a high degree of regulatory scrutiny and that scrutiny will likely play out over an extended period as the regulator and organisation go through the various stages of dealing with the issue. These situations are intense times for any regulatory relationship, however, there will be a common priority. Initially, the focus will be on minimising the impact, ensuring it is contained, and providing as much support and contingent arrangements as possible to provide the best response to those impacted by the situation. These are times that demand open, honest, and frank conversations, a high degree of transparency, and frequent interaction to ensure the organisation and its regulator are entirely in sync as they both respond to their respective audiences and stakeholders.

Once the immediate situation is under control, focus will naturally progress to ensuring fixes remain sustainable and resilient and normal operation can be resumed (resilience we will cover further later). The consideration of further remediation and redress activities, together with a wider consideration of risk that may remain, will likely become the subject of regulatory interactions. Questions over what could have prevented such issues, their root cause, risk, and control framework effectiveness in failing to identify or mitigate issues, and ongoing actions to reassure the regulator that lessons have been learned and material risks have been surfaced will all be under consideration. The clear focus will be on ensuring a repeat of the same or related issues is not going to arise and that there has been a rigorous read across to try and identify and therefore prevent other issues impacting the organisation.

Whilst the steps described above provide a general and broad approach, each issue or incident will have its own implications that will drive appropriate activity given the situation.

For significant issues, the ramifications can ripple out much further than the incident and its immediate aftermath or associated assurance work. Regulators may seek independent external reviews of what unfolded, its root cause, the effectiveness of response and wider control, governance, and decision making of the organisation. The relationship in these situations can be under intense scrutiny, not only due to the parties feeling the challenge of each other's needs as they attempt to respond to the issue, but also due to the wider stakeholder attention and requirements given the significance of issues. Media attention, political interest, consumer group focus, and claims management industry attention are just a few of the areas where interest can lead to further pressures on the parties. The tail of implications from such events can run far and wide, which ultimately leads to answers being established for the questions raised by any issue, and the associated accountabilities being understood. These are the most difficult of situations, they test the relationships to the extreme and they demand the highest levels of focus and attention to navigate what is often a very difficult terrain.

There are a couple of areas that warrant additional attention. The first is the area of resilience and the second is that of technology. As the pace of technological advancement increases and the fusing of new technologies, processes, procedures, skills, and practices to old capabilities take shape, the complexity and pace of change pose challenges, especially when being deployed at greater speed and agility. From the Board down, skills and capability need to adapt quickly to ensure businesses can move at pace on secure and resilient footings.

RESILIENCE AND TECHNOLOGY   The fusing of the new with the old (or older) capabilities has always been a challenge for organisations, however, if we consider the velocity and breadth of change, the challenge in front of us becomes clearer. These challenges show no signs of relenting and, organisationally, we are seeing the development of skills and capabilities built specifically to enable this pace of change (e.g., *agile* practices). Suffice to say, all periods of organisational development will have had their challenges, however, the rationale for emphasising technology and resilience and its potential impact on regulatory relationships is twofold. Firstly, regulators are increasingly showing their interest in this area (see Figure 6.2), secondly, the level of integration of systems and connectivity we now enjoy with our customers means that a lack of resilience has the potential for impact on a scale not experienced in the past[5].

Martin Stewart (2020) provides a good example of the shift in both pace and focus regulators have seen in terms of technology, recognising that this is becoming a growing area of interest and one in which they are building their skills and knowledge.

The downside of a lack of resilience, and the interest, therefore, of regulators in an organisation's overall picture of resilience, is only likely to increase. Given the potential downside of a lack of resilience, understanding the resilience right across the organisation and its various systems and controls is likely to be an assessment your regulator will want to understand. The key question is will organisations know and be able to evidence it across the breadth of their organisation so that they can avoid issues.

Consumer Feedback, Consumer Organisations, Complaint Resolution Services, Whistle Blowing, and Competitors

Feedback for any organisation is a rich source of insight, as it holds up the mirror to the organisation and provides the stakeholder view of how the organisation delivers across its entire interaction with the customer. Their views may cover a whole array of topics, like the products and services and whether they live up to the marketing claims, how easy the organisation is to deal with, how reliable your products and services are, the availability and ease of use of the channels they access, the people serving them, the level of service provision, the sales approach or their view on your environmental impact, and your approach to social responsibility. Along the journey, there will be positive and negative feedback and, of course, the regulator will be interested in how the organisation deals with the feedback it receives. Satisfying the regulator may entail providing data and information on complaint levels and outcomes, as well as understanding the root cause insights and what is being done to improve on the positives and remove the negatives that may drive complaint and dissatisfaction.

Furthermore, the regulator can, of course, receive insights from consumer organisations or competitors eager to comment on the track record and performance of any organisation, as well as complaint resolution services that may share data on key areas of consumer dissatisfaction and complaint. All this insight can be extremely valuable, but like most insight, it will often come down to how organisations read its signals and what weight they give them in terms of importance and urgency of action. If we take the vehicle emissions scandal for example discussed in Chapter 3, whilst the figures in brochures on fuel economy generally across manufacturers were useful as a standard of comparison across brands and models, there was always the perception that they did not mirror real driving conditions and, therefore, real performance indicators. Should this fact alone have not been enough of a signal that better performance measures were required and that in a world becoming ever more concerned over emissions and pollution, greater importance and urgency should be placed on the efficacy of this key indicator for the consumer? Please excuse the pun, but to put it another way, the *smoke signals* were quite literally there for organisations to see in terms of the bar rising in this area and regulatory scrutiny intensifying. Boston and Sloat (2015) provided a sobering summary of the scale and impact of the issue for Volkswagen, highlighting how the International Council on Clean Transport had raised concerns and providing estimates by the manufacturer that up to 11 million cars could be impacted, with potential costs running into billions of dollars.

In the example above, the interplay between the organisation, its consumers, consumer groups, and the regulator all played out. Ultimately, the organisation suffered on every level, from their brand and reputation to the financial impact and attention of the regulator in terms of enforcement action.

Overall, the feedback from the customer, whether it is direct or indirect, helps the regulator understand the path the organisation is treading regarding customer satisfaction[6].

Improvements in organisations leading to higher levels of consumer satisfaction and lower levels of complaint can be investigated for the drivers of improvement and the potential for your organisation to share best practice. Alternatively, growing dissatisfaction and climbing complaints may attract attention for what improvements and investment is needed to turn around a situation. Whatever the situation, the regulator can set these insights against the broader story your ecosystem of information is emitting to understand if overall the organisation is heading in the right direction vis-à-vis its regulatory objectives. Such evidence provides the regulator with a very clear view of whether outcomes are aligning to the messages the organisation itself is claiming regarding customer outcomes and the status of customer satisfaction or dissatisfaction.

National and International Regulator Insight Sharing

As our world has advanced with the march of capabilities in technology, communications, and transport, it has also become a seemingly smaller place. As these developments have unfolded, some businesses have grasped the opportunities that multi-national or global operations provide. Their markets and the distribution of their products and services have expanded across geographical boundaries, allowing them to grow in ways we have not experienced before.

For organisations operating in regulated industries, such supranational expansion introduces the challenge of ensuring that they are able to satisfy the regulatory requirements of differing global regions. This challenge is also present for the regulators in reverse, that is, ensuring all that operate within their markets do so with appropriate standards in place. Whilst regulators can be part of global standard-setting organisations, agreeing minimum standards for regional regulators to take account of in their own codes and rules means connectivity across regional regulatory bodies remains key. Such interoperability across geographical regions means regulators will often share insights on their respective standards, best practice, and common interest work, together with how organisations within their regions are operating. It may well be that an organisation is *registered* with one regulatory body in a given region and *licenced* to operate in other regions, however, the importance of knowing how a given organisation is performing across its breadth of operations will often involve regulators sharing insight between themselves.

From a regulatory relationship point of view, multinational and global businesses can, therefore, present significant challenges. Organisations may be required to maintain relationships across different regulatory bodies, in different geographical regions, for different types of businesses. Maintaining a relationship with a coherent and consistent thread of insight across a diverse ecosystem of operation can be a challenge. In these situations, areas of the organisation that provide direction, assure standards, and permeate the fabric of the organisation will be key signals to regulators. Thus, strategy, risk appetite, governance, control systems, and that binding cultural adhesive will all be keen areas of interest in terms of insight. Knowing large and complex organisations are innately set up well will be a fundamental starting point.

Applications for Company Officer Approval

One area of the ecosystem of insight provided to regulators is usually raised more by regulators themselves in discussions, rather than by organisations that are regulated: the process of approval for individuals. Regulators may have powers to approve individuals to conduct certain activities in an industry or firm. For example, in Financial Services in the U.K., the Financial

Conduct Authority will look to be satisfied that individuals are fit and proper to perform certain functions within an organisation. This involves understanding an individual's honesty, integrity, reputation, competence, capability, and financial soundness (FCA 2022).

Such applications provide the regulator with insight on the nature of key personnel organisations are attracting. It provides insights on the responsibilities and the breadth of accountability they will hold. It allows the regulator to see first-hand the type of team an organisation is building and provides the opportunity to understand their history, their reputation, their achievements and their competence, capability, and skills. Set against the information they have on the firm concerned, it provides a sense of how these individuals are being positioned to fit into the story of the organisation, from the messages on Board priorities, the appetite for risk being espoused, and the strategy being articulated to achieve the organisation's objectives.

Such powers are useful for the regulator. Like many of the areas we have discussed so far, such processes provide a view in on the organisation, in this case, into key appointments to enable them to gain comfort the right people are in control of organisations.

Industry Conferences, Speeches, and Interviews

Across different industries, you will often find a programme of conferences underway spanning the calendar year. These are gatherings of industry professionals brought together to discuss a whole array of issues and topics with speakers invited from organisations spanning the industry. Indeed, it may be that regulators and organisations share the same platform at the same time as issues of importance are discussed and debated.

Whether organisations are involved in discussions, debates, speaking on matters of importance to their organisation, or delivering industry speeches, seminars, or workshops, these public expressions of sentiment, opinion, policy, action, or inaction are all important points of insight in the regulatory relationship. The key is for the organisation to be comfortable with the messages it is sending and be cognisant of how they fit with the broader relationship approach being pursued.

For organisations, regulators presenting at such events will provide a useful source of insight. It provides an opportunity to hear about the regulator's priorities, to understand their concerns, and hear how they intend to progress on matters of interest. These signals can be early pointers for organisations to start considering how their organisation aligns, what challenges it may have, and what action it may need to take.

Industry Body Insight Sharing

Across many industries, representative bodies work with their member organisations in the advancement of their industry. They may perform the functions of being the voice of their industry or trying to proactively advance the industry through the setting of industry agreed standards (e.g., self-regulatory provisions, rules, and standards). They may cooperate on common industry issues and share best practices for the benefit of all and the progression of the industry. Membership of such bodies can be an important signal to regulators that the organisation is promoting the advancement of improved standards and the responsible development of the industry. Through these industry bodies, the views of the industry can be quickly gathered and understood to put forward industry viewpoints to a variety of stakeholder groups, including the political party of the day or regulatory bodies.

For the regulatory relationship, these bodies can provide a good signal of the overall direction of travel an industry is taking. It can also provide a useful conduit through which a regulator can share its views so that they can be quickly disseminated to the membership organisations on any topic under discussion. Similarly, if the industry body is pressing down a particular path the regulator is uneasy about, it may seek to understand where such a view is arising through bilateral discussions with members of the industry body. Conversely, if there are developments that the regulator is pleased to see unfolding, they may wish to seek out who is driving such ideas with a view to establish how their combined efforts could bring those opportunities to life.

Industry organisations, therefore, provide an important conduit for insight. That conduit will often involve discussions at a broader industry level, providing a level of anonymity to members whilst allowing views to be shared on matters being progressed either by the regulator or by member organisations. From a regulatory relationship point of view, understanding the items on the agendas of the organisations you are affiliated with and the discussions they are having with regulators can be useful to ensure you are ready to engage on those subjects bilaterally with your regulator should the subject arise.

Politicians

Politicians, as publicly accountable individuals, have an important role to play in ensuring the fair and orderly operation of society, including industry, trade, and commerce. It will not be surprising, therefore, that organisations or industries that capture political attention, whether for positive or negative reasons, will often feel the attention in the relationships with their regulators. Politicians will often look to regulators to ensure appropriate regulatory rules and controls are at play to assure the effective functioning of an industry in line with regulatory powers the political process has bestowed upon the regulator.

From a regulatory relationship perspective, the tone, intensity, and nature of political interest in any particular industry or organisation may see changes in the approach taken by regulators as they execute their duties. Where an industry or organisation is seen as problematic, both regulators and the organisations themselves will be under political scrutiny to understand and respond to the challenges they face. Where an industry is seen as an opportunity, that pressure may be to enable progression, remove red tape, and allow organisations to operate more freely. Where challenges arise, that scrutiny may be around whether further legislation or regulation is required and whether regulatory powers need to be strengthened. However, not all challenges are straight forward. Some pose increasingly difficult dilemmas, as the report by Pagliery (2016) on CNN Business demonstrates. The report highlighted that Apple was refusing to comply with a court order to allow access to an iPhone in a high-profile case. Apple CEO Tim Cook (2016) responded with a message to customers calling for a public discussion on the implications.

Sometimes clashes arise between the wider freedoms we all enjoy, the powerful and exciting opportunities that technology enables, and the need to protect us from those that would use such technologies against us. These examples demonstrate how products designed for social good, when used for detrimental outcomes, can have significant implications across stakeholder groups[7]. As new technologies have developed, become rapidly adopted and connected millions of individuals worldwide, they have attracted attention for how they are used with both positive and negative outcomes as well as started the conversation of how social media should be regulated to protect all users.

More and more such lessons point toward a need for anticipating potential detriment and designing in safeguards to ensure your objectives for the product or service cannot be easily undermined and misused. Such approaches will allow not only for the core capability of the new technologies to develop at pace, but also the protections they provide.

The key point to consider from a regulatory relationship point of view, is what the political dynamics of the industry and your organisation look like. This can be a useful insight into how the regulatory relationship may develop, the type of agenda you may well be called upon to discuss, and the challenges and opportunities that may face both parties as the relationship develops forward.

Annual Financial Statements and Market Announcements

From a regulatory relationship point of view, the rather clinical commercial realities of annual results, financial statements, and market announcements may seem unexpected ground to tread in terms of being a key part of the ecosystem. For some industries, this may matter more than for others, however, not only do these activities provide an indication on the financial performance of the organisation, financial statements and market announcements can cover a whole wealth of information on non-financial matters of interest or provide insight on the plans and direction the organisation is calling out to its shareholders. Within the detail of such voluminous publications, regulators may see statements of concern or contradictions they may wish to discuss further or satisfy themselves that such items do not pose undue risk. Like many areas of our discussion, ensuring such messages chime and are consistent with what is being discussed with the regulator is key. Even more important is that they do not contain significant surprises, as finding out about matters that should have been raised with the regulator that are buried in an annual financial statement is never a good opening agenda item for your next meeting with them!

ECOSYSTEM – A COHESIVE PICTURE

In previous chapters, we discussed what sound footings may look like for a regulatory relationship. In this chapter, we have considered the broad array of points of interaction or insight that could inform any given regulator, with the suggestion being that organisations need to develop a dynamic approach to their regulatory relationship based upon what is happening in their organisational ecosystem as a whole. Being tuned into the signals their organisation emits, as well as being able to respond and quickly place context around those signals to help make sense of such messages is a necessity.

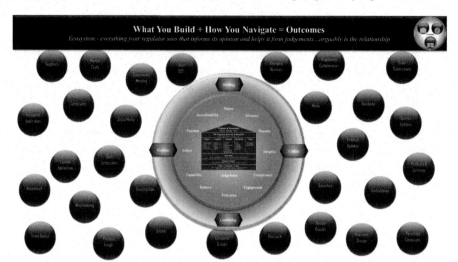

FIGURE 6.5   What You Build + How You Navigate = Outcomes

Figure 6.5 pulls together a picture of the ecosystem as we have discussed it.

This lays out the key factors we have considered to help bring to life how all the moving parts come together and how each can act as a source of insight connected in some way to the others.

Having the benefit of a sound basis for a relationship with the regulator and an understanding of where and how your regulator will tune-in to how the organisation is conducting itself is very useful. However, there is still one aspect that needs further attention. As your regulator interfaces with the variety of touch points that will exist across your ecosystem, it is crucial to ensure those interactions are positive ones. How interactions with your organisation are executed can also have an impact on the view of the regulator toward your organisation. In the next chapter, we consider some of the areas in which you can ensure your interactions are positive. As we walk through the practical considerations of engaging positively with regulators, consider how your own organisation goes about such matters. Stories you have heard, experiences you have had, and observations you may have made in the past can all be useful reflections. Again, this is not an exhaustive account, and the examples are illustrative, but this is where *the rubber hits the road* in regulatory relationship interactions, and as such, forms a crucial element in ensuring maximum traction in the relationship is achieved.

NOTES

1. See also Rusu (2021), "Drivers of change in the financial services industry and how we are responding".
2. For an example of a regulator asserting the importance of data and information, see Rathi, N. CEO of the Financial Conduct Authority and his comments on both the importance of data and the investment they are committing to data capabilities. Rathi, N. (2021), "Transforming to a forward-looking, proactive regulator".
3. See for example the U.K. Office of Gas and Electricity Markets (OFGEM 2004) Factsheet 30.

4. C.f. The following provides insight on Ofcom's view of the treatment of customers who wished to leave their contracts early. Ofcom (2018), "EE and Virgin Media fined for overcharging customers".
5. C.f. The following example references provide background reading in areas related to this subject. Ahmed (2017), "Five Corporate IT Failures That Caused Huge Disruption"; Buck, T. and Hollinger, P. (2017), "BA Faces £80m Cost For IT Failure that stranded 75,000 passengers"; B.B.C. News Report (2019), "BA Faces £183m Fine For Data Breach", and the related ICO fine, ICO (2020), "ICO Fines British Airways £20m For Data Breach Affecting More Than 400,000 Customers".
6. C.f. CNBC News Report (2017) – "Ryanair bows to UK regulator demand on passenger rights".
7. C.f. B.B.C. News Report (2019) – "Instagram biggest for child grooming online – NSPCC finds".
8. c.f. Financial Times article in the references section by Robin Vince, the Chief Executive and President of BNY Mellon. As blockchain was attracting the attention of regulators, Robin Vince writes on the challenges and opportunities this new technology presents, not least for regulating this new capability.

REFERENCES

Ahmed, M. (2017), 'Five corporate IT failures that caused huge disruption', [online], Financial Times, 28 May 2017, available: www.ft.com/content/270563ee-43b9-11e7-8d27-59b4dd6296b8

Bailey, A. (2018), Annual Public Meeting Speech, [online], Financial Conduct Authority, 11 September 2018, available: https://www.fca.org.U.K./news/speeches/andrew-bailey-speech-annual-public-meeting-2018

B.B.C. News Report (2019), 'British Airways faces record £183m fine for data breach', [Online], 8 July 2019, available: https://www.bbc.co.uk/news/business-48905907

B.B.C. News Report (2019), 'Instagram biggest for child grooming online – NSPCC finds', [online], 1 March 2019, available: www.bbc.co.U.K./news/U.K.-47410520

Boston, W. and Sloat, S. (2015), 'Volkswagen emissions scandal relates to 11 million cars', [online], Wall Street Journal, 22 September 2015, available: https://www.wsj.com/articles/volkswagen-emissions-scandal-relates-to-11-million-cars-1442916906

Buck, T. and Hollinger, P. (2017), 'BA faces £80m cost for IT failure that stranded 75,000 passengers', [online], Financial Times, 15 June 2017, available: https://www.ft.com/content/98367932-51c8-11e7-a1f2-db19572361bb

CNBC News Report (2017), 'Ryanair bows to U.K. regulator demand on passenger rights', [Online], 29 September 2017, available: https://www.cnbc.com/2017/09/29/ryanair-bows-to-U.K.-regulator-caa-demand-passenger-rights.html

Cook, T. (2016), 'A message to our customers', [online], 16 February 2016, available: https://www.apple.com/customer-letter/

Financial Conduct Authority (FCA) (2022), 'Fitness and propriety', [online], 25 May 2022, available: https://www.fca.org.uk/firms/approved-persons/fitness-propriety

Hudson, A. (2013), 'Is small print in online contracts enforceable?', [online], B.B.C., 5 June 2013, available: https://www.bbc.co.uk/news/technology-22772321

Information Commissioner's Office (ICO) (2020), 'ICO fines British Airways £20m for data breach affecting more than 400,000 customers', [online], available: https://ico.org.uk/about-the-ico/news-and-events/news-and-blogs/2020/10/ico-fines-british-airways-20m-for-data-breach-affecting-more-than-400-000-customers/

Innovative Medicines Initiative (2017), 'Report from The IMI-EMA-FDA Regulatory Science Summit – Collaborative Research Through Public-Private Partnership in Support to Advancing Regulatory Science', [online], 4 December 2017, available: https://www.imi.europa.eu/sites/default/files/uploads/documents/news-events/press-releases/RegulatorySummit2017_report.pdf

Mezher, M. (2020), 'Coronavirus: FDA, FTC warn seven firms over deceptive claims', [online], Regulatory Affairs Professionals Society, Regulatory Focus, 9 March 2020, available: https://www.raps.org/news-and-articles/news-articles/2020/3/coronavirus-fda-ftc-warn-seven-firms-over-deceptiv

Ofcom (2018), 'EE and Virgin Media fined for overcharging customers', [online], available: https://www.ofcom.org.U.K./about-ofcom/latest/media/media-releases/2018/ee-virgin-media-fined-overcharging-customers

OFGEM (2004), 'What is a price control?', [online], available: https://www.ofgem.gov.uk/publications/what-price-control-update

Pagliery, J. (2016), 'Apple is refusing to comply with a court order to break into the iPhone owned by one of the San Bernardino shooters', [online], CNN Business, 18 February 2016, available: https://money.cnn.com/2016/02/18/technology/apple-encryption/index.html

Proudman, J. (2018), 'Cyborg supervision – the application of advanced analytics in prudential supervision', [online], Bank of England, 19 November 2018, available: https://www.bankofengland.co.uk/speech/2018/james-proudman-cyborg-supervision

Rathi, N. (2021), 'Transforming to a forward-looking, proactive regulator', [online], Financial Conduct Authority, 15 July 2021, available: https://www.fca.org.uk/news/speeches/transforming-forward-looking-proactive-regulator

Rusu, J. (2021), 'Drivers of change in the financial services industry and how we are responding', [online], Financial Conduct Authority, 2 November 2021, available: https://www.fca.org.uk/news/speeches/drivers-change-financial-services-industry-and-how-we-are-responding

Stewart, M. (2020), 'Technology comes under the spotlight', Financial World, December 2019/January 2020, p.13

Syamnath, D. (2019), 'Australian watchdog says Uber Eats will amend "unfair" contract terms', [online], Reuters, 17 July 2019, available: https://U.K.reuters.com/article/U.K.-uber-australia-regulator/australian-watchdog-says-uber-eats-will-amend-unfair-contract-terms-idU.K.KCN1UC04L

Vince, R. (2022), 'Time for a reset of the crypto opportunity', [online], Financial Times, 2 December 2022, available: 5568bd6b-99df-4c8b-91bc-e0b49011da80

CHAPTER 7

Engagement
The Practical Considerations When Interacting with Regulators

CHAPTER SUMMARY – LET'S GET PRACTICAL

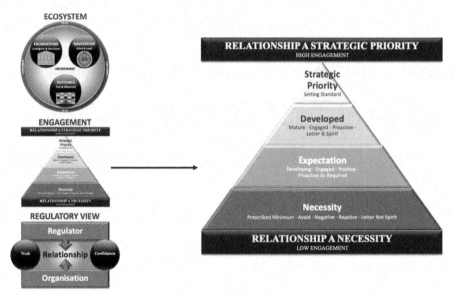

We begin by considering the importance of understanding your organisation's regulatory strategy, their approach toward their regulatory relationships along with your regulator's objectives, and the context in which engagements are to take place. These key factors provide a good backdrop against which we can judge how to appropriately prepare, respond, and engage to achieve the best possible outcome. As we will see, the context within which we engage and the objective the regulator pursues can have a significant effect on the manner, velocity, and breadth of how engagements take place.

Having considered the context, we move onto the most fundamental of principles that underpin relationships, that is that they involve people – and people form judgements. Here, we remind ourselves of the importance of considering our conduct and behaviour and the impact this can have in terms of

DOI: 10.4324/9781003297963-7

the conclusions that form based on our interactions. We explore the basics of etiquette, explore real examples where simple errors of judgement set the wrong tone, and explore how this *human factor* in the relationship is so fundamental to building a positive and effective relationship with your regulator.

With context and the need for appropriate conduct established, we move into the more practical considerations of how we prepare and deliver appropriately on our commitments. From the fundamentals of accountabilities and planning, rigour of preparation, art of communication, and robustness of delivery, we step through critical areas of focus and explore examples of where the basics can be missed at great cost.

THE CONTEXT OF YOUR REGULATORY RELATIONSHIP STRATEGY

In Chapter 1, we covered how organisations have fundamental choices in how they approach their regulatory relationships, what strategy will be followed, and what level of commitment they intend to direct toward it. Figure 7.1 illustrates how organisations can calibrate how they engage and the level of commitment they invest in their relationships.

Here we demonstrate how some organisations may approach their relationship strategy in terms of only committing to that which could be described as the minimum prescribed or required by their regulator, favouring low engagement (even avoidance) and a preference for delivering to the

FIGURE 7.1 Regulatory Relationship Strategy

letter rather than spirit of the rules. By contrast, we also illustrate the graduated scale toward having the regulatory relationship as one of the organisation's key strategic priorities, demonstrating high levels of engagement, proactivity in setting standards, and delivering the spirit as well as the letter of compliance. Wherever your organisation is on this scale will influence how you approach each of the considerations we cover throughout this chapter. It is, therefore, an important and influential factor in how organisations approach their regulator and their engagements and one that those engaging should be well versed in. Your regulatory strategy choices are some of the most important decisions you will take in terms of their impact on your regulatory relationship.

THE CONTEXT OF YOUR ENGAGEMENT IS IMPORTANT

As you would expect, there is no *one size fits all* approach to regulatory engagement.

Before you can begin to plan out how you will engage, it is key to understand the context in which that engagement is to take place. That involves understanding your regulator's objectives (overall objectives and focus for the engagement at hand), and the context and *mode* (see Chapter 1) in which that engagement is taking place (e.g., as a regulator undertaking a supervisor visit, enforcement, etc.).

Having an open dialogue to establish exactly what your regulator's expectations are in terms of your organisation can be a useful way of ensuring nothing is left to chance in this respect. Once understood, delivering to those expectations is of vital importance.

Across industries, organisations will enjoy different regulatory relationships. Some may see intense ongoing levels of scrutiny given their high risk and complex activities, others may have very limited interaction given their lack of complexity, scale, or risk that is posed. As well as the nature of the organisation itself, there will also be the context in which the regulator wishes to interact. Broadly, across industries, regulators seek engagement for a variety of reasons, some very specific to the organisation, others more generic and industry wide. The context of that engagement is important to understand, along with how your own engagement needs to align. For example, a regulator undertaking a study across all organisations on a particular aspect of industry practice will demand a far different response to an organisation experiencing a regulatory investigation that is seeking to assess if there is widespread non-compliance or wrongdoing (see Chapter 1).

In Chapter 6, we covered a host of sources of interactions, information, and insight for the regulatory relationship to operate around. To demonstrate such interactions, next are examples taken from across industries to provide a little food for thought as to how regulatory engagements may arise and how they vary. These aim to provide insight into the level of scrutiny an organisation may feel under, the intensity of the interaction and tone of such engagements, together with a sense of the pace at which they move. The key point being that context to the engagements you are embarking upon is key to be able to appropriately prepare, respond, and engage. To use a natural sciences analogy, the environment in which an organism exists often determines how that organism develops and interacts with its surroundings. Whilst a regulatory relationship may operate one way in an environment of low risk, slow progressive predictable change, or benign economic conditions; it may need to operate in a totally different way when risks rapidly escalate, change is significant, and economic conditions are challenging and changeable (see Chapter 8). Therefore, a one-size-fits-all *standardised approach* is unlikely to be appropriate. A more adaptive, responsive, and progressive course of regulatory relationship engagement will be more beneficial in ensuring you are always appropriately focused and prepared.

Scheduled Engagements and Ad Hoc Interaction

Arguably, the times when organisations are engaging proactively with regulators to discuss matters that arise in the normal course of their business, or, engaging on scheduled visits, are the best times in which to build the relationship. These interactions often involve the regulator and organisations spending more time together on matters that provide opportunities to discuss, explain, and understand their perspectives in greater detail. Organisations can assist regulators by providing additional context on items regulators may see, but by virtue of being one step removed, may not have as full or informed picture as the organisation concerned. This type of engagement builds understanding. It also allows the regulator to get a better reading of how the organisation operates, which if positive, can build a degree of regulatory credit for when issues arise. Mistakes will happen from time to time (organisations nor regulators are immune from this reality), but as we shall see from examples, there is a good chance that organisations demonstrating they are less than proactive and running against the spirit of the rules are likely to receive the full weight of sanction when things go wrong. Developing a positive, proactive, and constructive relationship can therefore provide real benefits.

Market Studies

Market studies involve specific requests across all market participants, or a sample of them, to help the regulator understand how a particular aspect of the market is operating, what the potential risks could be, and how the consumer could be affected. Supporting such studies and taking an outside-in view yourself can be an enlightening experience. Many market studies have found issues or undue risk in the outcomes that consumers experienced and provided the foundations for an alternative approach (e.g., passenger security standards in civil aviation and P.P.I. in financial services).

Consultations

Consultations involve engagement on aspects of an industry for which the regulator is considering or proposing changes and potentially new rules. These are ideal situations to engage with regulators in a constructive way. Not only do you have an opportunity to influence the path of a particular subject, but there is also the opportunity to help the regulator, for example, identify the implications of the proposals, suggest constructive refinements that may help, and explore any unintended consequences. In this respect, it offers the opportunity to help both your organisation and the regulator achieve their objectives in a way that builds the relationship and helps the regulator see how the organisation is trying to help the path of progress for consumers, the industry, the regulator, and the organisation alike.

Investigations

Investigations involve engagements where the regulator or their appointed representatives are investigating the firm, and possibly associated organisations and individuals. Clearly, where the regulator is investigating an issue, there remains an opportunity to demonstrate how the organisation operates and engages, which can lead to better outcomes for the organisation in terms of regulatory benefit[1].

Alternatively, your regulator may conclude that you have failed to be open and cooperative and may publish the fact for all to see, providing a clear indication that how you approach such situations can result in very different outcomes for the organisation[2].

These interactions can be intense times as broad and detailed levels of enquiry unfold in tight timescales. Where the relationship is already built on strong, open, and engaging foundations, these are times where events can cement that opinion. However, in times of scrutiny, it may also be where behaviours can be tested, so they are key events in which to show the organisation's true colours.

The above situations provide a variety of example contexts in which interactions can take place. In reading what follows, it is important to keep the subject of context front of mind as it will be an important guide in ensuring the response is appropriate. For all interactions, it is important to know the foundations of the relationship, how it has been formed, what the relationship is like now, what the purpose of the current interaction is, and how you would ideally like the engagement to play out and build foundations for future interactions. Donaldson and O'Toole (2007, p.33) provide a useful reflection on relationships in this regard, as they point out that relationships are not discrete transactions, but processes that we are engaged with over time.

Before You Take a Step, Try on Different Shoes

Regardless of the context within which your interactions take place, considering the perspective of the regulator is a common thread that should also be kept in mind throughout each section of this chapter. It is important in any relationship to consider who you are dealing with and the perspective they may hold so that you can adequately prepare and make the most of interactions.

As we noted earlier, it is an assumption that you have a good understanding of the regulatory objectives for your industry (Chapter 2 provides examples from aviation and financial services). This is important, as it provides an insight into the challenges the regulator faces and the subjects that are likely to be of interest. This, together with current industry areas of focus and the subjects or agenda items raised for any interaction, paints a useful picture in terms of areas of likely engagement. In short, knowing who you will be dealing with and their background, together with the issues currently being faced, is key. It will also allow you to think around the agenda and *read between the lines* on what may arise or what you could impart that would be useful.

Having equipped yourself with this insight, it is important to walk in the shoes of your regulator, try and put yourself in their situation and understand the perspective they will bring to your interactions and what their objectives are likely to be. Similarly, being clear on your organisation's position and the perspective you intend to take into the meeting is equally important. It will allow you to think through ahead of any interaction where the points of agreement, disagreement, and compromise may be as well as what questions may arise, what the answers are if you have them, and who you may need to cover such areas.

The more that all parties to the relationship can anticipate and focus on areas that can facilitate mutual progress, the more likely productive interactions will arise. So, try those different shoes on before you walk together... and remember, perspectives can change from different viewpoints, or as the philosopher Friedrich Nietzsche stated:

> *"There are no facts, only interpretations"*.

ETIQUETTE – DON'T FORGET THE BASICS!

Having considered the context within which the engagement with your regulator is taking place, it is worth, for a moment, to consider how those engagements will be conducted. As we navigate through the chapter and consider some of the practical points to remember when engaging, another common thread that should be considered across all that follows is etiquette. Respecting the conventional rules for accepted standards of behaviour is a critical starting point, suffice to say for now as we consider etiquette next, these expected conventions can have a powerful influence on the relationship.

Why is it important? Our judgements are often influenced by the standards we expect to see and the observations we make as to whether those standards are apparent in our interactions. Some of these expectations may be individual to oneself, some may be more customary in nature, or are generally accepted standards of polite and respectful behaviour amongst members of society or professional groups. Such etiquette is important – it can set the tone for interactions, it can undermine engagements, and it can send the right or wrong signals about you and your organisation.

We can all think of examples where we felt people have fallen short of standards we would expect, given a certain situation. Furthermore, as standards often develop over time, there may be occasions where we have felt that standards have slipped from that which we have come to expect. Being tuned into these expectations is important and demonstrating them is essential. Where businesses operate across national boundaries, being aware of geographic differences is also useful to ensure you are operating within the expected and accepted standards for that geography. At its most basic level, all engagements should be executed with the respect and standards that would reasonably be expected by the parties to the engagement.

From the hello to the goodbye in any type of interaction, ensuring that professional common courtesies are extended to the stakeholders is very important. What's more, that expectation is often made very clear by the regulator themselves (see Australian Prudential Regulation Authority 2020, p.8).

It may be simple, and it may seem obvious, but undertaking all reasonable expectations to ensure all guests are generally well looked after is fundamental to making their engagement effective and professional throughout. Common courtesies really do cost nothing, however, as you will see, how you engage matters, as the stories give testament. These recollections were used to illustrate points when discussing different aspects of how relationships work at times. What struck a chord was a sense of surprise that such basics were missed by those involved and how their actions had left the wrong impression, which stayed with those on the receiving end of that interaction. The basics matter and simple pitfalls are to be avoided – regardless of the nature of your engagement (see Figure 7.3), there is always an opportunity to impress…and disappoint! Furthermore, issues of neglecting common courtesies are not only the domain of the regulated organisation. We are all human and from time to time will make errors of judgement when it comes to our interactions, regardless of which side of the table we happen to sit, as Figure 7.2 demonstrates.

An agenda is an important document, it focuses the attention of those engaging in an interaction on the important ground to be covered at the meeting. Where supplied in advance, it also allows for preparation, which allows for the most productive of meetings as participants come furnished with all the information required to facilitate the discussion. So, imagine turning up to a regulatory meeting to learn that the agenda, which has been provided by your regulator, has been changed to an entirely different one rendering the preparation wasted. Gladly, these situations don't arise often, but it has happened and of course doesn't leave the best impression.

FIGURE 7.2   When an Agenda Is Not an Agenda

The supply of data to regulators is a common requirement, whether it involves regular returns, answering specific regulatory requests, or helping with market studies. What is required is often made clear in the request, however, how it is provided can often be left to the submitting party. Imagine what impression a regulator would get of organisations despatching data in response to a request that is excessive in volume, lacks focus in terms of distilling key data elements of use, is poorly organised, has little by way of explanation of what is contained and how it relates to the request, or is simply unrelated data that was not requested. It often happens, and for those that supply information in this way, it often leads to further extensive engagement to get to the actual data required, get to the understanding required, and get to the bottom of what the data means. Being focused on the basic customary and appropriate behaviour when interacting is key, and that goes as much for what you send as what you do.

FIGURE 7.3   You Asked for Data, So We Sent You Data…

In such examples, the organisations failed to make the task simple for the regulator and provide the data in a helpful, well ordered, organised way with appropriate context. However, these situations often resulted in re-work and further engagement with the organisation, as it not only raised questions about the data provided on the subject of enquiry, but often triggered further broader questions. The lesson here is: across all your engagements, including the simple supply of data, place yourself in your regulator's shoes (see also Figure 7.4). Help them do their job well, make it simple for them, and be respectful of their time.

> The provision of information to the regulator can involve many areas of an organisation and be extensive. However, ensuring there is consistency of message and ensuring your submissions align is crucial if you are not to face the obvious question…which version or information is the truth?
>
> Organisations have recounted numerous examples where their regulator has reviewed processes that spanned, for example, a particular function or a discipline across their organisation. Often, reviews looked at how areas or processes impacted the customer and the quality of the outcomes they receive. Typically, as part of their review, management information was requested that cut across the area of focus and picked up on key parts of the processes or function concerned. Common themes were that organisations diligently compiled and provided a vast amount of management information that covered both business unit operational information and escalated management information that had passed up and through the organisation's governance processes. What organisations often failed to do thoroughly enough was review that information holistically themselves (often having relied on various areas doing their own due diligence) to ensure there were no errors or inconsistencies that needed explanation. As a result, questions were raised on the information provided as the regulator often noted the inconsistencies or inaccuracies and sought explanations along with confirmation of which version or information was correct. In responding, themes that arose were that organisations often had to explain that some reports provided were drafts (instead of final versions), some were unnecessary as they were not directly related to the request, some of the draft reports never got to final versions due to the issues called out in them being disproved and the matter closed (and as such should not have been provided), and on thankfully rare occasions, some information was simply incorrect. The key lesson from such experiences is that quality assurance and review of information holistically is crucial before providing it.

FIGURE 7.4   Which Version of the Truth Do You Want?

Whether it is contradicting information or discussions in meetings that don't align to the data submitted, having mismatches across your management information, data submissions, or meeting discussions raises far more questions than you would imagine, including the quality of decisions being made given the lack of veracity of the information being used. All are questions that can be avoided by ensuring the management information system is robust and your messages align across your business. In these examples, imagine being a regulator who has just reviewed a host of information and effectively informed the organisation of issues in its own data, having reviewed information they needn't have reviewed as they should not have received it, and realising that information had been provided without looking across it for such issues before sending it to the regulator. It doesn't provide the best impression to the regulator that your organisation's governance and standards are where they need to be.

The examples above were selected to illustrate a variety of simple pitfalls to avoid for those on both sides of the regulatory relationship table. To wrap up this section, Figure 7.5 provides a final example for dramatic effect of how some of the most basic of considerations can be missed.

When regulators have a need to be on your premises, good etiquette involves providing a professional environment and facilities for them to use whilst on site. We are back to the common courtesies again.

However, recollections of regulators being provided with rooms that had more in common with cupboards than a professional working space, being left with little access to basic facilities or people to help them complete their work, and generally having a poor working environment were reflections that provide good simple examples of the impact of common courtesies. If you make your regulator's job more difficult and uncomfortable than it needs to be, by not providing them with the common courtesies as discussed and generally treating them like an inconvenience, then you sow seeds of a less than optimal regulatory relationship.

FIGURE 7.5   That's Your Room Over There (No... It's Not a Cupboard)

Our Vice the Device

A section on etiquette would not be complete without a word to the wise about device protocol. Modern business life is facilitated by an array of devices aimed at improving our efficiency and effectiveness at work. However, what is acceptable use to one individual, may be an annoyance to another. When engaging with others be mindful of what is acceptable behaviour when it comes to the presence (on the table/left in your desk), status (on or off), and use (to read and tap or not to read and tap, that is the question...) of such devices. We have all experienced people using devices whilst we've been talking to them, and it is one of the areas that can be fascinating in terms of what is deemed acceptable use or abuse of such capabilities. Ensuring the regulator is always assured of your attention, no annoying vibrations, and no tones or screens lighting up with messages to glance at is likely to be the most sensible route. This is an area everyone will have their own approach toward, however, one thing to keep in mind: when someone wants to speak to you, they expect your attention.

Now like every approach, there will be exceptional circumstances and from time-to-time things will crop up. Should you be required to be on call for any reason where it is not possible for someone else to cover things for you, be sure to explain this at the start of the meeting or before, if possible. Suffice to say, wherever possible, it is better to schedule meetings and interactions with regulators where you can give them your full attention.

Basics: Professional Respect Is a Reciprocal State

Regardless of the type of interaction, showing respect and supporting the efforts of the regulator is an obvious and fundamental requirement. We are all human and our responses to inappropriate treatment will vary, but one thing is likely, it won't be as positive as our responses to good, respectful interactions.

Ensure you don't forget the basics of etiquette and thread them through all your interactions. The previously mentioned examples are just a few (of the many!) to bring to life some of the most basic of errors that can creep into interactions in the twists and turns of professional life. They all have one thing in common, they were all used as examples of the most basic of failings, the common-sense items that, in the rush of the day, somehow got lost or forgotten. However, all of which were remembered by those on the receiving end of them as examples of what not to do.

Much of what has been covered here comes down to the individuals who are engaging in the relationship. Their interactions in whatever form are important, as is how they go about what they do. In the next section, it is worth for a moment to consider the people in the room. As the front line in whatever interaction is taking place, it is important they are ready to build positively on the relationship you have with your regulator.

THE HUMAN FACTOR – THE PEOPLE IN THE ROOM

Although the premise of this work is that the regulatory relationship is influenced by a whole ecosystem of insights from various sources, there can be no denying the importance of the *people in the room* or *human factor* on any interaction. This *human factor* in any relationship should not be underestimated and, as such, this next section takes a closer look at the importance and impact the people in the room can have on regulatory relationships. Building and sustaining regulatory relationships relies heavily on the interactions between individuals in respective organisations and how they develop their working arrangements to achieve their objectives in line with regulatory frameworks.

What do we mean by the *human factor*? The easiest way to think about this is in its fundamental terms as the very real, basic yet influential nature of human traits in the operation of any interaction, including attitudes, feelings, emotions, instinct, and bias. In any relationship, such traits will be at play and, as such, anticipating, understanding, accepting, working with them, or allowing for them become important considerations in how you interact or respond, as one industry leader reflected:

> *"What we have got to remember is you are dealing with human beings, and they form judgements, and they deal with you in the same way as any other relationship develops..... Sometimes we miss the subtleties in the way we set the regulatory relationship up".*

We all interact with people every day and how we do that can have a significant impact on those we interact with.

Theory also provides interesting perspectives on the importance of relationship building, Sin et al. (2002) point out how strong personal relationships are important to the development of organisational relationships and Hawkins, Gravier, and Powley (2011) highlight the importance of relationship development for building sustainable relationships and the building of trust as part of that development (Jeffries and Reed, 2000; Webber and Klimoski, 2004). Furthermore, Lindgreen (2001) suggests the foundations of relationship management encapsulate a need for trust and confidence, commitment to the relationship and its goals, cooperation, communication, and shared values.

Clearly, our approach matters. If we are aggressive, arrogant, biased, and dismissive in our relationships, we will likely elicit one type of response, and if we are open, friendly, supportive, and helpful, we will likely elicit a totally different one. Every interaction we have will leave an impression and this applies not only to what we say and how we say it, but also to our body language and what we do after the meeting (e.g., follow up on our commitments or not). All such interactions build a picture of what the organisation and/or the individual is like to deal with and what the drivers of such a picture may be, for example, a great culture. As Matsumoto (1996, p.18) references, there is an individualistic and psychological construct of culture as well as the broader social construct of culture.

This sentiment of the importance of the human interaction and the emotions that are tied up within any relationship engagement was well captured by Mintzberg, Jorgensen, Dougherty, and Westley (1996, p.62). In discussing the relationship between parties attempting to collaborate, they wrote of the importance of differing forms of communication interaction, noting the more interpersonal the method, the richer and more nuanced that communication becomes.

There, of course, is no magic formula here. We are all individuals and, as such, we will all approach interactions in our own unique way. However, there are threads of insight to share, gained from discussing with both practitioners and regulators over many years. As you would expect, there are traits that have a positive influence and there are traits that negatively impact. What is fascinating is that people enter such engagements at times with entirely the wrong outlook and attitude (yes, it happens!).

The key for your own success in engaging with regulators is to understand one very simple and fundamental fact. As individuals, we all have things that trigger negative and positive responses that we are sensitive to. In being individuals, we have expectations of those we deal with, and we all have our own standards by which we judge. To this end, never underestimate the influence your behaviour can have on those you engage with. How the relationship unfolds, what outcome results, and how much support and engagement happens along the way are all subjective matters. They are human decisions, they are malleable, can all be influenced positively or negatively, and they all can have significant implications for organisations. Relationships need to actively recognise, understand, and manage this dynamic during interactions and at every level, from the Board to the newest recruit selected by a regulator to speak with them.

The value and costs of our interactions also should not be underestimated. As we interact with regulators, we help them form views and opinions, build a picture of ourselves and our organisations, and ultimately come to conclusions and make decisions that may impact us. As one industry leader reflected:

> *"Organisations who have effective relationships will find it beneficial. Good relations, permits the regulator to streamline and simplify supervisory oversight. For the organisation good relationships and compliance reduce risk of regulatory sanctions. It enhances their own and the industry's reputation for compliance and competence. Likewise, this enhances the reputation of the regulator".*

If you were ever in doubt about the importance of how we interact and communicate with regulators (something we come back to later), let's use an example. Granted, this example looks at written communications, however, the point carries regarding how important and how much effort this regulator has put into understanding how its communications land with recipients. The Prudential Regulation Authority (P.R.A.), according to Proudman (2018), has used advances in machine learning to analyse the letters it writes to firms on the risks they face. The P.R.A. quantified several qualitative features of these letters, for example, how blunt the regulator is in its messaging, how personal it is in terms of to whom it addresses the letter, and the overall sentiment expressed by the letter. The P.R.A. then used a machine learning model to detect whether amongst other things, for instance, the P.R.A. writes to firms differently than the prior regulator, the F.S.A. (It turns out that it does.) On the back of that project, the P.R.A. has built an application that now enables supervisors to analyse their written communications for its impact. Supervisors can use the app to analyse any of their draft documents before they are sent to firms to ensure they have the desired impact.

Communication is crucial, whether it's written, verbal, and in the case of face-to face-or video interactions, let's not forget non-verbal. The *people in the room* on any type of interaction matter, as does what they say and do and how they say and do it.

What you do in your dealings with regulators will of course always be important, but that alone is only part of the story. *How* you interact will be just as important to forging a good regulatory relationship built on mutual respect.

PREPARATION

The term preparation may imply you have a specific duration, resource, and focus for an event that will happen at some point in future. That indeed may well be the case and is the context we cover in many of the comments below. However, in many industries, the regulator may well make it clear that unannounced visits or contact will be part of their approach. Here, organisations will need to be prepared for such situations, that is, always prepared to welcome and accommodate the regulator as they exercise their duties, even where they are at short notice. A key test of such visits can be to understand how the organisation operates in its normal rhythm of executing its business, which will offer the regulator a window on what we have covered in previous chapters (foundations you have, how you navigate, outcomes you drive, how you engage), and it will provide that view real-time.

In addition to the unannounced aspect of preparation, there is also the possibility that regulators don't think about or consider that organisations may be trying to prepare for and satisfy the requirements of multiple regulators at the same time. Whilst many regulators may try and coordinate activity, it can be the case that clashes arise resulting in attempts to satisfy requests on multiple fronts. As regulators will often have different areas of focus and priority, this can place demands on organisations attempting to support the needs of their regulators as they try and tailor the provision of information to the specific need and interest of each regulator at the same time. As a further complication, it is not always the case that regulators will align in their views and approach to a given subject as they consider it from their specific perspective, and, as such, this can pose challenges where opposing or conflicting views face the organisation from different regulators. Good preparation, however, can help in all such situations. Knowing what your position on a matter is, why you take that position, and the evidence you have used in determining your conclusions on a matter can all help the discussion.

Preparation can also be a very different concept depending on how the interaction(s) arise. Below, we will cover the various aspects of preparation, accepting that some of these may be more applicable than others depending on how the interaction arises.

In beginning preparations and having considered the insights of the previous chapters, you should have a good understanding of your foundations. The organisational *attitude* toward regulation and regulators will be clear to us through the strategy, culture, leadership, and organisational expectations of employees in terms of engaging with regulators. You will have a good understanding of the messages the organisation sends out across the ecosystem in which it operates and will hopefully (having done your homework) know what the organisation's hot topics of discussion are going to be with the regulator. You should also have a good understanding of whether there are any other items not on the agenda that may arise, i.e., you have reviewed the organisation's risk radar for items of interest that may be discussion points. So, you are ready to engage! Let's take a practical look at the preparation that can help those engagements work better for all parties, and a quick look at how leaders summed up their preparation approach in Figure 7.6 to get us started.

Reflections of industry leaders provide useful insight on some of the approaches to regulatory interaction.

Leaders referred to ensuring they had a good 360-degree view of their organisation and the market at the time of the interaction. Of course, they would focus on the key points of the interaction and agenda and prepare diligently for that, however, their approach was to also ensure that they had a comprehensive "health check" of what they understood to be the position beyond the formal agenda. So, for example, whilst they may see management reports on complaints and summarised views of information…they may seek to understand a little more by reviewing things a regulator may review, such as social media and consumer websites. They would review information about their organisation in the public domain along with industry challenges and hot topics. In effect, they attempted to walk in the regulator's shoes for a while and took their perspective from insights they may gather.

Finally, leaders would often refer to the more human side of any potential interaction. If they did not know the regulator, they would try and find out a little about them and their background. They may try and understand a little more about their area of expertise or interest and their style and approach, for example.

The overriding question they appeared to be trying to answer in preparation was, what does the regulator need from this interaction and how do I help them and help me in terms of a good outcome for both parties?

FIGURE 7.6   A 360-Degree View of the Organisation…A Stroll in the Regulator's Shoes

Preparations Should Be Context Specific

Like most important things in life, it is crucial to understand what preparation is required and ensure the action is put in place to deliver it. That is not to say that every interaction with a regulator should drive significant levels of preparation, on the contrary, some interactions could seem too contrived if overly prepared, which is where context is again important. Preparation is, therefore, a context specific activity. The extent of preparation will be driven by the nature of the interaction, its purpose, the objectives that have been set, and, as a result, the level of activity required to deliver them, i.e., preparation should be appropriate for the type of interaction. If there are day-to-day conversations underway, having the basic preparation in place to make those interactions as effective as possible will be key. However, if you are in the middle of a major investigation with significant potential implications for the organisation, their consumers, and the shareholders that invest, then a high degree of preparation is likely to be the requirement. No matter what the interaction, being organised and well prepared is a baseline for engagement. The next sections draw out some of the key elements of interacting with regulators and consider some of the pitfalls and areas where you can ensure a good interaction takes place. As relationships cover a whole gambit of interaction, some aspects of preparation will be of more use to certain types of interaction than others. Therefore, the sections should be seen as a toolbox of insight. Select the right tool for the right interaction ahead of you and use them in the appropriate combinations for the situation. Let's make a start.

Clarity of Objective and Accountability

At the heart of all preparation is the fundamental understanding of what exactly you are preparing for, as successful interaction with regulators will usually involve the achievement of a clear objective. This may seem obvious, however, it is clear from insights provided that this is not always clarified to achieve the level of understanding required (see Figure 7.7).

Imagine one day you receive a letter from your regulator regarding issues you have been engaging on that must be addressed by the organisation. The regulator has formally set down in writing their expectations of you and laid out the timescales that they expect the relevant actions to be completed by. All very clear so far. However, what if those expectations were not all that clear? What if your discussions or previous communications had not been as clear as they could and led to misunderstandings or misinterpretation and this had now manifested itself in an ask of you that is less than clear? What if the ask could be interpreted different ways, would you clarify? It is hoped you would, however, that is not always what is done. On occasions, individuals have confided, that due to not wanting to bother the regulator, antagonise or make an already difficult engagement worse, people will sometimes go ahead and provide what they anticipate the regulator is looking for, even if that means that something that may not be strictly necessary is undertaken. The challenge with this approach is that it runs the risk that what is provided misses the mark for the regulator, potentially perpetuates a view the regulator has that may not be the best it can be, and, of course, you end up undertaking work that is a wasteful use of resource that could be focused on ensuring the valid asks of the regulator are handled. Being clear on the objective is, therefore, in all parties' best interests. It can be a good point to clarify meaning, focus on actions of greatest value to both parties, and avoid misunderstandings further down the line. If in doubt...clarify upfront!

FIGURE 7.7 Thank You for Your Letter, Can I Just Clarify...

Once you are clear on what you are preparing for, it is useful to have a view of the objective of both parties (assuming there are only two in play for now). This allows you to shape your preparation to ensure that you are considering the perspectives of both parties and deliver preparation that supports both in the process of interaction.

Finally, no matter what the objective, it is crucial that there are clear lines of accountability to ensure all aspects of preparation are delivered in good time and to the required standards. It is seldom good enough to simply know who is accountable for the overall relationship or interaction, as often that could be the most senior of executives who may be several steps removed from some of the detail that would be required to make for a successful interaction on any given aspect of the organisation's operation. Instead, accountability should be clear across every aspect of what is to be delivered, right down to the individual items of data, insight, action, or meeting agenda item coverage. Knowing who exactly is responsible for delivering what and by when will allow for a smooth accumulation of insight on a timescale that allows sufficient review and agreement. This way, you have time to ensure everything aligns, and everyone knows what is to be covered and their role in it.

Don't Forget the Plan

How often have you heard people quote the wise old saying *fail to prepare… prepare to fail*? However, in the clamber to deliver to the regulator, often the fundamentals are forgotten. If we assume for a moment that your next regulatory engagement is a significant one (sufficient to warrant a good degree of planning), then some of the following fundamental steps may well be part of your planning process, and if they are, it is key that you provide (where possible) the time and resources to ensure they are well executed to give you the best chance of a good regulatory interaction.

Plan – As fundamental as it is, laying out the events that need to take place to deliver to the regulator's expectations whilst ensuring what you deliver to them has passed through the right processes to ensure it is fit for purpose is key. As you plan the activities, think about what the drivers of success will be and ensure you capture them as part of your preparation. You may need specific expertise, resources to be made available for data gathering and review, compliance to review the materials and provide an opinion, or time and people to overview the quality and alignment of information. Whatever the core elements will be that drive the success of the plan, ensure they are captured with clear accountability lined up so everyone who is party to the plan knows who is doing what aspects and who they need to engage with to ensure the pieces come together. Keep in mind, also, that plans need to be adaptable and refined as events progress, so be prepared to build in a degree of flexibility and anticipation of what could go wrong or may need to change. A good, well-thought-through plan with regular calibration and alignment with those engaged with the plan sets out your stall well for delivery. Given the importance of preparation, good planning, and clear accountability, let's break this down a little further.

Accountabilities – Ensuring someone is overall accountable for the delivery and its quality is a key first step. Like any plan, there should be clarity as to who is leading the work and accountable for its outcome. In addition, ensuring everyone working toward the plan is very clear on what aspects they are accountable for will be critical to ensuring there are no surprises when the team gets together to join up all the moving parts of the story for the regulator. Regularly checking across the team that each is clear on what they are and are not delivering is essential to ensure the components remain aligned. The benefit of being clinical about ownership in this way is that clarity will flush itself out as the team engages with what they think they are and are not accountable for. It allows for early resolution and avoids items falling through the cracks as you rule out assumption and replace it with fact.

Resources – Linked to the earlier point about the *people in the room*, it is worth noting that those you assign accountabilities to need to be capable of holding and executing that accountability. The regulator is a key stake-holder, and your people should be ready for such interactions and be able to provide what is required to the appropriate level of quality and with the appropriate level of rigour. It may go without saying, but ensuring the right skills and capability are around your plan will be a key factor in its success.

Timescales – In the rush to deliver quickly to the regulator, many organ-isations, as we have seen from the examples, miss the fundamentals, provide information that is not to the right standards, or miss the mark in terms of what the objective is. Regulators will allow a reasonable amount of time for organisations to get things right as, clearly, it is in their best interests also that what you provide is appropriate. Building reasonable timelines that facilitate the ability to compile what the regulator is seeking and ensuring it is of an appropriate quality and any approvals or oversight prior to release are complete is crucial. Pace is important, but so too is getting the job right first time.

Alignment Across the Organisation and Accuracy Across Your Information

When it comes to regulatory interactions, it is important to have a *house view* on the subject you are discussing with the regulator. Where that view may be supported by a variety of information sources showing a situation through different lenses (e.g., via different management reports), it is crucial that the organisation is aligned on what the *house view* is, how you got there, and why the information you see across the organisation supports that view. It is also, therefore, very useful to be clear on what is being sent to the regu-lator and where there are variations or anomaly, that these are pointed out and explained to aid the regulator in their understanding of the information before them. This not only saves regulators a lot of time and effort, but it dem-onstrates you are across your organisation's information, understand it, can explain it in the context of your conclusions, and, importantly, are trying to help them wherever you can in their understanding. One obvious but impor-tant point to make in terms of that view is that it must be *authentic, balanced and reasonable*. Even where you may not have all the answers or a complete view, be clinical on what you do and don't know, as Friedrich Von Hayek (1974) put it in his Nobel Prize lecture:

"I prefer true but imperfect knowledge, even if it leaves much indetermined and unpredictable, to a pretence of exact knowledge that is likely to be false".

© The Nobel Foundation 1977

Such a correlation and alignment will also help build trust and confidence in the mind of the regulator that the information you are supplying is complete and accurate and its implications are understood, i.e., there should be *no surprises* regarding what they are seeing.

Whilst having a good cohesive story is essential and would demonstrate alignment around the key aspects of the business in which the regulator may have interest, the proof points must also be available within the organisation to demonstrate that this story reflects reality. One regulator reflected on this, making it clear that in personal interactions with staff, they are looking for a consistency of message up, down, and across the organisation:

"I'm keen organisations put me in front of the right people, and that those people will be the people who can talk me through whatever subject is the focus of our attention. So, what I like, is to talk to the Executive and Senior Managers, and then talk to some of the people doing the job on the front line. What you are looking for is that you are getting a message that is consistent between those different layers of the organisation about whatever it is that you are testing or interested in".

As well as ensuring you have a clear house view on what you provide (see Figure 7.8), what you provide also needs to be accurate and aligned across reporting sources. Concerns are raised when information sent from differing parts of the organisation's governance system say different things due to inaccuracies, or where regulatory returns have one set of data, yet a specific regulatory request or market study results in a different set of data and information being provided with no context or explanation.

As well as commenting on the importance of data and information accuracy, it is also worth a word to the wise on version control while we are on the subject. Some organisations have very good version control, others not so good, however, from a regulatory perspective such tracking needs to be an organisational strength. For example, there have been situations recounted where internal reports have been sent to regulators that have not been the latest view, have been early reports on a suspected (unproven) problem, or in one instance, turned out not to be an issue at all, and, had the correct version of the report been issued to the regulator, it could have saved time (and plenty of questions) all round. Ensuring the accuracy of what you provide, making sure it is timely, and, of course, the latest version is crucial to building trust and confidence in what you do (and how you do it) as an organisation.

Having a clear objective and accountabilities understood is such an important aspect of engagement. Often individuals describe that with the best of intentions, they speed ahead to pull together the information for the regulator and, as a result, the focus and threads of insight necessary to satisfy the regulator are either diluted, lost, or omitted.

By way of examples, organisations having been told there would be a regulatory overview of an aspect of their business, often describe diligently pulling together representatives they would need to satisfy the request. Individuals were often assigned aspects of the regulators ask in terms of gathering data, reports, and information that would be stored centrally or coordinated by a central contact point. Periodic meetings across the internal teams were often put in place with one party or department taking accountability for coordinating activity. Activities were diligently checked to ensure the information was being gathered in good time and progress monitored. However, organisations recount how often the focus seemed to centre almost entirely on demonstrating good progress and performance across the areas of the business in terms of gathering evidence to meet a deadline. With such a focus, there was often a reflection of parties operating in isolation to provide information and reports, but with limited discussion on the common story that all could attest to and provide insight toward as all this information came together. Similarly, whilst progress was checked in terms of searching for items of evidence, information, and insight, there was a theme of limited read across of the information to ensure information was consistent, fitted together well, built an overall picture in line with the objective, and was complete and accurate. Often, accountability was present for the coordination of activity and delivery of information in line with timescales, but less clear in terms of who would create the overall picture or "house view" that resulted from the insight gathered, let alone for the quality of the outcome prior to submission.

The implications of such scenarios were, for example, further questions from regulators across the variety of data sources where items seemed to contradict each other, the regulator needing to piece together the picture as it was less than obvious what the overarching story was, and further interactions, meetings, and discussions to supplement what was provided and help build the picture.

Such challenges were often reflected upon with a view that they could have been avoided with better planning, preparation, a clearer objective, and tighter accountabilities. For the regulator, it was felt that such situations would likely have been seen as demonstrating a lack of rigour and preparation, resulting in them awaiting further information as they formulated their view. From an outcome point of view, organisations could often demonstrate alignment to regulator's expectations, but recalled the route to achieving this could at times be better executed.

Providing a succinct, clear, and consistent message across the organisation, supported with complete and accurate information is a baseline requirement for engagements. If you are unclear on your story, how it fits together, permeates the organisation, and is evidenced, how will your regulator be clear?

FIGURE 7.8   Gathering the Information Is Just Part of the Answer...

Be Balanced in the Picture You Paint

Ensuring the accuracy of your data and facts also needs to take account of the potential impact of bias. As individuals, we will often weigh the facts differently, emphasise the story differently, and reach alternative viewpoints. Being mindful of our potential for bias is a key skill and being as clinical as we can in representing the facts faithfully is a commendable objective. Whether we are naturally inclined to give more weight to facts that meet our views (confirmation bias), give priority to recent events when looking forward or disregard events of the past as historic (recency bias), or become over optimistic in the benefits of our plans and understate risks and costs (planning bias), we need to check ourselves and the picture and position we are presenting. Underplaying issues that materialise and challenge the organisation or overplaying your ability to deliver due to inherent bias in the way you think about the items at hand will not fill the regulator with confidence.

One item that tentatively links to these ideas, is that care is needed when information is being specifically manufactured for the regulator. It is usually better to use your established management information where possible, as not only does this demonstrate you are indeed monitoring the issues you are discussing with the regulator, but it also ensures that there is limited opportunity for miscommunication (or bias) as you pull something specific together for the regulator. Using existing information also has the benefit of not seemingly controlling the flow or messaging to the regulator, which can raise questions as to why such action is necessary in the regulator's mind. Industry leaders have recounted stories of regulators making this very clear to them. The following quote was a very simple ask from a regulator with a simple solution:

> *"Just share with us what you see in your normal management system. So, now our rule is, we don't create anything specifically for the regulator".*

Accepting that your management information system will not always provide you with what you need and that, from time-to-time, specific items will be pulled together for submission to the regulator, care should be observed in ensuring such documents align and make sense in the context of other information the regulator may be seeing. Where what regulators are already seeing is of relevance, it is a good idea in any documents you are specifically creating to cross reference to such items. That way, you can demonstrate how what you are providing aligns to other items they may be seeing and that you are assisting them in making those connections.

As a final point, you will no doubt have heard the phrase *death by Power-Point*…that sinking feeling as page upon page of regurgitation unfolds in front of you…I'm sure little else needs saying on this. Suffice to say, however you present prepared information, keep it in line with the points we cover throughout this chapter, that is, clear, concise, relevant, etc. Ensuring you focus on the matter or agenda at hand whilst keeping a clinical control of insight and information is crucial to ensure you get the most out of interactions. Presenting the information is important, but so too is the time for discussion around the subjects. Provide sufficient time so that everyone can and is encouraged to contribute without anyone dominating with a *download of all they know*. At the end of any interaction, understanding is a key outcome. It allows all parties to process what they have learned and think about what is required next – what further information, what further actions, and what further follow up is necessary. However you intend to interact, ensure you think through how that interaction will unfold to ensure all who are party to it get what they need out of it.

Communication

Communication with regulators takes many forms, some you control (see Figure 7.9), some you don't. No matter what its source, all communication will have its place in the considerations of the regulator who will seek to understand the messages in the context of the organisation it is dealing with.

Also, all communication has the benefit of being able to be placed in context. Communication is crucial to the relationship an organisation has with its regulator and to the regulator's level of understanding of how the organisation is operating and its impact on their regulatory objectives. Whether the organisation is receiving poor publicity with customer complaints rising or

Regulatory visits that have been recounted as positive and useful engagements for both parties appear to have exhibited useful insights in terms of what they entailed and the actions taken by the parties involved.

First, information provided was often readily available from internal governance meetings (the regulators saw what the organisation used day to day). Little was specifically manufactured for the interactions and, often, information was supplemented with officials who would talk to the information and provide any context required. If further information was needed, it would be pulled together after the sessions to clarify specific points immediately, to effectively close and conclude on the area whilst it was being considered.

Second, all reporting provided was "read from the shoes of the regulator" by those providing the information. Often, this would be supplemented by specialists in an area where needed (e.g., compliance, legal, or maybe technical representatives depending on the subject) to provide challenge and suggest areas where further insight may be useful or further questions may arise that should be covered regardless of whether they were raised.

Third, meeting agendas were often worked through with a view to ensuring the information provided covered all aspects, but also to provide a list of who would attend each session. These were often provided to the regulator and the organisational teams engaging so everyone had clarity on what was to be covered and by whom.

In some instances, organisations sought to ensure questions or outstanding requests that flowed from one meeting were covered, where possible, in the next session. This ensured the regulator was fully informed as the meetings progressed and walked away with all they needed wherever possible.

Whilst this level of preparation for the organisations concerned was more structured and time consuming, they reflected how appreciative the regulator often was that such a focus was being placed on ensuring by the time they left the organisations, they had as much of the information they required as possible, had the opportunity to discuss that in detail, and had been provided with further insight not originally sought but relevant to the discussion.

FIGURE 7.9 Putting the Effort in to Get the Full Picture Across

is seen as the market leader with consumer interests driving its agenda, communication that places these items in context and provides a coherent summary for the regulator will be key. After all, organisations may be receiving poor publicity and rising complaints as they attempt to improve protection for consumers (e.g., queues at airport security), whilst those leading the market may not see the potential for longer-term consequences or risks (e.g., mortgage step-up products becoming unaffordable).

The importance of the organisational story is key. What's more, that story needs to align through every facet of the messages organisations and their actions generate. From the vision and strategy espoused by the Chief Executive to the messages back from the market in terms of consumer outcomes, there needs to be referential consistency. Similarly, that consistency needs to be apparent throughout the organisation. Having a stated intent in the strategy that is then undermined by the policies, procedures, and processes followed will do little to instil confidence in your regulator.

Language and Perspective in Communication

When it comes to dealing directly with the regulator, there are also plenty of basic pitfalls to avoid. The English language is fabulously rich in its descriptive possibilities, unfortunately, these aren't always used in the most appropriate ways or situations. As a general rule, keep the message simple, specific, and avoid terms that can be interpreted in different ways. Referring to items in loose terms can open all sorts of questions in the minds of those receiving the communication...in short, stick to what you know, be clear and concise, and don't use language that will *spook* the recipient.

As well as the language you use, the perspective you take is also very important. You and your regulator have common ground in that your customer is at the centre of your organisation. However, you may have different perspectives on how you look at issues or may have competing objectives in terms of where you focus your attention and how you view matters. It is still crucial that you consider how you communicate and how that will be read by the regulator. An organisation taking a purely financial view of an issue being faced and allowing itself to focus its actions to bias the pursuit of profit is unlikely to gain much sympathy from a regulator focused on the fair treatment of the customer. It is therefore crucial that you view your communication from different perspectives, not only to ensure you have considered the implications of your decisions in a rounded and considered way, but also because failing to do this may well be seen as a lack of balance and judgement in the consideration of your actions. As one regulator succinctly commented:

> *"Those people who had the right balance and who could talk to you and articulate what they were doing and why they were doing it, even if that might not quite be right in your eyes...but then could also have a conversation with you about where they might improve, they are the people you tended to have the best relationship with".*

One related, but tangential point that is worthy of mention, is the debate over where in the organisation the regulatory relationship and communication channels are owned (see Figure 7.10). If relationships are to be well managed and coordinated, then accountabilities need to be clear. However, it is a debate that needs careful consideration. Clarity of ownership is important, but so is the importance of a relationship that is not hindered or constrained by overly restrictive controls.

One point worth digressing on is the debate on whether the relationship and communication channels with your regulator should be "owned", and if so, by whom? It is an interesting debate and one where it is unlikely to have a single right or wrong answer. In a survey of financial services organisations in Australia by the Governance Institute of Australia (2019), the custodianship of regulatory engagement was split, 43% stating the compliance function, 34% stating risk management, and 23% reporting the legal function.

As a key stakeholder, it is important that organisations ensure their regulatory relationships are well looked after. Where this is done is likely less important than how it is done. In the U.K., many financial services organisations have adopted, for example, a three-lines-of-defence model for risk management. The first line being front-line business areas (as owners of the risks they run), the second line being risk management and compliance oversight, and the third line being traditional audit functions. In this model, again, it is often the same function as in the Australian survey that own the relationship. This brings somewhat of a dilemma, as it is the first line of defence that will often own the risks regulators will wish to discuss and who will be closer to the processes, and their risks, controls, and mitigants. Having areas that are one step removed from those owning the regulatory relationship and communication channels can cause issues of interpretation and translation where they act as a funnel for the organisation.

Given this common alignment, what is more important is that all understand how the relationship will be catered for and how they will ensure that the practicalities of owning the relationship does not impede what it is necessary to deliver to build the relationship in line with regulatory and organisational requirements. In practical terms, whilst ownership may involve regular dialogue, coordinating engagements, and tracking progress, it should not get in the way of, for example, open, transparent, and direct communication flows with regulators by those who manage the risks. Wrapped around this should be a clear plan of interaction and tracking of actions and deliverables, i.e., a full picture of how the relationship is unfolding and being managed. It is therefore important when setting out the strategy for regulatory engagement where the clean lines of accountability and responsibility lay across the organisation and what the principles of engagement will be for all parties. That way, you will have a clear understanding of how you will ensure an engaging and productive relationship develops, whilst also ensuring practical considerations are catered for.

Finally, as regulators seek to engage more broadly across each area and level of organisations, it could well be that a shift more toward a coordinated first-line ownership of the relationship is more appropriate. As an analogy, we are moving from an analogue in-series model of structured and pre-planned interactions with regulators to a digital, dynamic, and parallel array of interactions fed by sources of insight whose breadth has significantly increased. In such an environment, traditional command and control structures may not cope so well. "The regulatory web" construction is well underway and soon the distillation of a wide array of information will bring forward a far richer view of the organisational ecosystem for regulators to assess, which, in turn, may demand a more responsive and dynamic model of organisational engagement.

FIGURE 7.10   Owning the Relationship and Communication Channels

Structure, Balance, and Proportionality

We are taught the importance of structure in story telling from our earliest years of education, however, along the way, it is surprising how often some forget the importance of structure and helping the recipient follow the thread of information we are providing as we communicate with them. Yet structure is such a fundamental part of delivering a clear and concise message, allowing us to take the recipient on a journey of understanding in an orderly fashion. Whether you have a pre-defined approach that works for you or construct your approach based on the subject you are communicating, many approaches will work, but all will have key ingredients, such as building the story in an orderly way and providing context that is important to the recipients understanding. In short, communication needs to lead the recipient on a journey that answers fundamental questions and provides a balanced picture.

To take their literal meanings, balance and proportionality are about giving factors the correct weight and visibility in our assessment of them.

As you will no doubt have gathered, balance and proportionality are judgement calls, and as judgement calls, there will be situations where the call will be a difficult one. The more difficult the issue or decision to be made and communicated, the more we will often see a desire for more data, more information, more insight, more benchmarking, and, possibly, more in the way of *smoke signals* from our regulator to help us navigate with the benefit of their views. This *balance zone* is a difficult area, but it is one of the most interesting areas, as it is where you can read more about an organisation, how it approaches decisions, and its outlook. It is also in this difficult balance zone that a regulator can get a good reading of the organisation's culture. You may recall in Chapter 5 that we had an example reflection on the role of culture from the Financial Conduct Authority, and its role in conduct failings, its role in trust and confidence, and a need to demonstrate firms are working in the interests of consumers and the market as well as their wider stakeholder groups. In delivering on culture, it becomes as much about the spirit of the regulation and doing the right thing by consumers as it is the letter. How organisations go about making their decisions and communicating them will be of equal interest to the regulator as the decision itself. Why? Because if culture is about how an organisation inherently functions, it is in these judgement call areas that you get to see how the organisation sets about building its case for the decisions it makes. Here, we will see the behaviours that are dominant, the mindsets that are held, and the balance that is assigned to coming to the right decision. Here, the regulator is in the perfect position to see how different organisations approach such issues, across a whole spectrum of decision responses. We can be sure there will be a whole array, from those organisations that simply get on with something as *the right thing to do* to the other extreme where responses may look to prove no action is required – and everything in between (see Figure 7.11). Here, a regulator begins to see a natural bias in the approach to decision making and communication, and if such a decision is not balanced and proportionate, or, indeed, is based on spurious assumptions that are not tested, their further interest will likely arise.

As relationships progress, there will inevitably be times when the regulated party will need to raise issues where things have gone wrong. There will be times when strict regulatory *rules* may not have been broken, but where principles, conduct, or morality and ethics may be called into question. Whilst

At times, organisations face situations where their products, services, or processes fail to perform as expected. In such situations, identifying the issue and attempting to correct the problem will be a key focus for any organisation faced with such a scenario. Whilst issues faced by the customer can often be resolved, at times these solutions may drive significant costs for an organisation to correct. Here, organisations may seek to balance the cost of solutions, where all issues are not put exactly right, but where they satisfy legal aspects of their obligations. However, from a regulatory perspective, such a solution may be deemed insufficient or unfair, and the organisation may be challenged to put all matters right at their cost. The point of fact here being that just because something has a legal basis, does not mean it is sufficiently compliant when set against regulatory expectations.

FIGURE 7.11   Can I Introduce My Lawyer...

there will be times when legal opinions will be required, and in some cases expected by a regulator to have been sought, these should still be placed in the context of regulatory objectives. Just because the law says you can do something, does not mean you should. There is a balance to be struck, a judgement to be made, and a rationale to be developed in justifying your stance on issues. Simply *introducing the lawyer*, following the legal rule and falling behind that is unlikely to be an optimal position to take with your regulator. That's not to say the legal position won't end up being the path followed once all considerations have been made, however, decisions need context and perspective. After all, your regulator also has access to the same laws and to their own lawyers...and remember most courts up and down the land are filled with disputes on points of law where different perspectives on its interpretation and applicability are played out.

Balance and proportionality then are key elements that will shape how the relationship will function. Where an organisation is inherently biased toward sound and balanced decision making, taking appropriate account of all its stakeholder's perspectives, and coming to well-reasoned and evidenced judgements, there is likely to be little challenge or concern in the relationship on such matters. Where an organisation is heavily skewed in decision making, impacting negatively on the outcomes of consumers, there is likely to be increased scrutiny and direction from the regulator (see Figure 7.12). Balance and proportionality, like many of the aspects we discuss, are pieces

Situations have arisen where decisions have been taken that relied on interpreting the facts in a legalistic way. The decisions appeared to lack balance and provided more favourable outcomes for organisations than would otherwise have been the case had a broader, more balanced interpretation been the outcome of decision-making processes. The interesting point to surface from such examples, is they led to a consideration of the process of decision making by regulators, not just the decision. As such, questions were raised covering decision making and how that had worked in detail.

So, making the decision is only one aspect to consider. Making a well-judged, balanced, and proportionate decision in line with the appropriate authority to do so, and with the right visibility on the process of making it, are the other factors to be clear on.

FIGURE 7.12   Decision-Making Can Raise Further Questions...

in the picture that is formed for the regulator on how the organisation operates. Each presents a piece of an organisation's corporate persona and, as such, provides insight for the regulator to assess how it approaches the regulatory relationship.

In summary, when you think about the practical considerations of engaging with regulators, there is little in the items noted previously in the *Preparation* section we have covered that would be forgotten given the time to reflect and prepare properly. However, the challenge comes when the pressure of delivering in day-to-day working life stifles appropriate preparation. It is in that pressure that issues can creep in and undermine the quality of the interaction. Plan well and plan early, as the time always seems to move faster when the pressure is on to respond against the myriad of other commitments organisations may have.

DELIVERY

Having prepared well for your regulatory interaction and engaged with the regulator, there are likely to be several potential outcomes, one of which may be actions or commitments that have been made on your part that now need delivering. Here, again, the opportunity arises to delight or disappoint. Next are some of the areas to be mindful of when your organisation moves into delivery mode for the regulator.

Commitments, Setting Expectations, and Responsiveness

Like all commitments, ensuring that you can deliver on them is crucial. There is little point making commitments you cannot deliver on, as this will only lead to disappointment and set yourself or the organisation in an unfavourable light. Here are some simple areas of guidance in this area.

Clarity – Be clear on what you are committing to. Whether you have presented a problem for which you commit to a solution, or commit to deliver data or information, being clear and setting the right level of expectation is important. If you are to build confidence and trust, what you commit to must be delivered and should not disappoint or look totally different from the exceptions that were set. Clarity is key, use straight forward language to avoid misinterpretation. The use of jargon, T.L.A.s (the dreaded Three Letter Acronyms), and flamboyant and unnecessary verbose language is simply a recipe to drive up the risk that clarity is lost. Your starting point for any commitment is absolute clarity on what will be delivered and what is expected between the parties.

Chronology – Once you have defined the action with clarity, the next expectation to be set will be when that can be delivered. Here, there is often a tendency to over commit, however, remember that regulators understand that items take time, so depending on what you have committed to, a regulator will allow a *reasonable* time to deliver it. The key is that when it is delivered, it is correct and the expectation will be that the timeline reflects the work required and is commensurate with the commitment. For example, if you have committed to provide your business-as-usual management reports, it would be reasonable to expect these would be available immediately given they are already produced, available, and in use. However, where you commit to resolve a problem for which you are still working through the solution, there will, of course, be an expectation of expediency along with a realisation that this may take time. The key is balance and ensuring the timeline is commensurate with what is being delivered and the work involved to deliver it.

Accountability – Where you have a commitment and you have a timeline, you need accountability. Who is it that will commit to deliver and will ensure that delivery is to the right standard, meets or exceeds your commitment, and is on time or ahead of it? Ensuring this is clear is a key part of ensuring delivery happens. All too often a series of commitments may be made by an organisation and, at times, assumptions are made on who will deal with the ask. This may lead to problems if there is not absolute clarity on who is accountable for what actions, as one of several outcomes often occur. Either the assumption is correct, all know who is dealing with what action and all is well (assuming it's on time, in line with the commitment, and of the right quality), or as a worst case, an action is missed, or more likely to be the case, part-way through the timeline someone realises no action or insufficient progress is being made, meaning you now have less time to do what you committed to in the first place. Being clear removes any ambiguity and ensures the job is done with sufficient time to ensure it is to the right standard and quality.

Responsiveness – In all your interactions, your responsiveness should be focused and fast. Whether it's a quick call or email, picking items up immediately and getting back to the regulator quickly makes for the best basis upon which to build the relationship. Demonstrating that you are committed to helping the regulator as quickly as possible achieve what they seek to achieve is a good foundation from which to build.

Delivery Process – Having prepared what needs to be delivered, the process of delivery needs to be considered and allowed for in terms of time and resources. For example, it may be that you have committed to provide additional data or insight on a matter of interest to your regulator. Before such items are delivered, however, it is wise to ensure there is time to allow accountable individuals to review and approve the document and ensure it is of sufficient quality to supply. It is also wise to ensure that what is to be supplied is considered in the context of what has or is already flowing to your regulator. That way, any points of divergence or conflict with existing insights can be explained or discussed, again saving the regulator time and effort in raising such matters.

Delivery Tracking – To ensure that you are always across your commitments to the regulator, it is a good idea to have an approach to tracking your actions and commitments. Having a holistic view of this across the organisation allows for the appropriate allocation of resources to ensure commitments are delivered, whilst also ensuring there is a full view of the interactions so that any patterns or points where further assistance could be useful to the regulator are identified and provided.

Open and Transparent

There will not be a regulator that won't say that being open and transparent is fundamental to the relationship, principally, because regulators are unable to achieve their objectives efficiently and effectively without a good deal of cooperation from those that they regulate. Whilst a regulator may be able to access information through regular reporting and specific information requests, there is still the need to put those documents in context, which is achieved through dialogue and questions to aid a more detailed understanding. Vaccaro and Madsen (2009) describe a process they refer to as "dynamic transparency" in which information flows result in a continuous dialogue between companies and their stakeholders. The idea is that this has the potential for transforming stakeholder perceptions and practices due to the open nature of the interaction and continuity of contact. One regulator put this requirement very succinctly:

"For the relationship to work there needs to be quid pro quo. Firms keep regulators up to date and in turn the regulators keep the firm informed of their views and thinking".

Open and transparent communication flows are also fundamental to the building of trust between parties. It allows for a better level of understanding, a more accurate assessment of risk, and fewer surprises, all of which can reduce the time and effort for organisations and regulators. Trust cannot be fostered if one party feels they are only getting a limited view of the insight they need or that things are being held back. Being open and transparent is critical as is the need to ensure that messages are clear, specific, and balanced. There is no point in providing insight that is open to interpretation, vague, or biased toward your viewpoint to the extent that the true meaning is lost. This will only come back to challenge you later when the true facts finally surface. It is better to be clear and specific so everyone's time is not wasted through misunderstanding or clarification. Furthermore, providing information or supplementing it with insight that the regulator may not have asked for, but which may help their understanding, is a further way to build constructive engagements and relationships. In addition, regulators will often have rules that compel an approach, which underlines the importance of transparency. For example, the Financial Conduct Authority (2018c) prescribes in Principle 11:

"A firm must deal with its regulators in an open and cooperative way, and must disclose to the appropriate regulator anything relating to the firm which that regulator would reasonably expect notice".

Non-disclosure, opacity, or providing misleading information is taken very seriously given what we have said about the importance of open engagement with the regulator. As a result, a lack of open and transparent engagement with regulators can contribute to adverse implications that regulators find against organisations[3].

Being open and transparent is however not about running to the regulator with every issue you think you may have or every risk that materialises. Organisations need to be clear on what their approach to disclosure will be. It can do this by using trigger events that provide a useful framework for disclosure, for example, items for notification to the Board that have a compliance or risk rating sufficient for escalation may also be notified to the regulator. Being clear on this is important, as the regulator will expect the organisation to be able to make reasonable and informed judgements on what is appropriate to disclose in terms of materiality. The order of magnitude of any issue, whilst it may be important to the organisation, needs the context of the risk considering to ensure items are appropriate to be flagged and are not seen as immaterial to your regulator.

Finally, be aware that *open* and *transparent* are very clear terms (excuse the pun!), so in your engagements, do not become victim to the pitfall of minimising the issue, omitting key facts, or playing down the importance of key aspects of items being disclosed. Be clinical about what you have found in a balanced and proportionate way. Where there are questions outstanding, be clear on these and what you are doing about providing the answers that you need.

Proactive

Being proactive in your engagements with the regulator is a further sound footing as you build regulatory relationships (see Figure 7.13). In a survey conducted by the Governance Institute of Australia (2019), almost 50% of respondents noted they have a defensive or reactive approach to engaging with regulators with little appetite for change. Clearly this is likely to be a challenge in a world where a more open and transparent engagement approach is being sought and where proactivity in disclosing items a regulator ought to be reasonably aware of is expected in many markets.

Being on the front foot to keep the regulator informed is also crucial if you are going to avoid embarrassing surprises hitting the regulator and the associated inquiry that would ensue. Making sure that key messages come from the organisation itself, with the appropriate context as previously discussed is important. It will also allow the regulator to consider the implications of whatever information is being shared in the context of their own objectives and

One example that provided a useful insight into the benefits of working closely and proactively with regulators was a situation that required both remediation of an issue and redress of the customers. Here, the organisation had committed to put things right, however, along that journey, regular updates were provided on progress, including a full run through of the approach taken to investigate issues and determine what detriment had arisen, the rationale for what would be redressed, and the approach to how that redress would be applied. These engagements were deemed extremely useful from the organisation's point of view, as it provided a continuity of discussion around the issues being resolved, an ongoing opportunity to update on key decisions and their rationale, and the ability to ensure there was a "no surprises" approach to all that the organisation was doing to try and put things right. Along the way, there were challenges, dilemmas, limitations on what could and could not be done, and, at times, a need for pragmatism. They reflected that the key to the success of how those difficult issues were resolved from a relationship point of view was how the organisation proactively engaged, was open about the challenges it faced, and sought views where broader industry insights or precedent may have arisen that could assist in ensuring appropriate outcomes were achieved.

FIGURE 7.13   Being Proactive Can Also Head Off Further Issues

the messaging you have been providing to that point. Either way, the earlier information is shared, the longer both parties have for a response. However, do remember it is a fine balance of judgement to know what needs to be disclosed and when and it is for the organisation to establish its own framework or guiding principles in this respect. The key is to ensure items are appropriate to be disclosed and that it happens in a timely fashion.

Remember, when the organisation has got something wrong once, the last thing your stakeholders need is to see its resolution poorly handled. Determining a balanced, fair, and reasonable response to issues can be a lengthy and difficult process, but such examples demonstrate it is worth the hard yards it takes to achieve. Only then can you be sure the matters are fully resolved. A read of regulatory enforcement notices from regulatory websites can provide an array of examples where organisations have committed to resolve issues only to be advised by the regulator that the steps have not satisfied requirements. Be clinical in your articulation of issues and ensure you understand the needs of all stakeholders in resolving such issues. Take the time to balance stakeholder perspectives and avoid over reliance on weighted arguments to ensure you have a rounded view in determining your decisions and arrive at a fair and balanced resolution (e.g., regulatory obligations and principles in letter and spirit, moral and ethical considerations, as well as industry practice). In short, ensure the methodology and methods followed are clear and robust so that you can articulate how you arrived at the decisions and demonstrate a fair and balanced approach.

Engagement, therefore, demands a good deal of judgement to assure a robust approach. Emotions can guide our behaviour at times, so being in control, confident, open to challenge, and professional in your engagement is all part of making the relationship work for you and your regulator. Having an open perspective and being adept at learning from the perspectives of others will be key, after all, the regulator sees a much broader picture of what is good and not so good in the operations of a particular industry, which can be an excellent source of insight for any organisation to tap into. One Director explained the approach their Board had adopted as they sought to lead the way in building a strong and mutually beneficial relationship with their main regulator. Their approach was to challenge the organisation to be proactive in providing insight to the regulator where they saw this as helpful. They saw this as fundamental to achieving what they had set out as their regulatory relationship strategy.

The benefits of the insights mentioned here are neatly and simply depicted in Figure 7.14 by Six (2013, p.176, building on the work of Murphy et al., 2009). Six presents a simple cycle of regulator trust and control that demonstrates

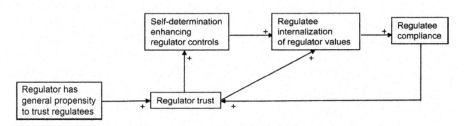

FIGURE 7.14 Reinforcing Cycle of Regulator Trust and Control (Six 2013)

how improvements in building trust as part of a change in approach can yield better compliance.

> *"If the way the regulator treats regulatees is perceived as procedurally just, regulatees are more likely to feel respected as part of the social group and are more likely to perceive that the regulator trusts them...regulator trust will have a positive effect on most regulatees' motivation".*

In conclusion, delivery is crucial, from setting down your commitments and the right level of expectation, to what you provide and how, delivery will set the tone and agenda for what comes next between your organisation and its regulator. Getting it right can, therefore, save all a great deal of further effort when handled correctly.

USING PEOPLE WHO ARE NOT IN THE ROOM

From time to time, your engagements with regulators may attract a level of importance where you feel that external expertise would be useful to help yourself or the team prepare. This can be a very good way of ensuring you are covering all the necessary areas given the subject of engagement.

Generally, these service providers will look at the objectives of the work and how you are approaching your responses to deliver to those objectives and assure that the quality of responses is sufficient and fit for purpose. Where there is an engagement aspect to the interaction, mock interviews or coaching may also form part of the preparation and readiness assessment to help individuals think about how they are to put over their messages and handle challenge and lines of enquiry. Such preparation can cover the best practice and pitfalls of being interviewed or engaging in regulatory meetings as well as conducting team-wide pre-interview calls to ensure the context and explanations are aligned.

In addition to the preparation, such interventions can provide insight on how the sequencing of engagement meetings and post-session debriefs can help anticipate lines of questioning and go prepared in subsequent sessions to help the regulator get the most out of the meetings.

Overall, these interventions help frame the engagements, they help the teams prepare, and ensure that, throughout engagements, they are focused on constantly assessing and taking the temperature of how things are going whilst adjusting to make them as successful as possible for all parties.

It is a judgement call on where such interventions are necessary, but often higher levels of preparation intervention are associated with those who have limited exposure to regulators, have run into some degree of challenge that they are keen to ensure is swiftly and appropriately addressed, or have fallen under the spotlight in terms of investigation or sanction. A key point to remember is whilst these services are a useful tool, in the final analysis, it is those in front of the regulator who will need to deliver and ensure the regulator and organisation are satisfied with the interaction and its outcome.

PRACTICALITIES OF APPROPRIATELY GOVERNED DISCLOSURE

Open and transparent disclosure, as we have discussed, is a central pillar of a good effective regulatory relationship. In fact, many regulators will have a specific provision to compel such an approach.

There will, of course, be situations where disclosure may need further governance to ensure that the interests of both parties are protected as well as those of related parties. In such circumstances, working with the regulator is crucial to ensure that both parties are clear on the issues they face and how they need to work together to ensure their objectives are met.

Organisations will, at times, need to be cognisant of other commitments and obligations they hold. These, for example, may be ones of data protection or areas requiring high degrees of confidentiality (e.g., market sensitive information, ongoing investigations, or restricted disclosure commitments). Similarly, the regulator may wish an organisation to restrict its actions whilst they undertake investigations, which may pose dilemmas where obligations exist to multiple stakeholders.

There is no *off the shelf* solution to such situations and often the right course of action will result as a consideration of balancing the following:

- The nature of the disclosure requested
- The context of the issue being faced
- The obligations the parties have to each stakeholder and the implications of disclosure given those obligations
- The legislative, regulatory (rules and principles), contractual, moral, and ethical commitments to which the parties are bound

As you work through the issues with your regulator, it could well be that there are solutions that allow both parties to operate without breaching such commitments. For example, using agreements to restrict disclosure, using legal privilege to allow parties to obtain advice that facilitates a suitable solution for both parties, or working through the sequencing of disclosure to ensure appropriate commitments are met whilst still meeting obligations to the regulator. Whatever the solution is that is considered, it will demand a practical and, at times, pragmatic working relationship. Only by working through the challenges both parties face can you ensure that your respective position is fully understood, and in doing so, all opportunities and avenues are explored. At the very least, through working together in such a way, there will be an appreciation that all that can be done is being done to allow the parties to resolve the situation.

PRACTICAL CONSIDERATIONS

This chapter has explored many of the practical considerations that ideally should be considered when engaging with regulators. From the context within which engagements are taking place, the professional and conventional considerations of etiquette, the impact and human influence of the people in the room, through to the practicalities of good preparation and diligence required when in delivery mode; these are all insights focused on helping you make your interactions as successful as possible from all perspectives. In addition, this practical walk through has provided examples to reflect upon, basics being forgotten, simple omissions, poor practice, due diligence, through to issues of perspective, balance, and transparency with the resultant potential implications in terms of regulatory response. There is a feast of history and practice gathered here for reflection. Remember, what is provided here is one view of practical approaches that can help the regulatory relationship develop positively, but it is by no means the only view. It offers the reader the opportunity for reflective practice to consider their own approach, to treat it as a buffet of insight from which to select, compare and refine their own approach, and in doing so, improve both engagements and their outcomes in future.

CLOSING COMMENTS

Having discussed the practical considerations of engaging with regulators, this marks a good point to consider the ground covered to this point.

To recap: in Chapter 1, we covered how regulatory relationships are traditionally approached, what we mean by a regulatory relationship strategy and why it is important, how relationships can operate in different modes, and how stakeholders can influence their direction, pace, and intensity. Before introducing a framework in Chapter 2 for building more effective relationships, we closed Chapter 1 by considering some of the drivers of change that impact and influence the path of regulatory engagement. In Chapter 2, the framework we introduced considered how a new perspective and approach to regulatory relationships could benefit organisations by taking a more holistic view of their whole regulatory ecosystem. Here, we considered how regulators are increasingly interested in how organisations are configured, how they are navigated, and, of course, what outcomes they generate across stakeholders. Chapter 3 considered the importance of building trust and confidence across your relationships, and how ensuring all aspects of your regulatory ecosystem align to earning that trust and confidence are a key to success. Here, we considered the implications when trust is lost and how the road back can be a long one for organisations where its loss is experienced. In Chapters 4 and 5, we started to explore the building blocks upon which trust can be developed. Here, we considered the importance of your organisation's foundations, its outlook if you like, and how the organisation's vision, strategy, and culture drive its approach to compliance, the regulator, and the regulatory relationship. Here, the foundations are laid, upon which the organisation functions and drives its activities as it delivers to the customer and balances the various stakeholder group needs. In Chapter 5, we took a closer look at the role of trust building through having an appropriate strategy, with good leadership and a well-tuned culture. The notion of how an organisation is navigated and its importance to the regulator was explored. It is at this point that we ventured into Chapter 6 and considered how the organisation's actions feed a whole ecosystem of insight the regulator is engaged with before considering in this chapter the practical considerations of regulatory engagement and building positive regulatory relationships.

In summary, we see that organisations that are well tuned into and aligned with the regulator's objectives, have developed sound organisational foundations, understand and actively manage the ecosystem with which they engage, and commit the investment of time into their regulatory relationships, can set themselves up to provide the best chance of avoiding the painful experiences of learning lessons the hard way.

Having considered some of the more practical considerations when engaging with regulators in this chapter, in Chapter 8, we pause. To this point, we have considered regulatory relationships through the lens of the past, the lessons, the events that unfolded, and their implications for the organisations concerned. However, the present has just provided one of the most significant events the world has experienced in modern history as a pandemic has gripped the globe. Next, we take the opportunity to look in on how organisations, their regulators, and wider stakeholders are responding and what it has meant for regulatory relationship strategy and in particular engagement and relationships.

NOTES

1. C.f. F.C.A. (2018b), Final Notice – Tesco Personal Finance PLC.
2. C.f. F.C.A. (2019b), "Final Notice – Tullett Prebon (Europe) Limited".
3. C.f. The following references provide background reading in areas related to this subject. F.S.A. (2013b), "Final Notice – Prudential Assurance Company Limited"; F.S.A. (2013a), "Final Notice – Prudential plc"; F.C.A. (2014), "Final Notice – Forex Capital Markets Limited ('FXCM Ltd'), FXCM Securities Limited ('FXCM Securities') (together 'FXCM UK')"; P.R.A. (2015), "Final Notice: The Cooperative Bank PLC (FRN: 121885)"; F.C.A. (2015c), "Final Notice – Threadneedle Asset Management"; F.C.A. (2015a), "Final Notice – Bank of Beirut (UK) Ltd"; F.C.A. (2015b), "Final Notice – Deutsche Bank AG"; F.C.A. (2016a), "Final Notice – Millburn Insurance Company Limited (in administration)"; F.C.A. (2016b), "Final Notice – Sonali Bank (UK) Limited"; D.O.J. (2017a), "Credit Suisse Agrees to Pay $5.28 Billion in Connection with its Sale of Residential Mortgage-Backed Securities"; D.O.J. (2017c), "Volkswagen AG Agrees to Plead Guilty and Pay $4.3 Billion in Criminal and Civil Penalties; Six Volkswagen Executives and Employees are Indicted in Connection with Conspiracy to Cheat U.S. Emissions Tests"; D.O.J. (2017b), "Deutsche Bank Agrees to Pay $7.2 Billion for Misleading Investors in its Sale of Residential Mortgage-Backed Securities"; P.R.A. (2017), "Final Notice: The Bank of Tokyo Mitsubishi UFJ Limited (FRN 139189) MUFG Securities EMEA plc (FRN124512)"; Federal Reserve (2018), "Federal Reserve Board fines Société Générale S.A. $81.3 Million for Firm's Unsafe and Unsound Practices Primarily Related to Violations of U.S. Sanctions Against Cuba"; D.O.J. (2018), "Wells Fargo Agrees to Pay $2.09 Billion Penalty for Allegedly Misreporting Quality of Loans Used in Residential Mortgage-Backed Securities"; F.C.A. (2018a), "Final Notice: Santander UK plc"; F.C.A. (2019a), "Final Notice: Bank of Scotland plc"; F.C.A. (2019b), "Final Notice – Tullet Prebon (Europe) Limited".

REFERENCES

Australian Prudential Regulation Authority (2020), 'APRA's Supervision Philosophy', [online], 6 October 2020, available: www.apra.gov.au/sites/default/files/2020-10/APRA%20Supervision%20Philosophy%20-%20October%202020.pdf, p.8

Bank of England, Prudential Regulation Authority (P.R.A.) (2015), 'Final Notice – The Co-operative Bank PLC (FRN: 121885)', [online], 10th August 2015, available: https://www.bankofengland.co.uk/-/media/boe/files/prudential-regulation/enforcement-notice/en110815.pdf?la=en&hash=8C725B400D0543C8E4E848A3374E73F09BCB7C3F

Bank of England, Prudential Regulation Authority (P.R.A.) (2017), 'Final Notice - The Bank of Tokyo Mitsubishi UFJ Limited (FRN 139189) MUFG Securities EMEA plc (FRN124512)', [online], 9 February 2017, available: https://www.bankofengland.co.uk/-/media/boe/files/prudential-regulation/enforcement-notice/en090217.pdf?la=en&hash=58442B59B07D7F5FB9A14CCD51224BE338BD0CF5

Donaldson, B. and O'Toole, T. (2007), 'Strategic Market Relationships: From Strategy to Implementation', 2nd edition, United States, Wiley

Federal Reserve (2018), 'Federal Reserve Board fines Société Générale S.A. $81.3 million for firm's unsafe and unsound practices primarily related to violations of U.S. sanctions against Cuba', [online], 19 November 2018, available: https://www.federalreserve.gov/newsevents/pressreleases/enforcement20181119a.htm

Financial Services Authority (F.S.A.) (2013a), 'Final Notice – Prudential plc', [online], 27 March 2013, available: https://www.fca.org.uk/publication/final-notices/fsa-pru-plc.pdf

Financial Services Authority (F.S.A.) (2013b), 'Final Notice – The Prudential Assurance Company Limited', [online], 27 March 2013, available: https://www.fca.org.uk/publication/final-notices/fsa-prudential-plc.pdf

Financial Conduct Authority (F.C.A.) (2014), 'Final Notice - Forex Capital Markets Limited ("FXCM Ltd") FXCM Securities Limited ("FXCM Securities") (together "FXCM UK")', [online], 24 February 2014, available: https://www.fca.org.uk/publication/final-notices/forex-capital-markets-limited.pdf

Financial Conduct Authority (F.C.A.) (2015a), 'Final Notice – Bank of Beirut (UK) Ltd', [online], 4 March 2015, available: https://www.fca.org.uk/publication/final-notices/bank-of-beirut.pdf

Financial Conduct Authority (F.C.A.) (2015b), 'Final Notice – Deutsche Bank AG', [online], 23 April 2015, available: https://www.fca.org.uk/publication/final-notices/deutsche-bank-ag-2015.pdf

Financial Conduct Authority (F.C.A.) (2015c), 'Final Notice - Threadneedle Asset Management Limited', [online], 10 December 2015, available: https://www.fca.org.uk/publication/final-notices/threadneedle-asset-management.pdf

Financial Conduct Authority (F.C.A.) (2016a), 'Final Notice – Millburn Insurance Company Limited (in administration)', [online], 1 February 2016, available: https://www.fca.org.uk/publication/final-notices/millburn-insurance-company-limited.pdf

Financial Conduct Authority (F.C.A.) (2016b), 'Final Notice – Sonali Bank (UK) Limited', [online], 12 October 2016, available: https://www.fca.org.uk/publication/final-notices/sonali-bank-uk-limited-2016.pdf

Financial Conduct Authority (F.C.A.) (2018a), 'Final Notice - Santander U.K. Plc', [online], 19 December 2018, available: http://www.fca.org.uk/publication/final-notices/santander-uk-plc-2018.pdf

Financial Conduct Authority (F.C.A.) (2018b), 'Final Notice – Tesco Personal Finance PLC', [online], 1 October 2018, available: https://www.fca.org.uk./publication/final-notices/tesco-personal-finance-plc-2018.pdf

Financial Conduct Authority (F.C.A.) (2018c), 'Principles For Businesses', [online], available: https://www.handbook.fca.org.uk/handbook/PRIN/2/?view=chapter

Financial Conduct Authority (F.C.A.) (2019a), 'Final Notice - Bank of Scotland plc', [online], 20 June 2019, available: www.fca.org.uk/publication/final-notices/bank-of-scotland-2019.pdf

Financial Conduct Authority (F.C.A.) (2019b), 'Final Notice - Tullett Prebon (Europe) Limited', [online], 11 October 2019, available: www.fca.org.uk/publication/final-notices/tullett-prebon-europe-limited-2019.pdf

Governance Institute of Australia (2019), 'Strategy for engaging with regulators', [online], available: https://www.governanceinstitute.com.au/resources/governance-directions/volume-71-number-7/strategy-for-engaging-with-regulators/

Hawkins, T., Gravier, M. and Powley, E. (2011), 'Public Versus Private Sector Procurement Ethics and Strategy: What Each Sector Can Learn from The Other', Journal of Business Ethics, Vol. 103, No. 4, pp.567–86

Hayek, F. V. (1974), 'The Pretence of Knowledge', © The Nobel Foundation 1977, [online], 11 December 1974, available: www.nobelprize.org/prizes/economic-sciences/1974/hayek/lecture/

Jeffries, F. L. and Reed, R. (2000), 'Trust and Adaptation in Relational Contracting', Academy of Management Review, Vol. 25, No. 4, pp.873–882

Lindgreen, A. (2001), 'A Framework for Studying Relationship Marketing Dyads', Qualitative Market Research: An International Journal, Vol. 4, No. 2, pp.75–88

Matsumoto, D. (1996), 'Culture and Psychology', Pacific Grove, CA: Brooks/Cole, p.18

Mintzberg, H., Jorgensen, J., Dougherty, D. and Westley, F. (1996), 'Some Surprising Things about Collaboration – Knowing How People Connect Makes it Work Better', Organisational Dynamics, Spring 1996, Elsevier Science Publishing, p.60

Murphy, K., Tyler, T. R. and Curtis, A. (2009), 'Nurturing Regulatory Compliance: Is Procedural Justice Effective When People Question the Legitimacy of the Law', Regulation & Governance, Vol. 3, pp.1–26.

Proudman, J. (2018), 'Cyborg supervision – the application of advanced analytics in prudential supervision', [online], Bank of England, 19 November 2018, available: https://www.bankofengland.co.uk/speech/2018/james-proudman-cyborg-supervision

Sin, L.Y.M., Tse, A.C.B., Yau, O.H.M., Lee, J.S.Y. and Chow, R. (2002), 'The Effect of Relationship Marketing Orientation on Business Performance in a Service-Oriented Economy', Journal of Service Marketing, Vol. 16, No. 7, pp.656–76

Six, F. (2013), 'Trust in Regulatory Relations', [online], Public Management Review, Vol. 15, No. 2, pp.163–85, available: http://www.tandfonline.com/loi/rpxm20, publisher Taylor & Francis Ltd, http://www.tandfonline.com reprinted by permission of the publisher, p.164, 170, 172, 173

U.S. Department of Justice (D.O.J.) (2017a), 'Credit Suisse Agrees to Pay $5.28 Billion in Connection with its Sale of Residential Mortgage-Backed Securities', [online], 18 January 2017, available: www.justice.gov/opa/pr/credit-suisse-agrees-pay-528-billion-connection-its-sale-residential-mortgage-backed

U.S. Department of Justice (D.O.J.) (2017b), 'Deutsche Bank Agrees to Pay $7.2 Billion for Misleading Investors in its Sale of Residential Mortgage-Backed Securities', [online], 17 January 2017, available: www.justice.gov/opa/pr/deutsche-bank-agrees-pay-72-billion-misleading-investors-its-sale-residential-mortgage-backed

U.S. Department of Justice (D.O.J.) (2017c), 'Volkswagen AG Agrees to Plead Guilty and Pay $4.3 Billion in Criminal and Civil Penalties; Six Volkswagen Executives and Employees are Indicted in Connection with Conspiracy to Cheat U.S. Emissions Tests', [online], 11 January 2017, available: https://www.justice.gov/opa/pr/volkswagen-ag-agrees-plead-guilty-and-pay-43-billion-criminal-and-civil-penalties-six

U.S. Department of Justice (D.O.J.) (2018), 'Wells Fargo Agrees to Pay $2.09 Billion Penalty for Allegedly Misreporting Quality of Loans Used in Residential Mortgage-Backed Securities', [online], 1 August 2018, available: www.justice.gov/opa/pr/wells-fargo-agrees-pay-209-billion-penalty-allegedly-misrepresenting-quality-loans-used

Vaccaro, A. and Madsen, P. (2009), 'Corporate Dynamic Transparency: The New ICT-Driven Ethics? Ethics and Information Technology, Vol. 11, No. 2, pp.113–122

Webber, S. S. and Klimoski, R. J. (2004), 'Client–project Manager Engagements, Trust, and Loyalty', Journal of Organisational Behaviour, Vol. 25, No. 8, pp.997–1013

CHAPTER **8**

Pandemic Crisis
Relationships Matter!

ECOSYSTEMS CAN HAVE A DRAMATIC EFFECT

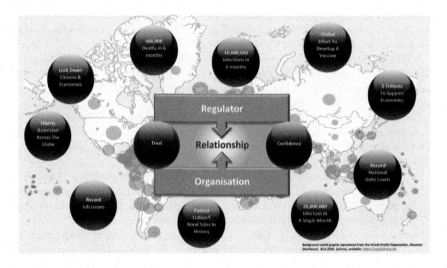

On 31 March 2020, the British summer had just commenced, and the first draft of this book was about to be issued for review. However, given the significance of what was unfolding around the world, this chapter on crisis situations was an important interjection – a point at which to pause and consider how regulatory relationships adapt as the world started to experience the acceleration of the pandemic relating to Covid-19. As one of the biggest global issues being faced, history was being written day by day, and whilst this would make conclusions difficult to draw, it enabled observations as events unfolded. This chapter, therefore, is dedicated to taking an opportunity to reflect on how a change in the environment can rapidly change the organisation's regulatory relationships and the ecosystem in which it operates. It demonstrates in the real and challenging events that unfold, how important that wider ecosystem is to regulatory relationships for the regulator, the regulated entity, and those they aim to serve, particularly in times of crisis.

DOI: 10.4324/9781003297963-8

COVID-19: A PUBLIC HEALTH EMERGENCY

Covid-19 was declared a public health emergency of international concern by the World Health Organisation (W.H.O.) on the 30 January 2020 and a pandemic on the 11 March 2020 (W.H.O. Timeline, 2020c). Subsequent action saw populations around the world being instructed to restrict their liberty as infections and the related death toll increased. To this point (mid-2022), it continues to be a crisis that is universal, as it cuts across nations, their industries, and their populations. It is a unifying fight, as every impacted nation (more than 200 globally) and their constituent organisations and populations have an aligned goal: the protection of people, limitation of harm, and prevention of the loss of life. A crisis of this scale, of course, has huge implications in terms of the human cost, which we are seeing every day.

Our interconnected way of life faced an abrupt and rapidly escalating level of disruption. As individuals travel, they carry with them the potential to transport a virus from one physical environment to another. Our ecosystem lit up across the globe as infections of Covid-19 continue to progress and, in response, countries around the globe limit movement to help prevent the spread of the virus. The world has for many years been described as becoming increasingly volatile, uncertain, complex, and ambiguous, and, as we look out across the world in recent times, all of those descriptions have and continue to apply to many aspects of our individual daily lives all at once. Whilst we have had warnings over the dangers of infectious disease from scientists over the decades and experienced warning signs with remarkable regularity (SARS in 2002, MERS in 2008, Ebola in 2014, and now Covid-19 in 2020), this outbreak has shown a velocity and trajectory the modern world has not experienced. The fragility of the world around us has suddenly come into sharp focus.

The charts below from the W.H.O. painted a troubling picture for us as the progression of the situation by the end of June 2020 demonstrates (W.H.O. 2020d).

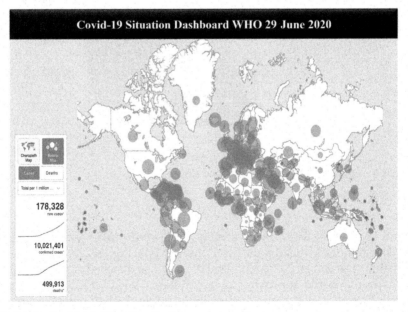

FIGURE 8.1   Covid-19 Situation Dashboard

The charts demonstrated how *volatile* the situation had become as different regions around the world experienced the impact of Covid-19 on their society; how *uncertain* the outcome was as we watched in despair at the rise of confirmed cases across the globe; how *complex* the situation was as we grappled to understand patterns of transmission and strategies for dealing with those infected; and how *ambiguous* things had become as we sought to understand what we should do next in the fight against the virus and what the evidence is pointing to.

By 29 June 2020 (c. 6 months in), the pandemic had passed a sombre landmark and provided the following facts according to the World Health Organisation (W.H.O. 2020a):

- More than 10 million cases confirmed across the globe (see Figures 8.1 and 8.3)
- Approaching half a million deaths reported (see Figures 8.1 and 8.3)
- More than 200 countries, areas, or territories with cases (see Figure 8.1)
- An acceleration of infections (see Figure 8.2)
- Record numbers of new cases being reported daily (see Figure 8.3)

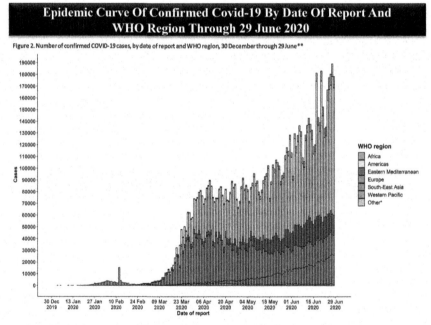

FIGURE 8.2   Epidemic Curve of Confirmed Covid-19

Around six months later, by December 2020, confirmed cases had reached circa 80 million and deaths circa 1.7 million (W.H.O. 2020b). A further 12 months on (December 2021), confirmed cases had reached circa 288 million and deaths numbered approximately 5.4 million (W.H.O. 2022). By December 2022, confirmed cases exceeded 640 million and deaths had passed 6.6 million (W.H.O 2022a)

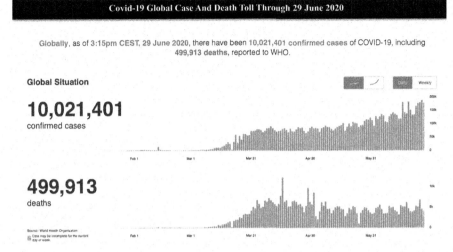

FIGURE 8.3   Covid-19 Global Case and Death Toll (W.H.O. Situation Dashboard 2020)

The scenario provides a stark example, of how the increased interconnectivity of an ecosystem facilitates the transmission where contagion exists, and with it, what can be devastating effects. As this example demonstrates, this can start with a trace concentrated in an area, but, with time, can accelerate in both frequency and breadth of where it strikes as we are seeing every day.

It also reminds us that we cannot always predict its path, its pace, or its ultimate impact, but what we know is we would rather not have that contagion in our midst.

This context we find ourselves in is devastating and provides a sombre reminder that highly interconnected ecosystems can be quickly undermined and heavily impacted when the system becomes polluted, i.e., the ecosystem itself, once impacted, can have a significant effect on the outcome in unpredictable and complex ways. To articulate it another way, as the Board charged with investigating a totally different complex disaster (the Columbia space shuttle explosion) concluded:

"Complex systems almost always fail in complex ways. (CAIB 2003)".

CRISIS AS A DRIVER OF CHANGE – RELATIONSHIPS, THEORY, PRACTICE, AND CONVENTION

Throughout this text, we have looked at the importance of thinking about regulatory relationships as an ecosystem of communication between all that an organisation impacts and its regulator. We have explored what a regulatory relationship is, what it entails, who the stakeholders are, and captured examples of the theories of regulation that drive its context (see appendix I). In periods of crisis, it is an interesting point to consider how theory, practice, and convention can be challenged. For example, theory can provide us with principles and ideas that help us explain a situation, but often periods of crisis introduce a crossroads where new decisions are required, often for situations we may have considered theoretically possible, but which are situations we have never faced.

One example the crisis provided was the debate regarding what steps would be acceptable to trial, and what level of sacrifice would be tolerable in our efforts to head off the pandemic (Bloomberg 2020). Crises (as we saw with the Global Financial Crisis) can lead to a wholesale review of how an industry operates, the legislation and rules that govern it, the organisations and how they operate, and the protections for consumers and broader stakeholders. When crises unfold, it is often what we learn and how we respond that inform the next wave of necessary changes. Our relationships in such times are critical and our swift actions often become the fulcrum between success and failure. In this context, theory, practice, and convention serve as guidance, which as events unfold may see themselves redefined.

Whilst the picture of the pandemic continues to be updated daily, captured below are some of the changes we see unfolding in this crisis. As changes take place across industries, the level of interaction and engagement between organisations and their stakeholders, particularly regulators, ramp up as both focus on responding to the challenges faced and both bring ideas, insight, and solutions to the table to achieve their goals. These are fascinating times and present an excellent example of how regulatory relationships adapt to the circumstances and environment in front of them with implications for all parties. Taking several of the subjects we have covered throughout this text, next we explore a few examples of how the pandemic has driven changes in the way organisations and their regulators are monitoring the ecosystem, adjusting their approach, and engaging to accelerate action. It provides a perfect lens through which to look at how regulatory relationships are operating and developing. Here, we look in on a live example of one ecosystem pitched against another. One being the ecosystem of the natural world as the virus transfers across the globe, and the other being nations, institutions, organisations, regulators, and people as they use their relationships and resources to fight back.

THE REGULATORY ECOSYSTEM *LIGHTS UP* – A DASHBOARD OF INSIGHT

In Chapter 2 we introduced the concept of thinking about regulatory relationships as an ecosystem. The argument being that, in understanding that broader system, we gain a better view of the influences on the regulatory relationship, including how these can rapidly change based on what the regulator and organisation faces.

The crisis has brought into sharp focus the benefits of having this *ecosystem* view. Every day, new pieces of data, information, and insight are being provided across those systems, each of which both the regulator and the regulatee are assessing for their impact and influence on the next set of actions they should consider.

A few simple examples, taken from across different industries, provide a view on how different aspects of the ecosystem lit up. Figure 8.4 highlights (red boxes) these areas of activity in the ecosystem, along with the general response of the industry and regulators. Those sources of information have been varied, from product announcements and media, consumer comments that have concerned the regulator due to the spurious claims of organisations,

Regulatory Relationship Ecosystem Impact Example					*Example 1 (Medical: Product Announcement) – US Food and Drug Administration (FDA) warns firms for selling unapproved products with fraudulent claims regarding Covid-19. Industry marketing, consumer feedback, media & social media all areas of insight. (FDA 2022)*
Academic Research	International Regulator Cooperation	Annual Financial Statements	National Regulator Cooperation	Market Announcement	
Product & Service Announcements	Marketing Campaigns	Political Insight	Interviews	Media	*Example 2 (Finance & Technology: Suppliers) – Supplier decided to engage with the regulator due to requests from clients for technology changes which could have regulatory implications for their clients. A proactive and preventative engagement by a supplier who had no prior regulatory relationship.*
Market Studies	Industry Body Insights	Benchmarking	Consumer Organisations	Social Media	*Example 3 (Motorsport & Medical: New Suppliers) – UK F1 teams united around 'project pitlane' to assist with ventilator production following a call from Government for industry to assist in the fight of Covid-19 (Galloway 2020).*
Thematic Reviews	Industry Consultations	Business Change	Suppliers	Complaint Resolution Services	
Whistleblowing	Issues Incidents Breaches	Licencing / Applications	Industry Speeches	Dear CEO... Correspondence	
Regulatory Visits / Investigations	Supervisory Scheduled Meetings	Company Officer Approvals	Data Submissions	Consumer Feedback	

FIGURE 8.4   Regulatory Relationship Ecosystem

to the arrival of new suppliers to these regulated industries and the interventions of existing ones. From an organisation's point of view, each of these interventions has implications. Whether your regulator intervenes for deceptive promotional claims, your suppliers start building relationships with your regulators that they never had before, or your regulator allows new suppliers into the market without formal approval. Each of these wider dynamics potentially impacts the relationship with your regulator.

What is interesting as we consider some of these interactions is that we are seeing connections that are not typical. Such changes across the stakeholder map bring into focus how in times of change, the stakeholder map can immediately begin to change and shape new relationships and disrupt old ones. It is a time when organisations need to be vigilant to the changes taking place around their organisation and keep the regulator well informed of what challenges are faced and what changes they are making to address them.

IN IT TOGETHER – A SHIFT OF *MODE* CAN GREATLY ASSIST

The crisis has provided a scenario in which regulators and the organisations they regulate have faced a significant change of events, at high velocity, with an unknown trajectory. In response, we have seen examples where their combined reaction has been swift, coordinated, and significant, providing coordinated support to the regulated organisations and ultimately the end consumer. Their mode of operation has been calibrated to the scenario at great speed and with great effect. Under examples provided by Dame Deirdre Hutton (2015) of the Civil Aviation Authority (see Chapter 1), the crisis could be described as a blend of *partnership (wrestling with a current problem with a joint interest in a solution),* and the traditional position as a *regulator (oversight and ensuring our enthusiasm to respond still facilitates a minimum level of protection).* Government, organisations, and regulators are all keenly focused, albeit from different perspectives, on ensuring the combined response to the crises facilitates a path to minimise the impact across the many areas that this crisis affects.

Next, we build out further examples from across industries to continue our exploration and demonstrate how regulators and organisations have adjusted and continue to do so to facilitate a response to the crisis. These range from conserving resources to delaying implementation of rules all aimed at providing improved capacity to focus and respond. These examples give a sense of the partnership and co-working whilst also maintaining a degree of traditional regulatory oversight. It is a great example of how the context of the issue an industry or organisation faces can rapidly change the regulatory relationship approach of all parties.

Medical Manoeuvres

National Medical Regulators – Regulators across nations have moved to facilitate the flow of medical resources. Their efforts have ranged from easing import requirements on goods, relaxing rules on the distribution of medicines where approval is not yet formally held, through to supporting entrepreneurial efforts to build new devices that can help in the fight against the virus, such as personal protection equipment (P.P.E.).

U.S. Food and Drug Administration (F.D.A.) – The F.D.A. adjusted to ease the supply of resources to medical professionals. Examples include easing import requirements for medical devices and P.P.E. (Brennan 2020a/b/c; Mezher 2020a/b).

U.K. Medicines and Healthcare Products Regulatory Agency (M.H.R.A.) – The M.H.R.A. (M.H.R.A. 2020a) immediately set to work with healthcare partners and stakeholders to rapidly develop flexibility into regulatory guidance to support the medical supply chain. Examples include rapid reviews of clinical trials, ceasing routine on-site inspections (Eglovitch 2021; F.D.A. 2022) to free up resources, and prioritisation of all Covid-19 enquiries and clinical investigations.

Free Up the Finances

Central Banks – Central banks moved swiftly to use policy to provide financial relief. For example, the Federal Reserve in the United States cut interest rates to zero (F.T. 2020), The Bank of England reduced its Bank Rate by 65 basis points to 0.1% (Bank of England, 2020a).

In addition, there has been further coordinated action to support global liquidity across national central banks, as demonstrated by the following announcement from the Federal Reserve (2020):

> *"The Bank of Canada, the Bank of England, the Bank of Japan, the European Central Bank, the Federal Reserve, and the Swiss National Bank are today announcing a coordinated action to enhance the provision of liquidity via the standing U.S. dollar liquidity swap line arrangements".*

Bank of England – In the U.K., the Bank of England wrote to the chief executives of banks asking them to suspend dividend payments (Bank of England 2020b).

Such a move provides banks with a clear mandate to conserve resources in the difficult times and the *air cover* of the regulator to do that. In a crisis that continues to see a significant draw on financial resources, this provided a positive impetus to bank reserves. Only a matter of weeks later, as the reporting periods unfolded, bank loss provisions soared as billions in provisions were set aside across Europe.

This along with other examples across industries demonstrates the extensive efforts of regulators and supervisors to remove activities that would tie up important resources in the difficult times (Bank of England 2020c/d). This shows the refocus of attention and release of near-term regulatory requirements.

Aviation Amnesty and Assistance

Aviation authorities around the world, such as the European Union Aviation Safety Agency (E.A.S.A. 2020), responded to the exceptional circumstances caused by Covid-19 with an array of measures aimed at supporting operators as they adjusted to the impacts of the virus.

Federal Aviation Administration (F.A.A. 2020) – The F.A.A. in the United States advised they would not take enforcement action against certain pilots or flight engineers who fly with medical certificates that expire between specific dates to avoid the need for aviation staff to attend medical examinations, which would place further pressure on the healthcare system. One of many examples of aviation regulators attempting to remove burdensome requirements to help different (healthcare) but interconnected systems respond to the crisis.

Civil Aviation Administration of China – China's aviation administration moved to support the re-structuring and merging of airlines to help cope with the commercial impact on carriers due to the virus (Qiu and Goh 2020).

Along with aviation authorities in many jurisdictions, China has demonstrated its willingness to support industries directly impacted by the crisis. Such support helps prevent situations having a domino effect across organisations and, potentially, industries.

Information Commissioners Office – The I.C.O. (U.K.) demonstrated its ability to remain flexible in its treatment of organisations who have fallen short of their standards in the past. Here, they have demonstrated their willingness to take account of the broad situation being faced by airlines and calibrate their response accordingly in terms of the severity of sanction they imposed (I.C.O. 2020).

Help Right to the Front Line

Unprecedented times have brought unprecedented responses from authorities, all of which focused on ensuring the benefits of interventions get to those in need of support as much as possible.

In the U.K., for example, the U.K. Government announced a £350 billion lifeline for the economy (B.B.C. 2020a), whilst in the U.S. Congress approved a $2 trillion stimulus package to support the economy through the pandemic (B.B.C. 2020b).

Such was the commitment to support the economy in the U.K., for example, that significant milestones were passed according to the Office for National Statistics (2020a/b/c), with figures that were some of the highest since their records began. Public Sector Net Debt (excluding public sector banks) passed the £2 trillion level for the first time (Office for National Statistics 2020a, B.B.C. 2020c), making the size of debt larger than the size of the economy (B.B.C. 2020d). Borrowing hit record monthly highs as the government responded to the crisis, and the Gross Domestic Product fell at a record level of 20.4% in April 2020 (Office for National Statistics 2020b).

As the weeks passed by, gravity could not be avoided, and the U.K., for example, slipped into its first recession in 11 years (Office for National Statistics 2020c). By 25 November 2020, Rishi Sunak, (Chancellor of The Exchequer 2020) noted in his spending review address to the House of Commons, that the U.K. had suffered its largest fall in output in more than 300 years. Roll the clock forward a little over 12 months to January 2022, and major world economies face the emerging spectre of inflation. Rates are rising at a historically fast pace, reaching levels not seen in decades in the U.S. (U.S. B.L.S. 2022), and in the U.K. (Office for National Statistics 2022d) – focusing central banker attention on the balancing act of controlling inflation whilst protecting the fragile recovery as economies around the world recover from the pandemic. Furthermore, the historic ripple effects of the crisis were felt in wider markets, for example, stock market values plummeting around the globe and oil prices turning negative as the effects of policies limiting travel and locking down nations devastated demand and drove excess supply and storage issues, destroying prices.

As well as government interventions, regulators across industries also drove actions focused on supporting those they protect through supporting those they regulate.[1]

Examples of their support have included relaxing rules, instructing consumer support (F.C.A. 2020b), challenging business practices, delaying regulation, and extending permissions to name a few (F.C.A. 2020a, U.K. Finance 2020). In executing these activities, engagement, guidance, and clarification has been a constant two-way process as organisations and regulators have navigated the significant and fast-moving storm around them.

The examples of interventions represent a tiny fraction of the colossal efforts as we continue to see regulators and industry practitioners align on a common objective in a way and with a focus rarely seen. An excellent demonstration of a level of collaboration on a remarkable scale.

In summary, the stakeholder map has been in full flux. Power, influence, importance, and activities have all been a constant moving picture as relationships develop and actions unfold. As the movements of some of the key stakeholders above demonstrate, the response has been extensive, as has the creativity of some who have come to the fore to assist. Relationships with stakeholders, as we have seen in the most desperate of times, are key to how you respond.

STAKEHOLDERS – THEY CAN COMPLETELY CHANGE YOUR FOCUS

The importance of the stakeholder map on an organisation's regulatory relationship can be heavily influenced by the situation the organisation and industry faces.

When an issue with such significance as the Covid-19 pandemic strikes, stakeholder power can shift quickly. In the current situation, we have seen our environment change rapidly, and with it, governments move to influence whole industries to divert their attention and resources to the crisis. We have seen industry regulators direct the actions of organisations, provide regulatory relief, whilst at the same time adjusting their approach to consumer protection. Organisations have demonstrated their flexibility by totally changing what they produce, how they operate, and what they provide in terms of support to the consumer.

As well as the shifts in power, we have seen changes in the level of engagement and influence of stakeholders. The traditional regulatory relationship has seen an escalation in interaction as both parties attempt to ensure they are doing all they can to respond. However, we have also seen an increase in the engagement of indirect stakeholders. Whether this has been the direct intervention of traditional suppliers getting more involved in regulatory relationships, or totally new suppliers coming to the table to join the fight against the virus, such as Formula 1 teams building respirators (Galloway 2020), and brewers developing anti-bacterial solutions (Brewdog 2020). Finally, when we think about the broader influencers, this crisis has also seen an escalation in wider consumer, trade, and industry groups making their views known – whether that is calls for greater leniency of regulatory burden to assist organisations in responding or calls for greater protections for workers at the front line of the fight. The stakeholder map has come to life as all parties attempt to navigate action from their perspective.

FIRM FOUNDATIONS – IN CRISIS, THEY HELP YOU THROUGH THE STORM

Points of crisis can introduce significant pressure into the operating rhythm of any organisation. For some, it will represent a period of difficulty, an interruption demanding attention, but which should not lead to significant trouble or danger for the organisation. For others, such disruption can place the organisation in significant trouble. It may be that their performance has already demonstrated weakness in normal operating conditions and disruption is a tipping point event as resilience is tested beyond the point it can respond. As lockdowns took hold, the outlook for the high streets of cities across the world looked increasingly difficult.

In extreme cases, crises can also introduce a point of danger, a stretch on resources that undermines the ability to operate at a level that drives real danger to consumers of public services. With the Covid-19 crisis, that point of danger has been healthcare, and has seen calls from governments around the world for changes across society to prevent the spread of the virus to avoid healthcare systems becoming overstretched and unable to effectively treat those suffering.

It is in these periods that the strategy, culture, and leadership of organisations will shine through and drive an approach and ability to respond (see Chapter 4). Innovation and creativity along with adaptability to the circumstances being faced have been a daily occurrence as organisations respond to the twists and turns of the crisis. We have and will continue to see the emerging impact of these essential organisational foundations on the outcomes and actions of organisations. Crises can be times when we see the best in organisations as well as questionable behaviours. Suffice to say, when times get difficult, having a dynamic strategy that's able to respond, backed by a culture that is willing and driven to respond, and a leadership that can corral those strengths and lead the way through is essential. When the organisation is changing hour to hour and day to day, being on those firm foundations can be a robust and stable keel with which to tack your way through the storm.

In terms of the regulatory relationship, it is in these times of crisis that a great deal can be gleaned from the actions of organisations. Regulators will be on heightened alert in monitoring their areas of responsibility and will be in more frequent contact with the organisations they regulate. They will get a good sense of how organisations are making decisions and just as importantly what is driving those decisions (e.g., financial pressure, altruism, compulsion, capability limitation). They will be able to see how the organisation can handle the pressures placed upon them. This will include how their leaders respond, how their systems perform, how their processes adapt, how their policies are adjusted to assist their customers, how they seek to help their broader communities, and how resilient they are when all these demands are placed upon them in short order. It is a time when relationships can rapidly build or destroy opinion and where the foundations of trust can be laid.

WHO CAN YOU TRUST? WHAT CAN YOU TRUST?

As events unfold, with such a keen examination on the steps organisations take and the outcomes they achieve in responding to the events they face, the trust that exists in a regulatory relationship can quickly (relatively speaking) be influenced. Crises are times when relationships can be made or undermined, as organisations demonstrate their contribution to the issues faced through their day-to-day actions.

While it is still early days in the likely chronology of the Covid-19 crisis, these previously mentioned examples demonstrate how an ecosystem approach to regulatory relationships can help organisations ensure they are building strong trust-based relationships. Examples show how regulators can use the whole ecosystem to identify poor practice, even in times of crisis, and hold organisations to account, while also using that same system to anticipate the impact on organisations and provide support to ease the burden where justified.

Responding and successfully emerging from the crisis will rely heavily on a wide range of trust relationships across governments, regulators, organisations, and individuals. To a large degree, people's lives will balance on the trust that people will do the right things, for the right reasons, in the right circumstances. Day to day we are seeing trust being tested at every level, right down to the individual. For example, trust that our healthcare systems will be able to cope, trust that our places of work will afford sufficient protection, trust that the individuals in those services we rely upon diligently perform their duties to keep us safe, trust that the financial support systems will help us through, trust that people generally follow expert opinion and the rules to limit the damage the virus can do, and trust that our food chain will keep provisions flowing. Our framework of trust suddenly has more profound consequences, and with it our confidence, in relying upon that framework is being challenged. In a time when trust and confidence are tested, relationships really matter.

IN SUMMARY – WHAT WE HAVE SEEN
MATTERS TO THIS FIGHT

The velocity, trajectory, and impact of this pandemic on a global scale has taken the world by surprise. It has demanded responses across nations in every facet of their social and business infrastructures, tested their resilience, and touched every individual.

This brief pause has highlighted just a small number of the significant shifts that have taken place. Dramatic interventions of governments, pragmatic adjustment by regulators, and creativity in the help provided by organisations and individuals has seen the stakeholder map move to stand shoulder to shoulder in their response.

Regulatory strategies have been adjusted on both sides of the regulatory relationship, regulatory engagement has seen a step change in pace, frequency, and breadth, and relationships have intensified as their efforts step up a gear. It has provided an excellent example of our systems working collegiately on a common objective...protecting lives and society.

Relationships Have Responded Rapidly

A great deal of those responses as we have seen above have involved organisations and their regulators moving from a state of calm, controlled business operating rhythms to crisis. This has been a huge shift in the mode of operation, however, it has also been one where we can observe excellent responses between organisations and their regulators for the benefit of their customers and colleagues – all at a velocity that has made a significant difference to millions of people. Where regulators and organisations may have proposed, consulted, and refined new rules and practices over a period of months pre-crisis, during the crisis such timescales have been measured in days – and both regulators and organisations have adapted and collaborated to facilitate such changes in pace.

Relationships Have Been Proactive, Creative, and Flexible

The alignment of one stakeholder group (organisations and regulators) to support another (consumers and colleagues) has been remarkable.

Relationships are showing themselves to be more proactive and responsive as they try to anticipate what to do next. They've become more dynamic and flexible as they try to move at pace, often resulting in extensive changes to their normal working approach, and more supportive and creative as they attempt to focus on the key issues and remove the burden of items that, in the face of such a crisis, tumble down the priority list.

As we observe the response to this new immediate priority, it is a testament to all involved how well regulatory relationships are facilitating such a pragmatic and positive response. It may be that being faced with such a crisis of no one's making, closer ties have emerged and will be the foundation of a new relationship approach for many with their regulator.

Whatever the outcome, the way organisations and their regulators have worked to respond is evidence of just how far regulatory relationships have developed. If many of the traits of what we have seen in these months can translate into longer-term approaches, the path forward should be an easier one to tread...one in which organisations and their regulators are more in tune with each other's needs and requirements and more proactive, open, and transparent in their relationships.

DATES TO REMEMBER

As the efforts of the world have focused on navigating the situation created by this crisis on many fronts, one like no other, has had the world's attention. The path out of the crisis has rested on the search for an effective vaccine and the medical community has been steadfast in its search throughout, with the eyes of the world tracking its progress. Whilst both Russia and China have reportedly been using vaccines they developed, Western societies were awaiting their first approvals. On 2 December 2020, the Western world awoke to news that the U.K. regulator (Medicines and Healthcare products Regulatory Agency 2020b) had approved the Pfizer/BioNTech Coronavirus vaccine for widespread use. The implication was that vaccinations could commence within days and the U.K. would commence the largest scale vaccination campaign in the country's history (Roberts 2020). By the 8 December 2020, the first U.K. vaccination took place.

This positive news was very welcome, but beside it continued to flow a harsh reality check of what was being faced. As if to remind us that this situation is one that would continue to test us, December also provided us with further lockdowns across Europe as infection rates climbed, the cancellation of planned time bound relaxations to restrictions over the Christmas period, the discovery of a new more infectious variant of the Covid-19 virus, restrictions being placed on travel of U.K. citizens, record levels of hospital admissions that rose above the peak seen earlier in the year, and record numbers of daily infections being seen. The race was clearly not won on containment and vaccinations became the latest runners in the long list of answers societies could throw at the pandemic.

As the latest in the long line of challenges provided by Covid-19 was achieved, attentions turned to the challenge of how the world would accelerate and prioritise the vaccination of the entire human race. Discussions quickly turned to the next significant challenge: how you achieve herd immunity and how that could mean more than 5 billion people globally needing a vaccination.

Whilst these dates are points for celebration of the enormous efforts of industry, regulators, and governments globally, they are also a point at which the enormity of the challenge that continued to lay ahead became clearer to all. The times continued to prove themselves as being volatile, uncertain, complex, and ambiguous.

By the second quarter of 2022, an improved picture had emerged, but still one of continued success and challenges. Success came progressively as nations relaxed their restrictions and opened their borders, as the impact of their actions and vaccination roll out took hold. However, challenges remained as nations across the globe continued with restrictions tailored to their situation throughout 2022. For China, following the relaxing of restrictions, January the 22nd 2023, would see the start of their first New Year without restrictions since Covid-19 lockdowns began. For some it would be the first time they had seen family and friends for three years. What was clear was living with Covid-19 would remain a journey of discovery and adaptation to its unpredictable path.

NOTE

1. Whilst the challenges and impacts of Covid-19 are devastating, war in Ukraine would add further to the challenges the world faced and the impacts it would need to endure during 2022.

REFERENCES

B.B.C. News Report (2020a), 'Coronavirus: Chancellor unveils £350bn lifeline for economy', [online], 17 March 2020, available: https://www.bbc.co.uk/news/business-51935467

B.B.C. News Report (2020b), 'Coronavirus: US Senate passes $2tn disaster aid bill', [online], 26 March 2020, available: https://www.bbc.co.uk/news/world-us-canada-52033863

B.B.C. News (2020c), 'U.K. Government Spending Measures on Virus Pushes Debt To £2 Trillion', [online], 21 August 2020, available: https://www.bbc.co.uk/news/business-53859299

B.B.C. News (2020d), 'U.K. Debt Now Larger Than Size of Whole Economy', [online], 19 June 2020, available: https://www.bbc.co.uk/news/business-53104734

Bank of England (2020a), 'Bank Rate Maintained At 0.1% - March 2020', [online], 26 March 2020, available: https://www.bankofengland.co.uk/monetary-policy-summary-and-minutes/2020/march-2020

Bank of England (2020b), 'Letters from Sam Woods to U.K. Deposit Takers on Dividend Payments, Share Buybacks and Cash Bonuses', [online], 31 March 2020, available: https://www.bankofengland.co.uk/prudential-regulation/letter/2020/letter-from-sam-woods-to-uk-deposit-takers-on-dividend-payments-share-buybacks-and-cash-bonuses

Bank of England (2020c), 'Our response to coronavirus (Covid): regulatory measures for PRA firms', [online], 19 August 2021, available: https://www.bankofengland.co.uk/coronavirus/information-for-firms

Bank of England (2020d), 'Joint PRA And HMT Statement on the Delay to Implementation of The Basel 3.1 Standards', [online], 2 April 2020, available: https://www.bankofengland.co.uk/prudential-regulation/publication/2020/joint-pra-and-hmt-statement-on-the-delay-to-implementation-of-the-basel-3-1-standards

Bloomberg News Report (2020), 'Volunteers are Lining Up to be Infected with Coronavirus', [online], 18 June 2020, available: https://www.bloomberg.com/news/articles/2020-06-18/volunteers-are-lining-up-to-be-infected-with-the-coronavirus

Brennan, Z. (2020a), 'FDA EUA Allows States to Receive Unapproved COVID-19 Treatments', [online], Regulatory Affairs Professionals Society, Regulatory Focus, 30 March 2020, available: https://www.raps.org/news-and-articles/news-articles/2020/3/fda-eua-allows-states-to-receive-unapproved-covid?utm_source=MagnetMail&utm_medium=Email%20&utm_campaign=RF%20Today%20%7C%2030%20March%202020

Brennan, Z. (2020b), 'FDA Looks to Speed Access to Potential Covid-19 Treatments', [online], Regulatory Affairs Professionals Society, Regulatory Focus, 19 March 2020, available: https://www.raps.org/news-and-articles/news-articles/2020/3/fda-looks-to-speed-access-to-approved-experimental?utm_source=MagnetMail&utm_medium=Email%20&utm_campaign=RF%20Today%20%7C%2019%20March%202020

Brennan, Z. (2020c), 'FDA Speeds New Coronavirus Diagnostic Tests', [online], Regulatory Affairs Professionals Society, Regulatory Focus, 2 March 2020, available: https://www.raps.org/news-and-articles/news-articles/2020/3/fda-speeds-new-coronavirus-diagnostic-tests?utm_source=MagnetMail&utm_medium=Email%20&utm_campaign=RF%20Today%20%7C%202%20March%202020

Brewdog (2020), 'Sanitiser: Sharing what we have learned', [online], 6 April 2020, available: www.brewdog.com/blog/sanitiser-sharing-what-we-have-learned

Eglovitch, J. (2021), 'FDA clarifies potential actions when onsite inspections are infeasible', [online], Regulatory Affairs Professionals Society, Regulatory Focus, 18 May 2021, available: https://www.raps.org/news-and-articles/news-articles/2021/5/fda-qa-outlines-regulatory-actions-following-remot?utm_source=MagnetMail&utm_medium=Email%20&utm_campaign=RF%20Today%20%7C%2018%20May%202021

European Union Aviation Safety Agency (E.A.S.A.) (2020), 'Coronavirus Covid-19', [online], available: https://www.easa.europa.eu/the-agency/coronavirus-covid-19?page=5

Federal Aviation Administration (F.A.A.) (2020), 'Novel Coronavirus (COVID-19) Update', [online], 31 March 2020, available: https://www.faa.gov/news/updates/?newsId=94991

Federal Reserve (2020), 'Coordinated Central Bank Action to Enhance the Provision of U.S. Dollar Liquidity', [online], 15 March 2020, available: https://www.federalreserve.gov/newsevents/pressreleases/monetary20200315c.htm

Financial Conduct Authority (F.C.A.) (2020a), 'Coronavirus (Covid-19)', [online], available: https://www.fca.org.uk/coronavirus

Financial Conduct Authority (F.C.A.) (2020b), 'F.C.A. confirms support for customers who are struggling to pay their mortgage due to coronavirus', [online], 2 June 2020, available: https://www.fca.org.uk/news/press-releases/fca-confirms-support-customers-who-are-struggling-pay-their-mortgage-due-coronavirus

Financial Times (F.T.) (2020), 'Fed cuts US interest rates to zero as part of sweeping crisis measures', Financial Times, [online], 15 March 2020, available: https://www.ft.com/content/a9a28bc0-66fb-11ea-a3c9-1fe6fedcca75

Galloway, J. (2020), 'F1 teams in U.K. launch Project Pitlane to help in Coronavirus fight', [online], Sky Sports News, 27 March 2020, available: https://www.sky-sports.com/f1/news/12433/11964718/f1-teams-in-uk-launch-project-pitlane-to-help-in-coronavirus-fight

Hutton, Dame Deirdre. (2015), 'The Role of Stakeholder Relationships in Regulatory Excellence', [online], The Regulatory Review, 27 July 2015, available: https://www.theregreview.org/2015/07/27/hutton-regulatory-excellence/

Information Commissioner's Office (I.C.O.) (2020), 'ICO Fines British Airways £20m for Data Breach Affecting More Than 400,000 Customers', [online], available: https://ico.org.uk/about-the-ico/news-and-events/news-and-blogs/2020/10/ico-fines-british-airways-20m-for-data-breach-affecting-more-than-400-000-customers/

Medicines and Healthcare Products Regulatory Agency (M.H.R.A.) (2020a), 'MHRA regulatory flexibilities resulting from coronavirus (Covid-19)', [online], available: https://www.gov.uk/guidance/mhra-regulatory-flexibilities-resulting-from-coronavirus-covid-19

Medicines and Healthcare Products Regulatory Agency (M.H.R.A.) (2020b), 'Regulatory approval of Pfizer/BioNTech vaccine for COVID-19', [online], 2 December 2020, available: https://www.gov.uk/government/publications/regulatory-approval-of-pfizer-biontech-vaccine-for-covid-19

Mezher, M. (2020a), 'FDA Eases Import Requirements for Devices and PPE to Fight Coronavirus', [online], Regulatory Affairs Professionals Society, Regulatory Focus, 25 March 2020, available: https://www.raps.org/news-and-articles/news-articles/2020/3/fda-eases-import-requirements-for-devices-and-ppe?utm_source=MagnetMail&utm_medium=Email%20&utm_campaign=RF%20Today%20%7C%2025%20March%202020

Mezher, M. (2020b), 'FDA Lifts Requirements for Masks, Respirators, Looks to Reprocessing to Ease Shortages', [online], Regulatory Affairs Professionals Society, Regulatory Focus, 26 March 2020, available: https://www.raps.org/news-and-articles/news-articles/2020/3/fda-lifts-requirements-for-masks-respirators-looks

Office for National Statistics (2020a), 'PS: Net Debt (Excluding Public Sector Banks)', [online], available: https://www.ons.gov.uk/economy/governmentpublicsectorandtaxes/publicsectorfinance/timeseries/hf6w/pusf?referrer=search&searchTerm=hf6w

Office for National Statistics (2020b), 'GDP Monthly Estimate, U.K.: April 2020', [online], available: https://www.ons.gov.uk/economy/grossdomesticproductgdp/bulletins/gdpmonthlyestimateuk/april2020

Office for National Statistics (2020c), 'Coronavirus and the impact on output in the UK economy: June 2020', [online], available: https://www.ons.gov.uk/economy/grossdomesticproductgdp/articles/coronavirusandtheimpactonoutputintheukeconomy/june2020

Office for National Statistics (2022d), 'Consumer price inflation, UK: December 2021', [online], 19 January 2022, available: https://www.ons.gov.uk/economy/inflationandpriceindices/bulletins/consumerpriceinflation/december2021

Qiu, S. and Goh, B. (Reuters 2020), 'China's aviation regulator supports airline mergers amid virus outbreak', [online], Reuters, 12 February 2020, available: https://www.reuters.com/article/us-china-health-aviation/chinas-aviation-regulator-says-supports-airline-mergers-amid-virus-outbreak-idUSKBN2060B8

Roberts, M. (2020), 'Covid-19: Pfizer/BioNTech Vaccine judged safe for use in UK', [online], B.B.C., 2 December 2020, available: https://www.bbc.co.uk/news/health-55145696

Sunak, R. (Chancellor of the Exchequer) (2020), 'Spending Review 2020 Speech', [online], 25 November 2020, available: https://www.gov.uk/government/speeches/spending-review-2020-speech

U.K. Finance (2020), 'Lenders Grant 1.9 Million Payment Deferrals to Mortgage Holders in 3 Months', [online], available: https://www.ukfinance.org.uk/press/press-releases/lenders-grant-over-million-payment-deferrals-to-mortgage-holders-in-three-months

U.S. Bureau of Labor Statistics (U.S. B.L.S.) (2022), 'Consumer Price Index News Release', [online], 12 January 2022, available: https://www.bls.gov/news.release/cpi.htm

U.S. Food & Drug Administration (F.D.A.) (2022), 'FDA Roundup: January 4, 2022', [online], 4 January 2022, available: https://www.fda.gov/news-events/press-announcements/fda-roundup-january-4-2022

World Health Organisation (W.H.O.) (2020). 'Background World Graphic Reproduction', Copyright (2020), [online], 30 June 2020, available: https://covid19.who.int

World Health Organisation (W.H.O.) (2020a). 'W.H.O. Coronavirus Disease (Covid-19) Situation Report-161', Copyright (2020), [online], 29 June 2020, available: https://www.who.int/docs/default-source/coronaviruse/situation-reports/20200629-covid-19-sitrep-161.pdf?sfvrsn=74fde64e_2

World Health Organisation (W.H.O.) (2020b). 'Weekly Epidemiological Update – 29 December 2020', [online], 29 December 2020, available: https://www.who.int/publications/m/item/weekly-epidemiological-update—29-december-2020

World Health Organisation (W.H.O.) (2020c). 'Timeline: W.H.O.'s Covid-19 Response', copyright (2020), [online], 11 March 2020, available: https://www.who.int/emergencies/diseases/novel-coronavirus-2019/interactive-timeline#event-72

World Health Organisation (W.H.O.) (2020d). 'Coronavirus Disease Situation Dashboard', Copyright (2020), [online], 30 June 2020, available: https://covid19.who.int

World Health Organisation (W.H.O.) (2022). 'Weekly Epidemiological Update on COVID-19 – 6 January 2022', [online], 6 January 2022, available: https://www.who.int/publications/m/item/weekly-epidemiological-update-on-covid-19—6-january-2022

World Health Organisation (W.H.O.) (2022a). 'Weekly Epidemiological Update on COVID-19 – 7 December 2022', [online], 7 December 2022, available: https://www.who.int/publications/m/item/weekly-epidemiological-update-on-covid-19—7-december-2022

CONCLUSIONS

Areas for Future Focus

WHAT HAVE WE COVERED?

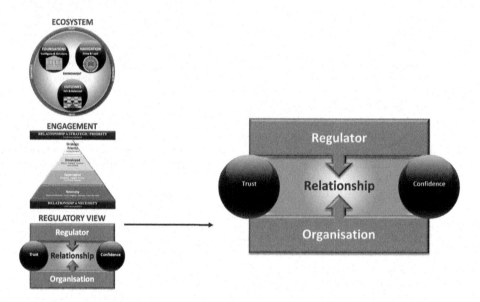

Our exploration of how to build more effective regulatory relationships has covered some considerable ground.

The overall concept we have explored is that organisations can achieve significant improvements in their regulatory relationships and their regulator's view of the organisation by thinking about regulatory relationships from a more holistic perspective. We explored this outcome you wish to achieve with your regulator by thinking about the approach using two broad

DOI: 10.4324/9781003297963-9

themes that drive the outcomes in terms of the regulatory relationship and regulatory view:

Theme 1: Your *Regulatory Ecosystem* and How You Engage with It

Theme 2: Your *Engagement* Approach with the Regulator

Outcome: The *Regulatory View* and Relationship You Enjoy, the Outcomes That Result

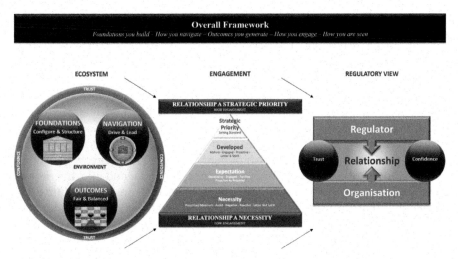

FIGURE A   Overall Framework

Theme 1 introduced the concept of taking a *regulatory ecosystem* approach, which involves organisations taking a broader, more holistic and strategic view of how they manage regulatory relationships, whilst Theme 2 focused on the practicalities of engagement, looking at everything from the fundamental considerations, through to common pitfalls and illustrations to underpin them. Within these two themes, we then broke each down into the elements that form the basis of the overall framework (see Figure A) and explored these in greater detail progressively throughout the chapters. In the next section, we briefly remind ourselves of the key messages and ground each chapter covered as the link to discussing what we conclude will be key areas of future focus that organisations, their regulators, and their relationships are likely to be required to navigate and place greater focus on.

WHAT ARE THE KEY MESSAGES FROM EACH CHAPTER?

This section summarises the ground covered and key messages chapter by chapter. It provides a useful recap on the range of subjects covered, an opportunity to place those subjects in the context of the overall framework, and a point to reflect upon and consider those areas in the context of your organisation.

Having reacquainted ourselves with the key areas, we move on to consider which areas are likely to continue to be the focus of organisations and regulators in future given the trends to date, the drivers of change, and recent events that have had a material impact on how businesses and regulators around the world have had to operate.

In *Chapter 1*, we started with exploring what we mean by regulatory relationships, how they operate, who the key stakeholders are, how they influence the variety of ways organisations establish their approach to engagement with regulators, and some of the key drivers of change that are likely to influence and shape regulatory relationships in the future. Here, we noted how an organisation's regulatory strategy is a key strategic choice and one that influences all aspects of regulatory engagement, including the outcomes the organisation achieves. Having laid some context and background, Chapter 2 discussed the scale and breadth of issues that can influence regulatory relationships.

Chapter 2 introduced the first theme of our overall concept by providing the framework that would help us as we worked our way through the rest of the book. Here, the idea of the *regulatory ecosystem* was introduced, which provided the opportunity for organisations to take a new perspective on their strategy and what their regulatory relationships entail. To facilitate an orderly exploration of this ecosystem throughout the book, the framework, made up of each component of the regulatory ecosystem, was introduced. Here, the framework highlighted the core components we would explore as part of our journey to understanding how to build more productive and effective regulatory relationships. These components are the *foundations* an organisation establishes, how the organisation is *navigated,* driven, and led, and the *outcomes* it generates as well as the impact each of these components collectively has on *trust* and *confidence*. It was at this point that we dove into each aspect chapter by chapter, starting with the most fundamental and underpinning foundation upon which all must be built…*trust.*

Chapter 3 began our exploration of each element of the regulatory ecosystem, beginning with that which wraps around all other elements and forms the lifeblood of regulatory relationships…the building of trust and confidence.

Here, we explored what we mean by trust and its role and importance in regulatory relationships, as well as how it develops and builds and the implications when it is lost. Reflecting on research and real examples, we demonstrated the centrality of trust to a positive and productive relationship, and how being trusted is as much about what you do and how you do it as it is about the outcomes you achieve.

Chapter 4 started our consideration of how the foundations an organisation builds are of significant interest to its regulator.

We explored how an organisation's purpose, vision, and the strategy it follows, along with the culture it creates, are fundamental in shaping how it approaches and engages in its regulatory relationships. In considering the importance of how organisations set themselves up and how they drive their business, we began to understand how these decisions shape the outcomes regulators see, and, therefore, how more and more regulators have become increasingly interested in these aspects.

More broadly, we considered many of the common elements that build the modern-day organisation and looked at how each of these may be of interest and impact your regulatory relationship. For example, these elements included the risk appetite an organisation has in pursuit of its objectives and the governance, systems, and controls it deploys to provide robust frameworks within which to progress. In short, we explored the broad organisational foundations and how important they are for regulators to understand in terms of the risks their failure could pose to consumers and to their own regulatory objectives.

Chapter 5 explored how regulators are increasingly interested in how the Board and leadership teams drive and lead their organisations.

We looked at how regulators consider the strategies, culture, and leadership of organisations as key barometers to understand how the organisation will be driven, and in light of that, how they consider the risk an organisation may pose in terms of the outcomes it may drive and the impact this could have.

In understanding how the organisation is being driven, we consider how this impacts a whole series of decisions and approaches that can fundamentally impact the regulatory relationship. Items include how the overall strategy and culture permeates the organisation and influences behaviour and actions, such as the approach to regulatory engagement.

Finally, we took a deeper dive into the more human areas of organisational make up, that of culture, the human factor, and dominant personalities as areas of increasing interest due to their potential impact on the direction, decisions, and activities of organisations.

Chapter 6 started to paint the picture of how the insight from across an organisation's ecosystem comes together to inform the regulator. Drawing on previous chapters, it explored how insight on the robustness of the organisation's foundations, the appropriateness of how organisations are navigated and driven, and the *ecosystem* of information and insight that flows to your regulator inform their regulatory opinion and help them make judgements on their approach.

We considered how the availability of data, information, and insight, has expanded in terms of breadth of source and accelerated in its immediacy of availability. Given this rich source of information is not always under the direct control of organisations, we also noted how regulators are in a perfect position to triangulate insights and build a rich picture of the impact organisations have in terms of the outcomes they drive. In this respect, we demonstrated how the relationship is being fed, and argued that, for organisations, taking the approach of considering all such information (or as much of it as they can access) themselves as part of the relationship provides the best chance of being able to keep your regulator fully and proactively informed. i.e., thinking about the *ecosystem* as the basis of your relationship is key to proactive and effective engagement. In other words, what informs your regulator's opinion, arguably, is the relationship. Finally, we looked at some of the sources of insight and examples of how they inform regulators in very practical ways.

Chapter 7 started to explore the practical considerations of engagement, beginning with the importance of understanding your regulator's objectives and establishing the context in which engagements are taking place.

Having established the context of engagements, we moved on to understanding the most fundamental of principles that underpin relationships and explored the importance of conduct and behaviour in building effective relationships. Here, we considered how the basics matter and how they are often overlooked. Exploring etiquette, considering examples where simple errors have negatively impacted engagements, and reflecting upon how this *human factor* can be so important provided us with a simple reminder that fundamentally relationships involve people, and people form judgements that are influenced by their engagements.

Having considered the context and nature of engagements, we moved into the more practical considerations of how to prepare and deliver on your commitments, from the fundamentals of accountabilities and planning, the rigour of appropriate preparation, the art of communication, to the robustness of delivery. We stepped through some of the more critical elements that often make the difference in engagements.

Chapter 8 took the opportunity to briefly pause as the world faced an incredible challenge. As the world faced a global pandemic, we looked in on the world of regulatory relationships and how they are adapting to the challenges they face. Here, we considered how the ecosystem of the business world we had described throughout this book was pitched in a struggle with the ecosystem of nature. We considered how, in times of crisis, rules, convention, and practice are often rewritten and how such times can fundamentally change how relationships work as all become focussed on a common objective.

As we observed the impact unfold, we saw how useful the regulatory ecosystem approach was in being able to identify and summarise multiple impacts across the field of regulatory relationships and frame how organisations can respond in unprecedented ways. To highlight the impact, we looked at examples of how the ecosystem *lit up*, how the *mode* of operation shifted, how the importance of trust was suddenly elevated, how stakeholder focus rapidly changed, and, ultimately, how the regulatory relationships responded with pace and increased proactiveness, creativity, and flexibility.

In summary, in the worst of times, we saw some of the best of times in terms of how regulatory relationships can work collegiately, achieve more as a collective, and work toward a greater good in a successful and pragmatic way.

CONCLUSIONS SURROUNDING AREAS FOR FUTURE FOCUS

Having recapped what we have covered throughout the book along with the key points raised in each chapter, now we turn our attentions more toward the future. In considering the ground we have covered, trends we see emerging, drivers of change, hot topics on the mind of industry practitioners and their regulators, and the consequences of recent events, we reflect upon those areas that are likely to be key areas of focus for the future. These focus areas for the future include a combination of items we have covered that are fundamental and warrant greater focus, items that appear likely to acquire a new level of importance given advances we are seeing, and items that may unfold from the challenging times the globe now finds itself in.

It is however worth noting that these views represent one perspective. From your industry perspective, you may see other trends and implications, you may attach greater or less importance to some of what we cover, and you may reach alternative conclusions. That is the beauty of the future, none of us has that illusive ball of crystal and we all see things from a different perspective as we consider the future. So now we take a view across the horizon to the future of regulatory relationships and focus on items (illustrated with further examples) that are likely to have further implications for the way we *build, navigate and engage* in future.

Make Strategic Choice a Priority

For organisations that wish to build positive and mutually beneficial regulatory relationships, taking deliberate steps to define their strategy and approach to regulatory relationships is key. Having a regulatory relationship strategy ensures organisations clearly set out how they will align the organisation to ensure they respect regulatory objectives in all they do, as well as setting out how they will work with such a key stakeholder in a positive and productive way. Being clear in these respects also allows organisations to ensure there is cultural alignment permeating the organisation to better set expectations and align the necessary resources, actions, and activities through all aspects of the business to achieve that strategy. In short, there is clear direction regarding your regulatory relationships and clear alignment of action focused on achieving the strategy. Strategy, therefore, not only makes it clear what will be done, it also, by definition, brings clarity to what should not be done.

Failing to have a regulatory relationship strategy or a lack of clear approach is not altogether unusual. As we saw in Chapter 5, Figure 5.2, a survey of financial services firms in Australia found only 60% of respondents had a strategy and only 82% of those that had one thought it was fit for purpose. Similarly, in research undertaken for this work, respondents on both sides of the regulatory relationship recount views that engagement and relationships are often driven incrementally in line with what the situation requires at the time, rather than in satisfaction of an overall strategy and plan. Failing to have a clear direction can have significant consequences for organisations. In Chapter 3, where we discussed the role and importance of building relationships in order to facilitate foundations of trust being established, we noted comments by a former Securities and Exchange Commission official, who reflected that where firms failed to build relationships and ran into issues, such organisations found themselves in a difficult position, with them noting how members of a firm's Board and management often were observed scrambling to get control of situations. Similarly, we have seen example after example of issues and incidents arising with a significant variance in terms of both response, resolution, and handling of regulators, all of which point to either a lack of a clear strategy or some aspect of their design falling short when it was needed most. It is often in the aftermath of such issues that focus is then placed on strategy, which too often is too late. So, in Chapter 1, Figure 1.4, we looked at some areas organisations should consider in shaping their strategy. As the world in which we operate becomes more complex, more connected, and faster paced, having a strategy around such a key relationship will only become more important as regulators become increasingly inquisitive around all aspects of an organisation that could pose a risk to its objectives. Helping them build their understanding, working with them to ensure what you deliver, how you deliver, and the outcomes you achieve are appropriate, as well as being prepared to respond regardless of the situation with a well-thought-through strategy and plan is fundamental to building high levels of trust and confidence in you and your organisation.

In conclusion, putting in place the right strategy is fundamental to how your regulatory relationship will form, function, and perform.

Stakeholder Sands Are Shifting – Calibrate Your Approach

In Chapter 1, we also considered the broad spectrum of stakeholders that exist around the regulatory ecosystem and how they can interact and influence both the regulator and organisation, and by association, the regulatory relationship you enjoy.

Given their importance and potential to influence, stakeholders are a key area that organisations should understand in terms of their impact.

Whether it is the march of your customers to the regulator's door, the need for greater transparency, the concerns of politicians raising questions of regulatory oversight or additional powers that may be needed, or the media and broader society raising questions on the impact your organisation's products and services are having, stakeholders as we have seen can have a significant influence on the organisation and its relationship with its regulator. In addition, that influence is dynamic and in these times of rapid and significant change, that changing landscape only serves to underscore the importance of stakeholder management.

As organisational stakeholders increasingly look to organisations to demonstrate value through positive contributions well beyond the bottom line, the long-standing challenge continues to be the relative power and influence of stakeholders and the prioritisation of their respective needs. Consumers and shareholders have generally been the most frequent beneficiaries of the prioritisation tug of war, with periodic interventions and adjustments in relative power and influence resulting from political policy and/or regulatory intervention. However, stakeholder sands are shifting and, along with it, the need for a shift in stewardship may well be the only way to navigate and satisfy stakeholder needs of the future. Today we appear to be entering a new era of expectation when it comes to corporate behaviour that could significantly disrupt the relative position, priority, and power of stakeholders (for examples in Financial Services, see Chapter 8, Task Force on Climate Related Disclosures [2017] and the related F.C.A. [2020a] proposals to enhance climate-related disclosures, PS20/17). If we look at just three of those stakeholders to emphasise the point, you can see how the landscape is shifting and how the demands on organisations to operate responsibly are rising:

First, consumers are increasingly interested in the fairness, openness, and transparency of organisations and their impact across their environment (e.g., climate change, resource exhaustion, pollution). The social responsibility of organisations is front and centre like never before. Whether it's their ethical behaviour, responsible sourcing of raw materials, or support for their communities, consumers wish to know that their dollar, pound, euro, yuan, etc., is not helping destroy the planet, exploit workers, or destroy communities.

On a national scale, countries around the world are responding to their citizens' demands for greater environmental protection, which, in turn, influences change throughout industry as the bar is lifted on commercial enterprise.

Along with their higher expectations, consumers are also enabled to act. They have more options in terms of supply, more channels through which to connect, and greater ease in transacting. They are a click away from becoming someone else's customer, and as the old saying goes, the consumer can fire everyone in the organisation where their needs are not met or are satisfied by the competition, substitutes, or replacements to what you stand for and offer. The consumer satisfaction bar is raising fast.

Second, government stake-holder power and influence around the globe has just taken a step change resulting from the Covid-19 pandemic, which has seen their intervention in corporate and business life explode – from forced lockdown, restricted reopening, imposed support to employees, financial support

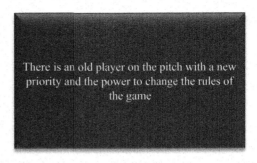

There is an old player on the pitch with a new priority and the power to change the rules of the game

to get organisations through the disruption, to changes in how markets are directed and regulated (e.g., regulators moving further into social protection). The political influence has rapidly permeated markets and organisations around the globe. There is an old player on the pitch with a new priority and the power to change the rules of the game. Governments are likely to seek to rebuild their economies in a way that can help repay the colossal financial support that has been provided, to advance in ways that build for the future, whilst at the same time building in resilience for future events that may arise. Their expectations on organisations could well take a step change, and much like the banking industry of a decade ago, look to ways of building better resilience in our corporate infrastructure. In addition, governments have the challenge of balancing this with calls to *build back better* and to build in a more sustainable way. An example of such sentiments is provided in the International Energy Agency Report (2020), who in their *Sustainable Recovery Plan*, point to the opportunity to boost growth and create millions of jobs, whilst at the same time putting emissions in structural decline. Should such an era unfold, it is likely to entail the rise in power and influence of governments keen to see a new level of social responsibility across businesses, a new level of retained investment in businesses, and with it, a reordering of stakeholder priorities in favour of consumers, employees, and political and regulatory priorities to rebuild at the expense of returns for shareholders. This sentiment on how such events have significant potential implications for the corporate world was captured well by the actions of British Petroleum (B.P.), who, in making billions of dollars of write downs, noted their expectation of an acceleration toward lower carbon energy as countries build back better as we progress through the crisis (B.B.C. 2020).

Third, shareholders and investors are increasingly concerned with the sustainability of investment in organisations and the environmental, social, and governance standards to which organisations operate. The question is how much are they willing to forego their returns to achieve it? Whilst shareholders have had decades of enjoying a favourable level of priority in the focus of Boards appointed to protect their interests, that priority looks set to be increasingly challenged as political and regulatory powers adjust to what is commonly being referred to as a *new normal* in which nations and governments set out to re-build their economies and develop greater resilience in their corporate infrastructures to face an increasingly uncertain world.

The stakeholder expectations and the relative levels of power and influence appear more than ever to be in a state of flux. The competing objectives of value for consumers, demands of government, higher regulatory standards, and the need to provide shareholder returns and invest in the business are being tested. With government support and intervention in many businesses, directions from regulators to retain profits and cease dividend payments, and consumers focused on supporting businesses that have demonstrated their values in the toughest of times, it seems likely the shareholder may have to wait a little further down the priority list in the years to come as the world recovers from the Covid-19 pandemic (see Chapter 8).

In such times, stakeholder influence on the organisation, its regulator, and, by definition, their regulatory relationship, look set to only intensify. A new era of stewardship may have arrived in which balance and judgement on serving the needs of multiple stakeholders is taken to a new level. In conclusion, the stakeholder map will need to be understood, closely monitored by both regulators and organisations, and navigated (a clear stakeholder strategy and plan) in line with what is now a very different future given Covid-19.

Relationships – Build Them Early

Throughout, we have discussed the importance of regulatory relationships from a variety of perspectives. We also reflected on the importance of *emergent relationships* and, in this respect, we highlight that a relationship can never start too early. There is always the opportunity to keep regulators informed of developments and always the opportunity to take the benefit of their extensive insight.

Taking the opportunity to build relationships early with your regulator is crucial. In fact, we are seeing more examples where regulators themselves are taking proactive steps to seize the opportunity to engage early to enable high levels of understanding to flourish and relationships to begin to build with organisations and across regulatory jurisdictions[1].

Regulatory relationships in such examples (see note 1) are taking a new course. Whilst regulators have always encouraged early engagement, these send a whole different message…engagement cannot be early enough. Through initiatives like these, the regulator is providing a whole range of opportunities for organisations to experiment, engage, and understand at the earliest stages of their thinking in developing new products and services. Proactively encouraging early engagement can provide a path to tap into a whole range of new areas of support and insight and avoid the issues of history repeating (whether on traditional products and services or new and innovative ones).

The rise of social media also provides an interesting case study in terms of the need for earlier engagement between regulators and organisations. It is a good example of how organisations can take a concept, develop it quickly and engage millions of consumers on a global basis without significant regulatory intervention or oversight. As that progress takes place, the implications and risks as well as the benefits start to materialise and, suddenly, all stakeholders are trying to catch up on understanding those risks, creating controls to mitigate them, and formulating a view on potential regulatory oversight and protections that are deemed necessary. Forward planning and anticipation of the potential impact of developments always allows for greater opportunity to understand, debate, and formulate what should be done before issues materialise. Taking Facebook as an example, in the face of calls for greater protection for users of social media, Facebook sought to open the debate on how a framework of regulation could look (Facebook 2020). Their opening comments put in perspective the pace and scale of adoption of technology along with the need for new regulatory frameworks for online content. It is an opportunity where all parties may have benefited from earlier engagement from all sides.

Consumers and regulators against this backdrop may demand a higher bar by which to measure value, fairness, and suitability together with the risks products and services pose – not just now – but over the useful life of the product or service. In addition, ensuring customers understand products, services, and associated risks will also likely be a rising evidential bar to meet. As the last few decades have demonstrated, things we may hold today as undisputable outcomes for our future can quickly erode and change, leaving risks we never expected to face. In determining what could pose future risks, there is likely to be a need for improvement in two key areas. Firstly, a need for organisations to demonstrate they have scrutinised that future well, scenario-tested products and services, and sought to underwrite potential risks. Secondly, no matter how comprehensive an organisation's *terms and conditions of use, key facts*, or *pre- or post-contract information*, understanding for many aspects of our transactions in this increasingly complex world is unlikely to be something that can be established in a one-way communication. Understanding is generally built based on two-way interaction. It is a level of engagement that implies greater responsibility on organisations to ensure what they put to their consumer is received and consumed in full knowledge and understanding of the risks it poses...not just now, but over the course of its use.

Ensure You Keep Focus on the Fundamentals

Building and navigating organisations is a significant undertaking and ensuring you are across your full ecosystem and the insight it is feeding your regulator can be challenging. It may well be that organisations focus on certain aspects of what we have covered throughout this book and choose not to cover all areas as the overhead is greater than they can commit to. Regardless of the strategy and approach taken toward your regulatory relationship, focus on the fundamentals will always be important, as will the need to work with the regulator and collaborate (see Woolard 2018 on the importance of collaboration).

Below are a couple of examples that bring home the importance of having sound fundamentals and highlight the impact a failure in such areas can have on an organisation.

THE FUNDAMENTALS OF RIGOUR, CONTROLS, AND TESTING   Fundamental lapses in your ability to deliver to expectations can have significant implications for your relationship. Not only does it undermine confidence, but such events can cause a *bleed of investigation* into other areas of the organisation to test the wider veracity of rigour through key control systems as well as affect the intensity, pace, and depth of scrutiny through the relationship. Even items as fundamental as reporting can have significant consequences where it falls short of regulator expectations[2].

The fact of the matter is, all things need to be understood for their risks and implications with controls designed and tested accordingly. A process may be simple, it may be automated and hold limited opportunity for human error, but even a simple and automated process can have a significant impact should it be incorrectly designed, tested, implemented, changed, or maintained.

There is an important point here in terms of how you *build* (see Chapter 4) – regardless of how simple things may appear, understanding the risk in terms of the potential impact is key.

THE FUNDAMENTAL REQUIREMENT OF RESILIENCE – DO WHAT YOU DO CONSISTENTLY WELL   As our world becomes more connected and complex, as we engage with new technology and adopt its opportunities, and as we share more of our valuable information, the need for greater resilience accelerates. The degree of interconnectivity and complexity means that failure in one part of these *systems*, at best, disrupts our access to services upon which we rely as consumers and, at worst, also exposes individuals, groups, organisations, markets, and infrastructure, to weaknesses that can be exploited. All such groups are increasingly seeing resilience and security of their own systems and those they interact with as a key priority.

Increasingly, regulators are engaging broadly to ensure that even at their regulatory perimeter, they are liaising to ensure those boundaries don't become vulnerabilities and that the combined efforts of regulators provide a good level of protection across the market.

Lifting standards in such a complex environment poses a significant challenge. It will rely on the standards of different organisations, different markets, and different technologies in different jurisdictions and geographies. Furthermore, it will involve organisations thinking about their new capabilities and governing them with a new breadth of consideration, for example, beyond conventional controls and processes and more focused on the principles and values that must thread through them. Increasing resilience will, to a large degree, demand ground-up consideration of how it can be designed, need greater consideration of the potential risks, a greater focus on mitigation, and an ability to provide controls across systems to provide the appropriate level of protection. An example of how thinking is changing and broadening in this respect is provided by Microsoft (2020) with its consideration of how to approach artificial intelligence and the ethical principles and broader considerations that need to underpin such developments[3].

As developments advance, thinking is already considering how the technologies should be governed and used and the underlying values, policies, principles, regulations, and laws that may be required to ensure its use is beneficial and its outcomes appropriate. In addition, the fundamentals of considering how systems can be operated reliably, safely, and consistently, even when under attack, are put forward as the fundamental underpinnings for having a basis of trust for their use. Whether we are considering a technology, process, or the financial underpinnings of the organisation…resilience is fundamental.

In this respect, organisations will need to ensure their capability and competence in disciplines for the prevention and recovery of significant issues are constantly challenged and checked as they progress. From how they invest in their capability and ensure change is safely executed to how they plan for crises and disaster recovery, it is likely such areas will require a more forensic approach to understanding whether capability and competence is at the required level. In the drive to deliver more, faster, and for less, the quality, robustness, and resilience will need greater consideration. Regulators will be keen to see those risks and issues organisations face are not externalised as simply events that *happen to them*. Instead, they will seek to ensure that a high degree of focus and action is directed to prevention, that where issues arise, the impacts are mitigated and corrected as quickly as possible, and appropriate attention is placed on learning the lessons to prevent future events of a similar or related nature.

A Rising Watermark Can Be Easier to Set Than Follow

Legislation, regulation, and rules cannot be written to define all areas of protection that are required, and to anticipate all harm or detriment that may unfold in an unknowable future. In an environment of such rapid change, there is likely to be a higher level of expectation and reliance on a new level of proactive organisational self-imposition of standards that go well beyond the backstop rules. As we saw earlier, drivers for such behaviour can be seen in how stakeholder expectations are changing, from consumers increasingly looking at organisational impact, governments demanding more in terms of social responsibility and contribution, regulators seeking higher standards, and shareholders looking to the future sustainability of their investments. It is a time when we are likely to see the magnification of the value of a strong reputation as well as failure in terms of cost, as your brand and reputation is under increasing scrutiny.

Against this background, establishing the standards offers organisations the opportunity to go beyond expectations, set the watermark for what good looks like, and do this as part of how they build their organisation and navigate it toward their objectives. Proactively defining and developing that future can, in many respects, be simpler than having the disruption of the imposition of standards, timelines, and expectations by legislators and regulators who are keen to deliver on their mandates. Here, a better alignment of regulatory and organisational objectives for what future protection should look like, offers the potential to carve the way forward and set the expectation for others to follow. In addition, it offers the opportunity to build a reputation, build value into the brand, build trust with key stakeholders, and set the organisation apart from those that see the watermark as something for regulators to set rather than organisations to raise.

Learn Lessons Fast

As we saw in Chapter 6, the ecosystem around organisations is rich in insight for both the regulator and organisations themselves. As you survey the ecosystem, there are any number of sources of insight that can provide great lessons from which to consider and reflect upon what your organisation can glean from them. Whether those sources are examples of new capability, examples of where things have not gone so well, speeches from regulators, notices regulators issue, or sanctions they have imposed, regardless of the source, there are insights that can be quickly cross referenced to your own business. Being adept at reading the *smoke signals* and anticipating the direction of travel is becoming increasingly important as the examples we cover below briefly demonstrate. What follows are examples to provide illustrations of the principle that learning the lessons of the activities of others, learning them fast, reading between the lines, and understanding the smoke signals and direction of travel of your regulator are skills that have become increasingly important and show no signs of abating.

TECHNOLOGY TRANSFORMATION AND TURMOIL – THERE IS MUCH WE CAN LEARN The world of technology we engage with has undergone a level of change that would have been unimaginable just a few decades ago. Through the advances in devices (our tools to connect), the growth, breadth, and availability of internet and telecommunications capability (our pathway to connect), and developments in software (what we use, and connect to), the pace of progression has been incredible.

As with all advances, there are implications to work through and plenty of historic examples, from the transformative use of technology to the turmoil it can cause. For organisations and their regulators, greater connectivity can elevate a myriad of challenges that can impact the regulatory relationship.

Expertise and Scrutiny – Given our greater reliance on technology across organisations, it is reasonable to expect a greater level of focus on the area by your respective regulators. That focus may take several forms. First, those you engage with from a regulatory perspective will increasingly include individuals with high levels of expertise and experience in the fields of technology you deploy. Second, regulators will look to ensure that the governance of organisations has sufficient experience and expertise at the key levels where risks are considered and decisions taken regarding technology, from the Board configuration down. Third, where organisations outsource such capability, regulators will increasingly show interest in how organisations assure their end-to-end service provision and what expertise they have in house to hold such providers appropriately to account for their performance.

Understanding – In Chapter 8, we briefly reflected on the challenges posed by operating at the cutting edge of technological development with a reflection by the Board of the investigation into the Space Shuttle Columbia disaster. Their poignant reminder that *"Complex systems almost always fail in complex ways"* (C.I.A.B. 2003), is a lesson that informs us for our future developments. Real risks exist at the cutting edge of advancement with, at times, disastrous potential consequences. Learning from the past and designing in deep levels of understanding of what we build and their wider implications will be crucial if we are to harness their power in a safe, resilient, and effective way. The complexity and connectedness of systems increases the challenge of understanding, whilst magnifies the potential impact of their failure. In such a situation, transparency of what we develop will also be crucial (see, Microsoft 2020) and with its technical complexity and significant possibilities, it makes prescient thinking increasingly important.

Resilience – Increasingly connected organisations are likely to see regulators focused across the field of resilience and across all fronts, for example, the resilience of services, infrastructure, and data. In other words, looking back to Chapter 4, what you *build* and how resilient it remains will likely receive greater focus where complexity within and around your organisation increases and the risks of failure grow. As the reach of technology increases and the implications of failure grow, so the focus upon its resilience will sharpen.

Security – As technology enables greater connectivity, its uses have been remarkable. However, so has the need to be able to connect in a safe and secure fashion to protect the end users. Whether we think about the security we need as we connect to our bank, the security in purchasing goods over the internet, or the security of devices we use around our homes, security is likely to remain a key focus area. Indeed, if we take the *internet of things* as an example, we see that regulators need to consider how to regulate for standards of protection that we once would have never considered. Who would have thought devices as routine as our televisions, our fridges, or our heating systems would have needed protocols and standards for cyber security…or even more unbelievable for those that medicine has provided the miraculous benefits of implanted devices…for security updates to the devices themselves (see Figure 1.10). The implications of such developments are both significant and challenging for organisations and their regulators. In these emerging fields, organisations and regulators not only have decisions on how to regulate, protect consumers, and adapt their regulatory relationships, but also on how to help shape how industries appropriately engage, communicate, explain, and inform of the risks such developments pose. For example, what is the appropriate way to communicate with a patient regarding the risks inherent in their implanted medical device, and who is accountable for that risk? Who should have that conversation – the tech company or the medical expert? How should those currently unknown cyber risks be framed and what standard of disclosure should organisations be held to? (See Figure 1.11.)

In terms of the regulatory relationship, organisations are likely to see greater scrutiny from regulators who are highly skilled in the areas of greatest concern regarding their technologies. The degree of scrutiny, depth of knowledge, and frequency of interaction will all likely increase as the risks and stakes increase.

UNDERSTAND THE PRINCIPLES AND CARRY LESSONS OVER TO YOUR SITUATION   Where organisations become adept at understanding the lessons different insights across the world of commerce have for their organisation and adjusting their course accordingly, they can avoid significant issues for their own business. Those lessons may not always be direct comparisons from which to draw conclusions and, of course, practices both within and across industries can be very different from organisation to organisation. However, whilst an organisation may not immediately see their own practices as problematic due to there being real differences in approach, it is often in the underlying principles of what is being undertaken where the similarities and issues exist. For example, practices in one industry may be similar to another, and where regulatory scrutiny has raised issues in one market, it can be prudent to review those practices for your own organisation.

Learning from the mistakes of others, checking you don't have similar or related issues, and correcting your course should you have concerns are all part of using the regulatory insights to prevent potential future issues.

Collaboration Will Increase (Along with Expectations on Engagement)

Technology has enabled a digital world that allows us to connect, share, and transact seamlessly. As we go about our lives, we increasingly share our information wider, transact with growing numbers of organisations, and connect with individuals, organisations, and institutions like never before. As a result, the information we share (or is created) about us is diffused across our digital lives. That digital life, in turn, touches an increasing number of organisations, geographies, jurisdictions, laws, regulations, and as a result, regulators.

For organisations and regulators attempting to protect consumers, ensuring that such protection is in place and works effectively end to end along the consumer journey is an increasingly difficult prospect.

If we take our data as an example (given it is a key currency to a digital life), as new technologies have arrived for us to engage with, more of our data has left us. We have found our data is requested more and our technology enables us to store more, all the while making the sharing of information easier. Over time, our appetite to share information has slowly increased as we are desensitised to the activity of sharing across the digital world. We now have more passwords than we can remember (often trusting devices to store, retrieve, and input them for us), we operate across multiple platforms designed to connect us to our friends and family, and we undertake many of the tasks and transactions that in the past we would have executed face to face across digital platforms.

We have arrived at a point where our data and information are scattered around our digital lives and is often accessible by a greater number of organisations or individuals than we would have historically been comfortable with. This development poses significant challenges for organisations and regulators alike. As individuals, we have entrusted our data to this new digital world, where we expect it to be protected, secured, and used for the purposes that each of us deems acceptable. Organisations and regulators have, therefore, had to work hard to ensure our trust is maintained by ensuring sufficient protections are in place and that these are resilient. This is especially important in a world where we rely so much on the technological infrastructure to deliver for us, or where criminals have increasingly moved onto these same platforms to attempt to exploit vulnerabilities for their own gain. Where these protections and the resilience of such platforms fall short, trust and confidence are fundamentally undermined.

By its very nature, our propensity to share is raising new challenges in terms of regulatory relationships. As organisations increase the complexity of their infrastructure to enable this increased connectivity in delivering their services, so they need to become more adept at satisfying regulatory needs across differing regulatory requirements, often in different markets or geographies. Their ecosystems are increasing as their reach, capability, and services extend. From a regulator's point of view, such complexity is equally challenging, as understanding where all the respective regulatory perimeters lie (accountabilities and responsibilities for regulatory oversight) and whether sufficient protection is being assured across end-to-end systems with which customers engage will be a growing concern.

Protecting end-to-end customer journeys will see a need for collaboration and proactive engagement increasing more and more as a baseline expectation. For organisations, their command and control of what they have built will be essential and will not be constrained by the walls of the organisation but by the full journey their customer travels. Where third parties are used in any form in that delivery, the expectation will be that those who have configured the journey will walk it and govern it from a consumer protection point of view.

For regulators, we are likely to see similar traits with greater collaboration across regulators to ensure consumers remain protected and do not fall between regulatory boundaries. Take our example of medical devices implanted in patients that are connected remotely for updates as well as the provision of information to clinicians. It is conceivable that we could cross the thresholds of many regulatory bodies and authorities and across different geographies, for example, the medical device regulators, data protection regulators, product standards regulators, telecommunications regulators, and law enforcement agencies should aspects of the end-to-end delivery of that solution to the patient fail at some point. The need for greater collaboration between regulators and other official bodies is likely to face the challenge of being able to respond and adapt quick enough to these rapidly developing advances.

The U.K. has already seen these moves begin with the development of the U.K. Regulators Network (U.K.R.N.), which is a member organisation formed of 13 of the U.K.'s sectoral regulators. Established in 2014, it provides a structure for regulators to consider common issues and policy projects with relevance across different sectors.

In specific sectors, regulators also collaborate across international borders, for example, the Financial Conduct Authority liaises with its international counterparts as regulators across the geographies aim to keep the global financial system operating efficiently, effectively, and in line with respective regulatory objectives. Furthermore, as noted earlier, collaboration also takes place in the more emergent areas of financial services, such as through the Global Financial Innovation Network, which sees 46 financial authorities engaging with market participants in emergent technologies to find solutions for cross-border challenges that arise as a result of such developments.

As fast as technology enables us and as boundaries blur between products, services, technologies, support services, and delivery channels, so the need for greater integration and collaboration of the activities of regulators is likely to increase. Perimeters between regulatory jurisdictions will likely become increasingly grey, and it is in the grey that the combined efforts and expertise of regulatory oversight will be most keenly needed if we are to continue to protect the consumer and avoid protections falling through the regulatory net. The regulatory web is likely to require a closer weave between the individual bodies if a seamless layer of consumer protection is to be maintained and the common statutory role to protect the interests of consumers upheld.

ENGAGE IN THE LETTER AND THE SPIRIT In an increasingly complex and connected landscape across which customers travel, the demarcation of rules, regulation, legislation, and industry codes can be complex, roles and responsibilities less clear, and an overall view of protection being afforded to the consumer end to end uncertain. If we continue the example of data and information, as the years have passed by and organisations have been capturing, storing, and using our information, legislators and regulators around the world have been attempting to shore up our protections with new laws and regulations.

Despite these significant efforts, we still have a situation where we don't truly know how our data and information are being used. Let's just pause for a second, and consider all the organisations you bank with, shop with, or take services from by way of example. Now simply try and think what data you gave them, if you know if they have kept it, if you know where and how they store it, what you allowed them to use it for, and how long they will keep it...it is yours after all. For most individuals, the answer to these questions would be that they have no idea, and that, to a large, degree goes to the root of this point. The letter of the rules may be written and organisations diligently following them, but regulators are likely to increasingly look to organisations to be able to demonstrate they are well within the spirit as well as the letter of their rules. Perhaps, when we get to a point where we know the answers to the questions above, we will truly be able to say we are in control of our data and organisations in the spirit of the rules are keeping us well informed and updated. Balancing what is fair and appropriate with what technically is allowed is always going to be a judgement call, but organisations should expect that their regulator increasingly will look to see how well they exercise that judgement across more areas. Greater collaboration with regulators to proactively discuss and set the bar ahead of the letter of regulation will see some organisations begin to forge the standards for industry to follow. Organisations stand to enjoy both brand and reputational benefits as well as regulatory credit in setting out to achieve such standards. In a world where consumers are increasingly looking for organisations that set high standards across the way they operate, greater control through collaboration across stakeholder groups offers potential benefit for organisations.

JOINING THE DOTS – ONE TO ONE OR MANY TO MANY As we discussed above, technology has enabled connectivity in a way that has seen organisations become increasingly modular, often resulting in the end-to-end delivery to the customer involving many organisations. Where capability increasingly bridges disciplines and industries, regulation and regulatory relationships will need to consider the entire customer journey, *the design risk* if you like, and each element that is crucial to protecting consumers as they travel it. For example, how should both the physician and medical devices manufacturing organisation engage with regulators to assure them their combined services culminate in appropriate patient outcomes with acceptable risks? How should the financial services organisation and the technology company upon which all its products are delivered engage with regulators? The interconnectivity of supplying services and solutions will drive a need to scrutinise questions such as these more deeply so industry can ensure the sum of the parts in these increasingly interconnected organisational systems assure the required standards of protection for consumers.

The implications for regulatory relationships may be that regulators will not only become increasingly collaborative with each other, but may seek engagement with all key organisations across the customer journey to ensure all who are involved, can satisfy the full range of regulators, so that the end to end journey does not threaten their combined objectives. Instead of one-to-one relationship interactions, one regulator to many service providers or many regulators to many service providers may become a feature of future interactions. What is more, collaboration will increasingly need to develop as a discipline between regulators and organisations as the broader stakeholder map participants come to expect improved outcomes facilitated by both parties working together to achieve them.

Democratised Risk – Be Prepared to Underwrite It

As progress marches on, considering some of that progress from the perspective of its impact on our lives as individuals and the risks we may face in future because of those changes can be enlightening. It is in this space that the regulator and regulatory relationships can provide important scrutiny, increased transparency and a higher level of protection or disclosure for the benefit of organisations themselves and their consumers.

As individuals, we are increasingly being placed in a position of responsibility for our own future in areas where traditionally that risk was born by the state or organisations with whom we place our trust. Examples cut across so many aspects of our lives, but to demonstrate the importance of regulatory relationships constantly needing to adapt in terms of their areas of focus, let me provide a few to consider.

Medicine – Medical advances like in so many industries have seen the increased use of technology, in this case to provide patients with life-changing treatments. As these developments have unfolded, new risks have arisen such as those highlighted previously, where the nature of medical advancement (e.g., implants and medical devices) has involved the adoption of connected technologies, which introduces the inherent cyber security risks such technologies suffer. The patient may well benefit from the medical intervention, but with it, they now face a different risk they ideally would rather not have faced. For both the organisations providing such services and the regulators governing their compliance, these new developments raise a whole range of new questions about how the patient is engaged on these new issues, is kept informed, and, most importantly, makes informed choices and is protected. Organisations and regulators may increasingly need to consider future potential risks, be engaged at embryonic development to understand potential risks, or think about how risk is migrated over time to ensure consumers have sufficient capacity to accommodate risk transfer.

Social Care and Pension Provision – In the U.K., the challenges of demographics have seen changes imposed upon individuals that fundamentally shift the balance of risk toward the individual. These include the expectation that, in old age, the state would support our care in full (which has fundamentally been challenged over the years) or changes in pension provision provided by employers that significantly impact our outcomes for retirement income or our pension planning ahead of it.

As such changes in expectation filter through, the implications for organisations and regulators can be significant. New future risks for individuals bring new requirements for communicating and understanding those risks, providing potential solutions, and ensuring sufficient protection is in place for consumers. For example, such changes as pension provision have seen a re-think across many aspects of retirement planning, from government policy in the U.K. with the introduction of the employer workplace pension schemes, pension freedoms being introduced for those approaching retirement, and the establishment of increased guidance for financial advisors on pension transfers.

This is not new ground, as the democratisation of such risks has been long recognised as a key challenge for consumer protection. The Organisation for Economic Co-operation and Development (2011), reflecting on the implications of such trends together with the advances in new technologies and advances in financial services markets, highlighted the importance of increased protection:

> *"This renewed policy and regulatory focus on financial consumer protection results inter alia from the increased transfer of opportunities and risks to individuals and households in various segments of financial services, as well as the increased complexity of financial products and rapid technological change, all coming at a time when basic access to financial products and the level of financial literacy remain low in a number of jurisdictions".*

As risk has continued to shift over time, lessons are likely to be learned regarding how earlier engagement can help mitigate their impact.

Data – With the explosion of data sharing, there have been great efforts to put consumers back in control of their data through new regulations (e.g., General Data Protection Regulation [G.D.P.R.], agreed upon by the European Parliament). Similarly, in areas such as financial services, Open Banking has allowed consumers to share their data with organisations other than their traditional bank…effectively giving you control on who uses that data for your benefit as opposed to it being your data locked in the bank's hands. Whilst these are extremely useful developments, it does necessitate a level of accountability being taken by individuals (which is good, where you understand the risks and understand the processes to adequately manage them). Think how often you are now asked how your data can be used, think how often you change, maintain, or update those settings, you simply accept rather than read the notifications, or start to read them but are overwhelmed by the verbose volume of unintelligible terms…then just click accept. Now consider the question of whether you feel in control? We may well be in a better place with organisations being restricted from having unfettered use of our data, but that risk is now in our hands in terms of the decisions and actions we take. In our increasingly complex interactions and relationships with organisations, it is easy to lose track of who has access to what and for what purpose.

As a related example in the way we have been enabled to share our data, also think about the technological advances in social media, these demonstrate how quickly a capability can materialise, develop, be adopted by millions of individuals, and cause sufficient concern about the need for protection before a meaningful response can be established.

What challenges does this pose for our regulatory relationships? Our pace of establishing and maintaining regulation and the regulatory relationships around them to oversee organisational activity may well need to accelerate. Indeed, being at the forefront of developments may well become the norm to anticipate future requirements and establish relationships at a more embryonic stage.

> Our pace of establishing and maintaining regulation and the regulatory relationships around them to oversee organisational activity may well need to accelerate

The examples above also bring to the fore a further challenge. That challenge is in the changing dynamic of how the advances we are seeing will impact the future expectations and outcomes for individuals. In the financial world, the examples of pensions and healthcare have fundamentally shifted the future expectations of both income and spending in retirement. These risks may raise questions of how we anticipate, provision for, or manage the transfer of risk between organisations and individuals over extended periods of time, and, importantly, underwrite those risks where appropriate. In the example of data, it may be that future relationships between organisations and their regulator need to consider aspects of capability more broadly. For example, whilst the ask on individuals from one organisation may be manageable in terms of controlling their data and maintaining security of access, in a world where individuals have a significant number of relationships with different organisations, that ask may become untenable when multiplied across all the relationships held. In such circumstances, consumers simply become overwhelmed or lose track (for example of passwords or what rights to data they have shared), resulting in a default to lower standards (for example, using one password across relationships or defaulting to allowing greater sharing of data). In such situations, it may be that higher baseline protections for consumers become the expectation of responsible organisations. Just because an organisation can do something by virtue of conforming to a rule does not mean it should not attempt to go well beyond that base standard.

The risks of democratised risk, as we have seen, can cover a broad range of issues with the potential for significant impact on individuals and is likely to continue the case for greater consumer protection. Where organisations transfer risks to consumers whether intended or unintended, they are likely to see greater scrutiny from regulators and a higher bar for why such transfer is appropriate, fair, understood, and accepted by the consumer.

Understanding the potential risks and the transfer of those risks to consumers may well see a trend for organisations and regulators engaging earlier on new product and service developments, and an expectation that risk is mitigated, where possible, or covered in terms of liability where mitigants are insufficient. Where *effectively* risk has historically been underwritten by way of remediation, redress, and fines, which send clear signals to encourage better protections, in the future, potential risks may well be anticipated, understood, and underwritten should they arise. A recent example of such a proactive approach to risk coverage can be seen with the TSB Bank in the U.K. openly declaring to its customers that the bank will cover the costs of fraud where their customers are deemed to have suffered loss. Such risks are difficult for customers to understand, difficult for them to avoid at times given the insidious nature of criminals, and difficult to completely mitigate. As such, they form a perfect example of an area where an organisation can step in and raise the bar of protection on their behalf.

Similarly, as the pace of development and change accelerates (see Figure 1.14 for an example of technological change and adoption) we are likely to see increasingly dynamic legislators, flexibility in the provision of regulation and powers to enable regulators to oversee fast developing markets and organisations, and an increasing reliance on principle-based pressures on organisations to stay well within the spirit and letter of expected standards, whilst ideally lifting and defining them.

Increased Public Scrutiny and Transparency Will Continue to Build

Over the last decade, the explosion of information availability has also led to an increased propensity for regulators to utilise this growing communication capability to disclose organisational news in the public interest, whether it is the misdemeanours of specific individuals, the practices of organisations, or the protections available to consumers. Not only does this lay out the issues for the industry to take note of, in terms of double checking, they do not operate in a similar fashion, it also provides a very powerful deterrent with such public punishment impacting the brand, reputation, and trust between organisations and their consumers, facilitating the legal principle of *caveat emptor*. Now, through both traditional media sources and the ever growing online and digital offerings, the reach, breadth, and immediacy of such news has taken on a new form and a new level of impact.

We will all be able to recount examples that have caught our attention when an organisation we have placed our trust in has been found wanting in their practices. For global financial services in the decade that followed the commencement of the Global Financial Crisis, there were a significant number and frequency of issues published by regulators that laid bare the extent of the issues with which financial institutions were grappling. From claims of misselling to manipulation, the industry faced a long period of poor practice exposure, record fines, and significant damage to brand, reputation, and trust, that to this day, is still being repaired and rebuilt. In fact, across many industries, issues that have challenged the trust between organisation, regulator, and its customers have continued to emerge and be placed in the public arena for all to note. From the motor industry with its emissions scandal, the fuel industry with its environmental record, or the social media companies use of our data, the challenges continue to unfold.

This trend of increased transparency is only likely to continue as consumers appreciate the extent to which their trust is placed with organisations. As consumers appreciate the potential impact organisations can have, they are likely to continue to demand higher standards of protection and resilience. Trust will become more central to those relationships, and this will be no different for the regulatory relationship. Helping regulators understand your organisation and how it functions and supports their regulatory objectives will be increasingly important. Open and transparent disclosure forms a significant part of trust building and will continue to be used by organisations, consumers, and regulators to greater extents.

Leadership – Increasing Expectations in Balancing Perspectives and Delivery

A thread throughout this book has been to reflect on the incredible pace of advancement being achieved in so many areas of modern society. Technological change has exploded in pace, its benefits and challenges are being seen everywhere from how we socialise and build relationships, to how we maintain our health, how we conduct our business, how we consume goods, and how we transact and manage our finances. Our world is seeing more automation and, with the development of artificial intelligence, the slide rule of what we as individuals need to take care of versus that of a machine is likely to keep shifting. Across all facets of our private and professional lives, this will mean we will continually need to adapt for such changes at greater pace and with potentially greater consequences whilst taking stock of what our role becomes as these developments take shape.

From a professional perspective, the skills future leaders will need will also change and develop. Stakeholders will increasingly look to ensure their trust is warranted, that leadership displays the highest levels of integrity and that organisations and the people within them deploy their products and services with an appropriate level of skill, rigour, understanding of risk, and sufficient control to protect them both at point of engagement and for the duration of that relationship. In such an environment, having the appropriate technical skills will need to be complimented with a host of capabilities, such as an ability to question appropriately, to understand complex situations that develop at pace, to determine and assess interconnected risks and controls, to assimilate broad sources of information, to apply judgement and balance in forming options, conclusions and taking decisions, and to be able to take stakeholders with you as you navigate and communicate the path forward. The skillsets of future leaders will need to develop and adapt to the growing ecosystem within which their organisations operate.

Trust in organisations and those that lead them is likely to be of increased importance – like a pillar around which its stakeholder's opinions will anchor. An organisation's brand, its reputation, and its success are likely to grow or decline around the strength of its ability to build and sustain trust. Internally, its values, standards, ethics, culture…the foundations discussed in Chapters 4 and 5, increasingly become the driving force for its external performance. An organisation that is healthy on the inside is much more likely to be able to carry that capability externally in all it does. From a regulatory relationship perspective, there will be few regulators who don't see these elements as crucial traits they would wish to see in organisations and their leadership. It is in these traits where value can be gained or destroyed…and there are many lessons in recent history where such factors have contributed to the decline of organisations and individuals within them.

That trust is also likely to come at a greater cost. We have already seen some industries move to bring greater clarity of accountability and responsibility as well as increased personal liability should things go wrong. Increasingly, senior executive accountability for harm will be sought. This can take both a path of personal financial liability and exclusion from practice should sanction deem them unfit for office. As the stakes rise, so stakeholders will look for the implications to move in a commensurate way. The lure of reward systems on behaviour will be countered more overtly by the reality of personal liability.

The ability to balance delivery and outcomes for a broader range of stakeholder needs and wants, with sound moral, ethical, and socially responsible underpinnings will be an increasingly demanding watermark for leaders to attain.

Pandemic – Implications, Questions, and Observations

Attempting to draw conclusions from what is an ongoing crisis is always going to be a perilous endeavour. So, whilst the comments that follow reside in this section that discusses conclusions, they are put forward as food for thought regarding the potential implications, questions, and observations we can draw from events thus far.

Chapter 8 provided a window through which to observe some of the implications that have unfolded during the current Covid-19 pandemic. It highlighted the impact we have seen on the relationships between regulated parties and their regulators. Those observations and developments are of course a *work in progress*. Every day, the parties in these relationships continue to respond and develop to an ongoing dynamic global situation.

Whilst the situation is still developing, there are immediate implications we can reflect upon, questions those implications raise, and observations about how, to date, the path of regulatory relationships have responded. What follows is by no means a comprehensive view given the complexity of what we have seen unfolding, but it may offer a good start to some of the issues many organisations will need to consider as events progress. From the macro level considerations of how the world responds and uses this as a inflexion point for action on global issues that the virus has passed a lens over; to the potential implications for businesses and their regulators as governments consider how they prepare their nations for a future in which pandemics are front of mind; to considerations of how societies and citizens better prepare themselves for such events in future, we consider just a handful of example areas where we can see the potential for future implications and broader questions, given what we have observed to date.

NEW DIRECTIONS AND DESTINATIONS   The Covid-19 pandemic forced the world into a significant detour in terms of its focus, with the direction of travel for more than 200 countries across the globe being disrupted to control the velocity of transmission of the virus.

One of the most significant implications of that detour has been the need for countries to adjust their levers of State to navigate the activities of society and industry in ways that support the prevention of viral transmission. This change in direction has been accepted as a critical step in the fight against the virus, with whole populations acceding to rules that have significantly changed day-to-day life. Such significant changes pose questions regarding what a future beyond the immediate crisis may look like. For example, how many of the adjustments made to take us in this new direction will remain in place in some shape or form? Will this period usher in a new era and new destination for the future direction of travel, i.e., will the detour become our new route forward altogether? For example, will governments expect more of businesses in terms of how they provision for crisis, how they contribute to its costs, and how they support environmental and social development in future? Will there be shifts in society's cultural focus toward a savings, healthcare, and provision for the future versus consumption? Similarly, will some of the steps taken to enable those who supervise and regulate to drive more into the realms of social policy and protection (e.g., homeowner support noted earlier) remain in place or progress further through changes in the statutory objectives of regulators?

POLICY, PACE, AND PROGRESS   Whole industries and their regulators during this pandemic have been thrust into situations neither group has faced before.

We have observed accepted methods and practices of developing and running businesses, along with regulating them, in a matter of weeks be re-written.

The implication of moves to adjust to the pandemic has seen a necessity for some organisations and regulators to respond at pace, both in terms of how policy and rulemaking developed and how the changes required to comply were executed.

Such changes will likely leave questions in their midst. For example, organisations have demonstrated their ability, as we saw in Chapter 8, to totally change the way they do business, change the type of business they do, and accelerate the pace at which change is executed to deliver to the immediacy of the situation. Where policy makers and regulators see the need for significant and rapid change in industry in future, the pandemic has provided an interesting frame of reference for just how quickly business can respond when the stakes are high. For regulated industries and businesses, their urgency of response to implementing regulatory requirements may well have a higher level of expectation in future.

Whilst globally we remain in the midst of the pandemic (or at least its impications) and organisations and regulators continue to calibrate their response as the situation develops, there will be a necessary point of reflection on what has been changed and implemented. The speed, breadth, and depth of change that has been delivered through new ways of working, may well have left its implications in its wake. Change control, risk mitigation and management, along with quality assurance will have all seen adjustments in their application. Organisations and regulators will no doubt ask questions of how they assure themselves that this period of *emergency state* operation and change is fit for the future and has not left simmering vulnerabilities and implications for the organisations and their customers. For example, a new policy direction, such as the creation of mortgage payment deferral options for millions of mortgage customers in the U.K., executed at pace by financial institutions, and progressed through rapidly developed solutions on systems that may not have been originally designed to work that way, will require scrutiny to ensure the intended outcomes are met both near and long term for customers.

A REPUTATION ON THE LINE   One of the implications of a crisis is that all who are touched by such a situation are often faced with difficult and challenging situations, where decisions are required, often in times when pressures are high, information is limited, and implications are significant.

Whether the reputation is that of a government, an industry, a regulator, a business, or an individual, what we do when the stakes are high can define the views of others for a significant time as actions and decisions become associated with an event of such magnitude.

The implications of the actions and decisions taken will therefore leave an imprint on the reputations of those parties. For regulated organisations, this can also be a significant source of insight for their regulator. How industries and the organisations themselves respond in times of crisis can help a regulator understand how the DNA of the organisation responds when times are challenging, and the stakes are high.

During the pandemic, as noted in Chapter 8, we have seen the best and worst of behaviour when in crisis, from organisations totally changing their business operations to support the cause to prevent the loss of life, to regulatory warnings over misleading claims that could lead to increased revenues and profits. It is in these times that reputations are made and lost and where regulators will tap into the DNA of the organisations they regulate.

REMOTE WORKING   As nations around the globe have imposed lockdown restrictions, whole societies have needed to adjust to the realities of restricted travel and access to certain premises. For organisations, this has often meant being unable to operate as normal from their business premises, necessitating adjustments in working patterns and working practices.

Regarding regulatory relationships and keeping the regulator informed, regulated organisations have needed to ensure that processes operating to satisfy the regulatory relationship have adjusted to new remote ways of working in order that engagement and information flows continue, albeit in new ways (e.g., virtual rather than physical engagement).

Indeed, for many organisations, this momentous shift in operating practices may well have raised questions for how the future operating models of organisations should be configured. Beyond the organisations themselves, society more broadly has also engaged on the implications of such changes in practice, with discussions as diverse as the impact on pollution levels and global warming as the world slowed down, through to the implications of isolation on well-being and mental health. The arguments for and against home-working and the degree to which organisations need a physical presence will likely continue. However, such considerations can have wider implications. Consider the question of how a regulated organisation that decides to move to a distributed home-working model satisfies its regulatory obligations. How does a regulator conduct its supervision or regulatory visits and oversight in a digital world? How does the organisation satisfy its regulatory obligations where a physical presence is a requirement of being regulated? How do those within areas of compliance and risk in such organisations need to adjust their approach to provide effective oversight and challenge? The implications of such significant shifts in operating rhythm and approach are far reaching and would need significant changes to how regulatory relationships operate by all parties.

Time will tell what the true future implications of this period will be, however, organisations and their regulators will need to monitor the *smoke signals* of how the pandemic continues to play out and consider whether the direction of travel is changing, and if so, what such a change could mean for their organisation and relationships in future. Government pronouncements of a need to *build back better*, global issues such as the increasing focus on the impact humankind is having on our planet, and the economic impact of the virus across the globe are just a handful of subjects that bring a need to consider how countries, their economies, populations, and industries consider what that new future beyond this pandemic entails and where focus and priority will be placed.

IN CLOSING

The premise that regulatory relationships need to operate by taking full account of the ecosystem is a broad view and is not without challenges, as it imposes an overhead in ensuring that ecosystem is fed, monitored, managed, nurtured, and understood. However, taking a more holistic view of the regulatory relationship in the context of an organisation and its environment provides a significant opportunity to ensure the organisation can gain a full picture on its impact, its outcomes, and how these align to regulatory objectives.

A relationship where proactive risk identification and mitigation, build trust through well understood mechanisms of engagement, that work together to head off risk at the pass through proactive, positive, open, frank, and trusted interactions between regulators and organisations, can only be beneficial in the long run for the parties concerned.

Achieving greater effectiveness in our relationships, however, does demand an investment by organisations and regulators alike. Being willing to invest more, open up more, and to engage more will, for some, feel an uncomfortable prospect. However, it is these very actions that will allow greater understanding, greater collaboration, and increased effectiveness in terms of avoiding difficult situations arising between the parties. That greater understanding can lead to improvements that can head off issues, help organisations improve what they have built, help shape how they will navigate, and improve the outcomes they achieve for the benefit of all stakeholders.

Whilst the past has many lessons, how we use the insights to help us progress in the future is more important. The areas mentioned previously have concluded where we might wish to place greater focus to help us achieve improvements in how our regulatory relationships work. These all fundamentally focus on areas where history has lessons for us, progress has challenges for us, and the direction of travel has messages for us. From the importance of the fundamental decisions on strategic priorities, the shifting demands of stakeholders, the importance of early engagement, the need to deliver the fundamentals consistently well, the need to set your own high standards, the imperative of learning lessons fast, the need to be adept at engaging and collaborating, the challenge of being prepared to underwrite your outcomes, the expectations of being transparent and welcoming of scrutiny, and the importance of leadership that balances all perspectives, there is a great deal that our future relationships will demand of organisations. Those that understand and engage with what their regulator is seeking to achieve, can read their ecosystems well, can align and adapt their organisations to respond, and can forge productive relationships across their stakeholder groups will have a far better opportunity to gain the full benefits of having close relationships with their regulator. Tapping into their regulator's insight, reaping the benefit of their input, and enjoying the positive impact of regulatory credit are all opportunities that can provide reduced regulatory risk to an organisation. Being open to the lessons of history, of others, and the insights of regulators who see the good, the bad, and the ugly across any given industry, can help organisations inform and drive-up competence, improve conduct and achieve positive consequences, not least ensuring they do not become a contributor to the billion-dollar history of failure.

We started this book with a reflection on the incredible times we live in, the amazing opportunities and advancements we see, the challenges they pose, and the impact they can have as well as the billions of dollars they can cost. Failure, we noted, can often be attributed to aspects of how organisations are built and navigated, and all have commonalities in that they call into question some aspect of competence or conduct that lead at times to devastating consequences.

Throughout, we have noted how organisations that understand their regulator's objectives and their ecosystems well have an opportunity to constantly calibrate their organisation's competence and conduct to ensure they are delivering for all stakeholder groups in a proactive and progressive way whilst avoiding the pitfalls others have suffered and the poor outcomes that have resulted. To this end, we have systematically stepped through the key areas of how organisations are configured, how they are navigated, and how they engage with regulators whilst also highlighting key areas organisations should consider in ensuring they drive the right outcomes from a regulatory relationship perspective. Whilst this has covered some considerable ground, it is intended to act as a body of insight from which readers can consider their own position and select those elements that can help them in achieving their objectives.

Whether it has reminded you, informed you, surprised and entertained you, or challenged you, the hope is that it leads to changes that allow you and your organisation to build a more proactive, constructive, and effective relationship with your regulators to enable broader stakeholders to benefit from what you achieve together in that new relationship.

NOTES

1. C.f. Commodity Futures Trading Commission (2020), "LabCFTC"; F.C.A. (2020b), "Fostering innovation through collaboration: The evolution of the F.C.A. TechSprint approach"; C.A.A. (2020), "Innovation"; Global Financial Innovation Network (2020), "About GFIN".
2. C.f. Ofgem (2011), "Notice under section 30A(5) of the Gas Act 1986"; D.O.J. (2012), "GlaxoSmithKline to Plead Guilty and Pay $3 Billion to Resolve Fraud Allegations and Failure to Report Safety Data"; F.C.A. (2019), "Final Notice – Goldman Sachs International", Bank of England, P.R.A. (2019), "Final Notice – Citigroup Global Markets Limited ('CGML') (FRN 124384) Citibank N.A. London Branch ('CBNA London') (FRN 124704) Citibank Europe Plc UK Branch ('CEP UK') (FRN 211646)".
3. Further discussions around this general area of advancement can be seen across a number of industries. By way of example in the medical and health arena, organisations are facing into the same challenges posed by technological advancement and developing out principles accordingly. See U.S. Food & Drug Administration (2021), "Good Machine Learning Practice for Medical Device Development: Guiding Principles", developed in conjunction with Health Canada, and the United Kingdom's Medicines and Healthcare products Regulatory Agency (M.H.R.A.) and Schneider, M. E. (2021), "Regulators release 10 principles for good machine learning practice for a wider context"; see also, World Health Organisation (2021), "Ethics And Governance Of Artificial Intelligence For Health" and Takawira et al (2022), "Ethical Governance of AI".

REFERENCES

Bank of England, Prudential Regulation Authority (2019), 'Final Notice – Citigroup Global Markets Limited ("CGML") (FRN 124384) Citibank N.A. London Branch ("CBNA London") (FRN 124704) Citibank Europe Plc UK Branch ("CEP UK") (FRN 211646)', [online], 26 November 2019, available: https://www.bankofengland. co.uk/-/media/boe/files/news/2019/november/pra-decision-notice-citigroup. pdf?la=en&hash=4030FC4D482DF4C330A367A7A1A97E4649FB2968

B.B.C. (2020), 'BP Takes Hit of up to $17.5bn as it Forecasts Cheaper Oil', [online], 15 June 2020, available: https://www.bbc.co.uk/news/business-53047894

Civil Aviation Authority (2020), 'Innovation', [online], available: https://www.caa.co.uk/our-work/innovation/

Columbia Accident Investigation Board (C.I.A.B.) (2003), 'Report of Columbia Accident Investigation Board' – Volume 1', [online], available: https://www.nasa.gov/columbia/home/CAIB_Vol1.html

Commodity Futures Trading Commission (2020), 'LabCFTC', [online], available: https://www.cftc.gov/LabCFTC/index.htm

Facebook (2020), 'Charting A Way Forward – Online Content Regulation', [online], February 2020, available: https://about.fb.com/wp-content/uploads/2020/02/Charting-A-Way-Forward_Online-Content-Regulation-White-Paper-1.pdf, p.3–4

Financial Conduct Authority (2019), 'Final Notice – Goldman Sachs International', [online], 27 March 2019, available: https://www.fca.org.uk/publication/final-notices/goldman-sachs-international-2019.pdf

Financial Conduct Authority (F.C.A.) (2020a), 'Proposals to Enhance Climate-Related Disclosures by Listed Issuers and Clarification of Existing Disclosure Obligations', [online], December 2020, available: https://www.fca.org.uk/publication/policy/ps20-17.pdf

Financial Conduct Authority (F.C.A.) (2020b), 'Fostering Innovation Through Collaboration: The Evolution of the F.C.A. TechSprint Approach', [online], 3 March 2020, available: www.fca.org.U.K./publication/research/fostering-innovation-through-collaboration-evolution-techsprint-approach.pdf, p.3, 5

Global Financial Innovation Network (2020), 'About GFIN', [online], available: https://www.thegfin.com/about

International Energy Agency (2020), 'Sustainable Recovery', [online], June 2020, available: https://www.iea.org/reports/sustainable-recovery

Microsoft (2020), 'Our approach to Artificial Intelligence', Microsoft Corporate Website, [online], available: https://www.microsoft.com/en-us/ai/our-approach-to-ai

Ofgem (2011), 'Notice under section 30A(5) of the Gas Act 1986', [online], available: https://www.ofgem.gov.uk/sites/default/files/docs/2017/04/final_ngg_penalty_notice_for_breach_of_licence_obligations_on_regulatory_reporting.pdf

Organisation for Economic Co-operation and Development (2011), 'G20 High-Level Principles On Financial Consumer Protection', [online], October 2011, available: https://www.oecd.org/daf/fin/financial-markets/48892010.pdf

Schneider, M. E. (2021), 'Regulators release 10 principles for good machine learning practice', [online], Regulatory Affairs Professionals Society, Regulatory Focus, 27 October 2021, available: https://www.raps.org/news-and-articles/news-articles/2021/10/regulators-release-10-principles-for-good-machine?utm_source=MagnetMail&utm_medium=Email%20&utm_campaign=RF%20Today%20%7C%2027%20October%202021

Takawira, G. et al. (2022), 'Ethical Governance of AI', [online], Chartered Governance Institute, available: https://www.cgiglobal.org/media/a0jdmqu2/ethicalgovernanceai.pdf

Task Force on Climate-Related Financial Disclosures (2017), 'Recommendations of the Task Force on Climate-related Financial Disclosures', [online], available: https://assets.bbhub.io/company/sites/60/2020/10/FINAL-2017-TCFD-Report-11052018.pdf

U.S. Department of Justice (2012), 'GlaxoSmithKline to Plead Guilty and Pay $3 Billion to Resolve Fraud Allegations and Failure to Report Safety Data', [online], 2 July 2012, available: https://www.justice.gov/opa/pr/glaxosmithkline-plead-guilty-and-pay-3-billion-resolve-fraud-allegations-and-failure-report

U.S. Food & Drug Administration (F.D.A.) (2021), 'Good Machine Learning Practice for Medical Device Development: Guiding Principles', [online], 27 October 2021, available: https://www.fda.gov/medical-devices/software-medical-device-samd/good-machine-learning-practice-medical-device-development-guiding-principles

Woolard, C. (2018), 'Prisoners, Wellness Programmes and the Rats of Hanoi: Why the F.C.A. Tests its Interventions', [online], Financial Conduct Authority, 5 October 2018, available: https://www.fca.org.uk/news/speeches/prisoners-wellness-programmes-and-rats-hanoi-why-fca-tests-its-interventions

World Health Organisation (2021), 'Ethics And Governance of Artificial Intelligence for Health', [online], 28 June 2021, available: https://www.who.int/publications/i/item/9789240029200

APPENDIX **I**

An Introduction to Regulatory Theory

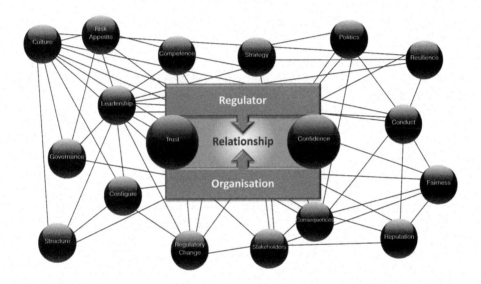

REGULATORY THEORIES

If we are to truly understand the role of the regulator, the regulatory relationship, and the regulations they govern, it is useful to consider some of the regulatory theories that aim to explain them and the catalyst for their existence.

As noted in Chapter 1, the outcomes, and regulatory objectives a regulator may have, form the foundations upon which the regulatory relationship will need to rest. Here, we look at examples of regulatory theory that seek to drive those objectives and shape regulatory intent. They are themselves an interesting weathervane in the ecosystem of the regulatory relationship, as they help set the backcloth against which the industry operates in terms of theory.

The theories of regulation also bring a tangential view, as there are some nuances of theory that cast different lenses on the relative importance of items, such as political appetite for intervention, the degree of industry influence that may exist, the consumer acceptance of market operations, and whether they

DOI: 10.4324/9781003297963-10

see value and utility in what is delivered. To this end, a key aspect of this section is not to provide a definitive summary of all theories, nor is it providing arguments for and against any model or theory of regulation in the examples provided here, but to show the subtleties and broaden our understanding that these theories have the potential to deliver different approaches and outcomes for stakeholders. These examples also serve to demonstrate that as the regulatory environment changes, so too do the appetite, influences, and activities of the participants.

The following sections act as a brief overview and introduction of a couple of the theories of regulation and their features to provide a little background. There is a significant body of insight surrounding the theory of regulation should readers wish to delve further, for which the references cited provide a trail that can be followed, explored, and expanded upon should they spark your interest. Suffice to say, here we only scratch the surface of the area as a signpost to the existence of a much broader body of insight.

Economic Theory of Regulation

The economic theory of regulation is predicated on regulators attempting to maximize a particular objective by delivering policies that deliver benefits for a given group (see Beard, Kaserman and Mayo [2003], Stigler [1971], and Posner [1974], for further discussion on the subject). As most regulated markets will have multiple stakeholders, delivering to one interest group is often at the expense of the relative benefits for other interest groups. To this extent, this theory, even at this most fundamental level, introduces trade-offs, relative bargaining or absolute power influences, and the importance and influence of the regulator's overall objective. In other words, the utility that it is driven to deliver.

If we reflect for a moment on the situation faced during the global economic downturn, the impact on the consumer, the scrutiny the industry and the regulator were put under, together with the enabling powers regulators had been granted under regulatory reform provided a powerful catalyst to shift the regulatory objective strongly in favour of the consumer. This shift in the utility to be delivered by the regulatory objective not only influences the application of the policies the regulator delivers, but also shifts the balance of influence and relative benefits to the stakeholder groups as appropriate. Given the events experienced in financial services, we should not be surprised at such shifts. Beard et al. (2003, p.604) explain how such changes in underlying market conditions can cause the regulatory equilibrium to shift.

Posner (1974, p.335) explained that two main theories of economic regulation have been proposed, one being public interest (the Global Financial Crisis as an example), which Posner explains is regulation that arises resulting from a public demand for a correction of market practices.

The other being capture theory, which is explained as regulation arising in response to interest groups.

Whilst such authors have also discussed the challenges with the theory, for our purposes, the above insights provide a taste of some of the considerations that underpin, provide context, and inform and influence the environment in which the regulatory relationship is playing out. The *public interest* example is a particularly interesting one, as many industries from financial services, aviation, to the new challenges emerging for social media seem to face a point in their chronology where the voice of public interest and the need for greater protection becomes so influential that an inflection point occurs in their direction of travel. For further insight on ideas of how the economic theory of regulation could be developed, see also the discussion on hybrid theories of regulation put forward by Blank and Mayo (2009, pp.233–235).

Taxation by Regulation

Posner (1971, p.22) proposed enhancements to the traditional views of regulation by proposing that these views did not explain some important phenomena. He argued that the traditional views argued two core perspectives, one being that regulation is there to protect the public against the potential detrimental impacts of monopoly situations, the other being for groups to effect regulation change or development for their own protection. According to Posner, neither of these views explains an important phenomenon of regulated industries, namely, how services are provided at lower rates and in quantities than would exist in an unregulated competitive marketplace.

Posner exposes some interesting examples where competitive advantages are undermined by an effective regulatory taxation where the activities of one organisation threaten the future of another. In the examples offered, the complexity of this regulatory intervention is surfaced in demonstrating how regulatory intervention is used where there are concerns over the protection of services to certain customers or groups of businesses that would otherwise not be served or fail (Posner 1971, p.32). Posner (1971, p.34) goes on to demonstrate that where such interventions exist, there is also often a feature over control of the market in certain ways, such as entry to it.

For our purposes, this example provides another interesting consideration regarding the backdrop, protections, and controls against which industries and organisations within them may find themselves. Having a radar for the way in which the environment is operating is useful to understand the likely direction both regulation and regulatory relationships may develop.

In summary, the regulatory framework, regulation, and the relationships that flow from these are not mutually exclusive. They are interconnected, they are plugged into the ecosystem of industry insight and, as such, are influenced by its outcomes. Theories of regulation are, therefore, important contextual considerations, as they can provide the early smoke signals of change when political and regulatory institutions begin to engage in contemplating how industries and markets are working for stakeholder groups and how they should develop for the future. By way of example, social media represents an industry facing into a period of contemplation regarding how the industry is working for stakeholders, whether it should be regulated further, and how that should take shape. As the debate unfolds, we see many of the above arguments across theories coming to the fore, such as, a political appetite for greater control; the relative bargaining power of stakeholders; the degree of industry influence; consumer perspectives and sentiment; the public interest conundrum with a consideration of the protection required versus a need to conserve our freedom of expression; the financial and economic power such organisations have amassed, and, finally, matters of considering the power and dominance of technology organisations. It is a debate as you can see that has many dimensions and demonstrates how shifts in sentiment can trigger a path that potentially leads to significant change for industries and their organisations. It is also a debate that is already influencing how regulatory relationships develop, with existing regulators thinking about the limitations of their current powers to regulate such an industry, whilst contributing to the debate about what could and should be done. Here, regulators are engaging more, debating more, and shaping more of what may unfold for the industry.

The brief exploration of example theories resonate with examples that have unfolded across industries and provide a reasonable alignment in terms of explaining what industries experience. They also provide a useful reflection point in terms of considering some of the ideas they put forward and how they may play out and influence the direction of regulation and regulatory relationships if they became a reality in your industry. In this way, they are useful, thought-provoking theories, the exploration of which can provide a broader consideration of how regulation may develop and what may form some of the key drivers for that development in your industry in future.

REFERENCES

Beard, T. R., Kaserman, L. and Mayo, J. W. (2003), 'A Graphical Exposition of the Economic Theory of Regulation', Economic Enquiry, Vol. 41, No. 4, pp. 592–606

Blank, L. and Mayo, J. W. (2009), 'Endogenous Regulatory Constraints and the Emergence of Hybrid Regulation', Science and Business Media LLC, Springer, pp. 233, 235

Posner, R. (1971), 'Taxation by Regulation', Bell Journal of Economics and Management Science, Vol. 2, No. 1 (Spring, 1971), pp. 22, 32, 34

Posner, R. (1974), 'Theories of Economic Regulation', Bell Journal of Economics and Management Science', Vol. 5, No. 2 (Autumn 1974), pp. 335–358

Stigler, G. (1971), 'The Theory of Economic Regulation', Bell Journal of Economics and Management Science, Vol. 2, No. 1 (Spring 1971), pp. 3–21

BIBLIOGRAPHY

Allen, F. and Carletti, E. (2011), 'New Theories To Underpin Financial Reform', Journal of Financial Stability, pp.1–8, Doi:10.1016/j.jfs.2011.07.001

Arrow, K. (1974), 'The Limits of Organization', New York, Norton, p.23

Axelrod, R. (1984), 'The Evolution of Cooperation', New York, Basic, p.12

Bank For International Settlements (2011), 'Basel III: A Global Regulatory Framework for More Resilient Banks and Banking Systems', revised version June 2011, [online], available: http://www.bis.org/publ/bcbs189.pdf

Barstow, D., Rohde, D. and Saul, S. (2010), 'Deepwater Horizon's Final Hours', [online], The New York Times, 25 December 2010, available: https://www.nytimes.com/2010/12/26/us/26spill.html

B.B.C. News Report (2014), 'Bank Culture "Will Take A Generation To Change" Says Report', [Online], 26 November 2014, available: https://www.bbc.co.uk/news/business-30190753

B.B.C. News Report (2015), 'Co-op Bank Escapes Regulatory Fine', [Online], 11 August 2015, available: http://www.bbc.co.uk/news/business-33859010

Bailey, E. and Coleman, R. D. (1971). 'The Effect of Lagged Regulation in an Averch-Johnson Model'. Bell Journal of Economics and Management Science, Vol. 2, pp.278–292

Basu, K. and Palazzo, G. (2008), 'Corporate Social Responsibility: A Process Model of Sense making', Academy of Management Review, Vol. 32, No. 1

Baumol, W. J. and Klevorick, A. (1970). 'Input Choices and Rate-of-Return Regulation: An Overview of the Discussion'. Bell Journal of Economics and Management Science, Vol. 1, pp. 162–190

B.B.C. News Report (2015), 'Bank of England was unaware of impending financial crisis', [online], B.B.C., available: http://www.bbc.co.uk/news/business-30699476

Bebenroth, R., Dietrich, D. and U. Vollmer (2009), 'Bank Regulation and Supervision In Bank-Dominated Financial Systems: A Comparison Between Japan and Germany', European Journal of Law and Economics Vol. 27, No. 2, pp.177–209

Black, J. (2004), 'The Development of Risk Based Regulation in Financial Services: Canada, The U.K. and Australia – A Research Report', London School of Economics and Political Science, London

Blank, L. and Mayo, J. W. (2009), 'Endogenous Regulatory Constraints and the Emergence of Hybrid Regulation', Science and Business Media LLC, Springer, p.233, 235

Blommaert, J. (1999), 'The Debate is Open', In J. Blommaert (ed.) Language Ideological Debates, Berlin, New York, Mouton de Gruyter, pp.1–38

Borio, C. (2013), 'The Great Financial Crisis: Setting Priorities for New Statistics', Journal of Banking Regulation, Vol. 14, p.306

Bradach, J. L. and Eccles, R. G. (1989), 'Price, Authority, and Trust: From Ideal Types to Plural Forms', Annual Review of Sociology, Vol. 15, p.97, 104

Braithwaite, J. and Makkai, T. (1994), 'Trust and Compliance', Policy and Society, Vol. 4, pp.1–12

BrightHouse (2020), 'Appointment of Joint Administrators', [online], 30 March 2020, available: https://www.brighthouse.co.uk/customer-care/joint-administration

Bronfman, N. C., Vasquez, E. L. and Dorantes, G. (2009), 'An Empirical Study for the Direct and Indirect Links Between Trust in Regulatory Institutions and Acceptability of Hazards', Safety Science, pp.686–692

Calton, J. M. and Lad, L. J. (1995), 'Social Contracting as a Trust-Building Process of Network Governance'. Business Ethics Quarterly, Vol. 5, No. 2, pp. 271–295

Cannata, F. and Quagliariello, M. (2011), 'Basel III and Beyond: A Guide to Banking Regulation After the Crisis', Risk Books, London

Civil Aviation Authority (2020), 'Covid 19', [online], 2 April 2020, available: https://www.caa.co.uk/Our-work/Newsroom/COVID-19/

Clarfelt, H. (2020), 'Wirecard Inquiry', Investors Chronicle, 4 Sep–10 Sep, p.6, 10

Conaghan, D. (2012), 'How QE Became Conventional', Financial World, London, June 2012, pp.15–16

Crawford, A. and Benjamin, A. (2019), 'Trust "Undermined" by Food Delivery Firms Over Hygiene', [online], B.B.C., 26 June 2019, available: www.bbc.co.U.K./news/U.K.-48705066

Darling, A. (2008), 'Storm Warning', [online], The Guardian, 29 August 2008, available: http://www.theguardian.com/politics/2008/aug/30/alistairdarling.economy.

Darling, A. (2010), 'Crisis Management and the Role of the Chancellor', [online], U.K. Treasury Department, London, available: http://www.publications.parliament.uk/pa/cm201012/cmselect/cmtreasy/874/87409.htm

Das, T. K. and Teng, B. (1998), 'Between Trust and Control: Developing Confidence in Partner Cooperation in Alliances', Academy of Management Review, Vol. 23, No. 3, pp.491–512

Deci, E. L. and Ryan, R. M. (2000), 'The "What" and "Why" of Goal Pursuits: Human Needs and the Self Determination of Behaviour', Psychological Inquiry, Vol. 11, No. 4, pp.227–68

Deloitte (2018), 'A Journey Through the F.C.A. Regulatory Sandbox – The Benefits, Challenges, and Next Steps', [online], available: https://www2.deloitte.com/content/dam/Deloitte/U.K./Documents/financial-services/deloitte-U.K.-fca-regulatory-sandbox-project-innovate-finance-journey.pdf

Department for Business Innovation and Skills (2010), 'Learning from Some of Britain's Successful Sectors: An Historical Analysis of the Role of Government', BIS Economics Paper No.6, London

Drage, J. and Mann, F. (1999), 'Improving the Stability of the International Financial System', Financial Stability Review, June, pp.40–77

Fasterling, B. (2011), 'Development of Norms Through Compliance Disclosure', Springer Science+Business Media B. V., p.75, 84

Ferguson, N. (2009), 'The Ascent of Money – A Financial History of the World', London, Penguin, p.50, 235, 252, 261, 274

Fildes, C. (2015), 'Secrets Worth Keeping', Financial World, February/March 2015, p.7

Financial Conduct Authority (2015), 'Principles of Good Regulation', [online], available: https://www.fca.org.U.K./about/operate/principles

Financial Conduct Authority (2015), 'Statement on Payment Protection Insurance', [online], available: https://www.fca.org.U.K./news/statement-on-payment-protection-insurance-ppi

Financial Services Authority (2010), 'Effective Corporate Governance – Significant Influence Controlled Functions and the Walker Review', [online], available: www.fca.org.uk/static/pubs/policy/ps10_15.pdf

Follet, M. P., Metcalf, H.C. and Urwick L. (eds.) (1940), 'Dynamic Administration', New York, Harper and Row

Ford, D., Hakansson, H., Gadde, L.E. and Snehota, I. (2003), 'Managing Business Relationships', 2nd ed. Chichester, John Wiley and Sons

Frank, R. H. (1988), 'Passions Within Reason: The Strategic Role of Emotions', New York, Norton

Frewer, L.J., Howard, C. and Shepherd, R. (1998), 'Understanding Public Attitudes to Technology', Journal of Risk Research, Vol. 1, No. 3, pp.221–235

Fukuyama, F. (1995), 'Trust: The Social Virtues and the Creation of Prosperity', London, Penguin, p.40, 41, 151, 153

Gambetta, D. (1988), 'Trust: Making and Breaking Cooperative Relations', New York, Blackwell

Garrow, N. S. (2012), 'An Examination of the Effectiveness of the Chairman and Chief Executive Officer in Mergers and Acquisitions in Australia', [online], available: http://hdl.handle.net/1959.14/221650, p.57, 58

Gemmell, K. (2022), 'Shell Faces U.K. Showdown Over Impact of "Cataclysmic" Oil Spill, Bloomberg, 26 February, 2022, [online], available: https://www.bloomberg.com/news/articles/2022-02-26/shell-faces-u-k-showdown-over-impact-of-cataclysmic-oil-spill

Ghosh, S. and Patnaik, S. (2012), 'The Independent Banking Commission (Vickers) Report: Squaring the Circle?', International Journal of Law and Management, Vol. 54, Issue 2, p.141

Gonzalez, F. (2005), 'Bank Regulation and Risk-Taking Incentives: An International Comparison of Bank Risk', Journal of Banking and Finance, Vol. 29, pp.1153–1184, Spain

Goodhart, C.A.E. (2008), 'The Regulatory Response to the Financial Crisis', Journal of Financial Stability, Vol. 4, pp.351–358, London

Granovetter, M. (1985), 'Economic Action and Social Structure: The Problem of Embeddedness', American Journal of Sociology, Vol. 91, p.491

Guiso, L., Sapienza, P. and Zingales, L. (2008), 'Trusting the Stock Market', The Journal of Finance, Vol. LXIII, No. 6, pp.2557–2600

Haldane, A. G. (2013), 'Constraining Discretion in Bank Regulation', Speech at the Federal Reserve Bank of Atlanta Conference on 'Maintaining Financial Stability', [online], available: https://www.bankofengland.co.uk/paper/2013/constraining-discretion-in-bank-regulation

Hall, S. (1996), 'Encoding/Decoding', In P. Marris and S. Thornham (eds.), 'Media Studies: A Reader', Edinburgh, Edinburgh University Press, pp.51–61

Hargreaves, D. and Huertas, T. (2011), 'Test under Stress for the EBA' Financial World, April 2011, pp.16–17

Higgs, M. (2009), 'The Good, the Bad and the Ugly: Leadership and Narcissism', Journal of Change Management, Vol. 9, June 2009, p.175.

HM Treasury (2011), 'A New Approach to Financial Regulation: Building a Stronger System', [online], February 2011, available: https://www.gov.uk/government/consultations/a-new-approach-to-financial-regulation-building-a-stronger-system, p.5

HM Treasury Select Committee (2011), 'Competition and Choice in Retail Banking', [online], Vol. 1, Ninth Report of 2010–11, available: https://publications.parliament.uk/pa/cm201011/cmselect/cmtreasy/612/61202.htm

Huxham, C. (1996), 'Collaboration and Collaborative Advantage'. In: Huxham, C. (ed.), Creating Collaborative Advantage, Thousand Oaks, CA, Sage Publications

Jackson, P. (2015), 'Banking is about Risk', Financial World, February/March 2015, p.6

Jenson, M.C. and Meckling, W.H. (1976), 'Theory of the Firm: Management Behaviour, Agency Costs and the Ownership Structure', Journal of Financial Economics, Vol. 3, pp.305–360

Kanter, R.M. (1989), 'When Giants Learn to Dance', New York, NY, Simon and Schuster

Kay, J. (2011), 'Dear ICB...', Financial World, April 2011, p.27

Kay, J. and King, M., 'Radical Uncertainty: Decision-Making for an Unknowable Future', London, The Bridge Street Press

Keynes, J. M. (1914), 'The Prospects of Money', Economic Journal, 24, p.633

King, Sir M. (2010), 'Banking: From Bagehot to Basel, and Back Again', The Second Bagehot Lecture Buttonwood Gathering, New York City, [online], available: www.scribd.com/doc/40114333/Mervyn-King-BoE-Speech

King, Sir M. (2011), 'Governor of the Bank of England Mansion House Speech', London, [online]. 15 June 2011, available: https://www.bankofengland.co.uk/-/media/boe/files/speech/2011/speech-by-mervyn-king-at-the-lord-mayors-banquet-at-mansion-house.pdf

King, Sir M. (2011), 'Financial Regulation: A Preliminary Consideration of the Government Proposals – Treasury', [online]. Last updated 27 January 2011, available: http://www.publications.parliament.uk/pa/cm201011/cmselect/cmtreasy/430/10072802.htm

King, Sir M. (2016), 'The End of Alchemy – Money, Banking and the Future of the Global Economy', London, Little, Brown, p.15

Lambert, D. M. and Knemeyer, A. M. (2004), 'We're in this Together', Harvard Business Review, Vol. 82, No. 12, pp.114–122

Lencioni, J. B. (2012), 'The Five Dysfunctions of a Team', 2nd ed. Wiley

Lindgren, C.J., Garcia, G. and Saal M. (1996), 'Bank Soundness and Macroeconomic Policy', Washington, DC, IMF

Llewellyn, D. T. (2000), 'Some Lessons for Regulation from Recent Bank Crises', Open Economics Review, Vol. 11, No. S1, p.70, 71, 106

Matsumoto, D. (1996), 'Culture and Psychology', Pacific Grove, CA, Brooks/Cole, p.18

Mayer, R. C., Davis, J. H. and Schoorman, F. D. (1995), 'An Integrative Model of Organisational Trust'. Academy of Management Review, Vol. 20, pp.709–734

Mayes, D. G. and Wood, G. E. (2007), 'The Structure of Financial Regulation', Routledge, Oxon

Murphy, K. (2004), 'The Role of Trust in Nurturing Compliance: A Study of Accused Tax Avoiders', Law and Human Behaviour, Vol. 28, No. 2, pp.187–209

Murphy, K., Tyler, T. R. and Curtis, A. (2009), 'Nurturing Regulatory Compliance: Is Procedural Justice Effective When People Question the Legitimacy of the Law?', Regulation and Governance, Vol. 3, pp.1–26

National Commission on The BP Deepwater Horizon Oil Spill and Offshore Drilling (2011), 'Deep Water – The Gulf Oil Disaster and the Future of Offshore Drilling', January 2011 [online], available: https://www.govinfo.gov/content/pkg/GPO-OILCOMMISSION/pdf/GPO-OILCOMMISSION.pdf

Nikolova, M. (2018), 'Bank of England Official Forecasts Development of Cyborg Supervision', [online], available: https://financefeeds.com/bank-england-official-forecasts-development-cyborg-supervision/

Ofgem (2020), 'Investigations and Enforcement Data', [online], available: https://www.ofgem.gov.uk/investigations/investigations-and-enforcement-data

Parliamentary Commission on Banking Standards (2013), 'Changing Banking for Good', London, The Stationery Office, Vol. 1, p.8, 57

Peltzman, S. (1976). 'Toward a More General Theory of Regulation', Journal of Law and Economics, Vol. 19, pp.211–248

Perman, R. (2013), 'Hubris: How HBOS Wrecked the Best Bank in Britain', Edinburgh, Berlinn, p. xi, xiii, xiv, xx

Pfeffer, J. (1994), 'Competitive Advantage Through People', Boston, Harvard Business School Press

Potter, J. and Wetherell, M. (1987), 'Discourse and Social Psychology: Beyond Attitudes and Behaviour', London, Sage, p.7

Power, M., Ashby, S. and Palermo, T. (2013), 'Risk Culture in Financial Organisations – A Research Report, London School of Economics

Ring, P. S. and Van De Ven, A. H. (1994), 'Developmental Process of Cooperative Interorganisational Relationships', Academy of Management Review, Vol. 19, No. 1, pp.90–118

Roll, R. (1986), 'The Hubris Hypothesis of Corporate Takeovers', Journal of Business, vol. 59, p.212

Roselli, A. (2012), 'Financial Structures and Regulation – A Comparison of Crises in the U.K., USA and Italy', Palgrave Macmillan, Hampshire, p. xii, 140

Rosengren, E. S. (2000), 'Modernizing Financial Regulation: Implications for Bank Supervision' Journal of Financial Services Research, Vol. 17, No. 1, p.12, 28, 121, Massachusetts

Rowland, D. and Higgs, M. J. (2008), 'Sustaining Change: Leadership that Works', Chichester, Jossey-Bass

Royal Commission into Misconduct in the Banking, Superannuation and Financial Services Industry (2019), 'Final Report', [online], February 2019, Commonwealth of Australia 2022, vol. 1, p. 433, available: https://www.royalcommission.gov.au/banking

Schelkle, W. (2012), 'A Crisis of What? Mortgage Credit Markets and the Social Policy of Promoting Homeownership in the United States and in Europe', Politics and Society, Vol. 40, pp.59–80, Sage

Shleifer, A. and Vishny, R.W. (1989), 'Management Entrenchment – The Case of Manager-Specific Investments', Journal of Financial Economics, Vol. 25, p. 134, 123–139

Slovic, P. (1993), 'Perceived Risk, Trust and Democracy', Risk Analysis, Vol. 13, No. 6, p.677

Stigler, G. and Friedland, C. (1962), 'What Can Regulators Regulate?', Journal of Law and Economics', Vol. 5, pp.1–16

Sydow, J. (1998), 'Understanding the Constitution of Interorganisational Trust in Trust Within and Between Organisations', In Lane Christel and Bachman Richard (eds.) Conceptual Issues and Empirical Applications, Oxford University Press

Syrus, P. (1st Century BC), 'Sententiae by Publilius Syrus', Bickford-Smith, Roandeu Albert Henry, 1859, London, Clay, [online], available: https://archive.org/details/sententiae00publuoft/page/xxiv/mode/2up

Taylor, M. (2011), 'Dismantle the Bloated Giants', Financial World, April 2011, pp.23–24

Vangen, S. and Huxham, C. (2003), 'Nurturing Collaborative Relations, Building Trust In Inter-Organisational Collaboration'. The Journal of Applied Behavioural Science, Vol. 39, No. 1, pp.5–31

Weibel, A. (2007), 'Formal Control and Trustworthiness: Shall the Twain Never Meet?', Group and Organisation Management, Vol. 32, No. 4, pp.500–517

Williamson, J. and Mahar, M. (1998), 'A Survey of Financial Liberalization', Essays in International Finance, No. 211, Princeton Department of Economics

Wolf, M. (2014), 'The Shifts and the Shocks: What We've Learned and Still Have to Learn from the Financial Crisis', London, Penguin

Zand, D. E. (1997), 'The Leadership Triad, Knowledge, Trust and Power'. New York, Oxford University Press

Zuckerberg, M. (2019), 'The Internet Needs New Rules. Let's Start in these Four Areas', Washington Post, 30 March 2019, [online], available: https://www.washingtonpost.com/opinions/mark-zuckerberg-the-internet-needs-new-rules-lets-start-in-these-four-areas/2019/03/29/9e6f0504-521a-11e9-a3f7-78b7525a8d5f_story.html

GLOSSARY

App.   Software application used in performing a computing task

B.A.C.S.   A subsidiary of Pay.UK, responsible for various payment services across the United Kingdom

Bank of England   The central bank of the United Kingdom

Board   The elected group of individuals that represent shareholders, whose key purpose is to ensure the company's prosperity by collectively directing the company's affairs

C.A.A.   The Civil Aviation Authority is the U.K. aviation regulator

Caveat Emptor   The principle that the buyer is responsible for checking the suitability and quality of goods

Capitalism   An economic and political system in which a country's trade and industry are controlled by private owners for profit, rather than by the state

C.F.T.C.   The Commodity Futures Trading Commission in the United States, responsible for promoting integrity, resilience, and vibrancy of the derivatives markets through sound regulation

Conduct   The manner in which a person behaves, especially on a particular occasion or in a particular context

C-Suite   Executive level leaders in an organisation that occupy chief status, such as Chief Executive Officer, Chief Operating Officer, Chief Financial Officer, and Chief Information Officer

D.F.S.   New York State Department of Financial Services supervises and regulates the activities of approximately 1,500 banking and other financial institutions and more than 1,400 insurance companies

Ecosystem   A complex network or interconnected system; a community of interacting organisms and their physical environment

Enforcement   The imposition of compliance with rules and obligations, which can be accompanied in some circumstances by a sanction (fines, permissions withdrawn, public announcements, warnings, prosecutions, etc.)

Ethics   Moral principles that govern a person's behaviour or the conducting of an activity

F.C.A.   Financial Conduct Authority is the regulator of financial services in the United Kingdom established on 1 April 2013. It regulates the conduct of more than 50,000 firms and is the prudential supervisor for over 48,000 firms

F.D.A.   Food and Drug Administration is the organisation in the United States responsible for protecting the public health

Federal Reserve   The central bank of the United States

F.I.N.M.A.   Financial Market Supervisory Authority (Swiss) is the organisation tasked with protecting investors, creditors, and policyholders through ensuring that the financial markets in Switzerland function properly

Fintech   Financial technology is used to describe new technology that seeks to improve and automate the delivery and use of financial services

FOREX (Foreign Exchange)   Refers to the foreign exchange markets in which the major currencies of the world are traded

Framework   The basic underlying structure of the book to aid the reader in their understanding of approaches and concepts covered in the text

F.S.A.   Financial Services Authority is the financial regulator that preceded the F.C.A. in the United Kingdom

F.S.M.A   The Financial Services and Markets Act (2000) provides the framework within which a single regulator for the financial services industry in the United Kingdom will operate

F.T.C.   Federal Trade Commission is an organisation that has the dual mission to protect consumers and promote competition in America. It champions the interests of the American consumer

G.A.O.   Government Accountability Office provides an independent, nonpartisan agency that works for the U.S. Congress and acts as the congressional watchdog, examining how U.S. taxpayers' contributions are spent

G.F.C.   Global Financial Crisis relates to the issues arising across financial markets that impacted countries and institutions across the globe. Widely reported as commencing during the years of 2007–08 when financial institutions started to experience difficulties in their ability to fund their operations

G.F.I.N.   Global Financial Innovation Network is a global network of 46 financial authorities, initiated by the Financial Conduct Authority in the United Kingdom. Its aim is to provide a way for regulators to engage with market participants and find solutions for cross-border challenges that arise resulting from the developments in fintech

House View   The conclusion arrived at as the sum of views, opinions, or analysis

I.C.O.   The Information Commissioners Office is the United Kingdom's independent body set up to uphold information rights

Internet of Things   The interconnection of computing devices embedded in everyday objects, using the internet to communicate and pass data

L.A.B.C.F.T.C.   The Commodity Futures Trading Commission LAB, which promotes fintech innovation and regulatory engagement in the United States. It also publishes papers in the broad field of innovation, such as artificial intelligence, blockchain, and digital assets

Leadership Team   For our purposes, this refers to the executive team charged with leading the organisation day to day in line with the wishes of the Board (see also C-Suite)

L.I.B.O.R.   London Interbank Offer Rate has historically been one of the main interest rate benchmarks used in financial contracts

L.S.B.   The Legal Services Board is the oversight regulator for legal services in England and Wales

Machine Learning   The process of computers changing the way they carry out tasks by learning from new data without a human being needing to give instructions

Metaverse   A virtual reality space in which users can interact with other users in a computer generated environment

M.H.R.A.   Medicines and Healthcare Products Regulatory Agency is the U.K. regulator for medicines, medical devices, and blood components for transfusion

Mode of Operation   The situation in which the regulatory engagement occurs, is experienced, or is undertaken

Modus Operandi   A particular way or method of doing something

Non-Fungible Token (N.F.T.)   A digital certificate that provides ownership and provenance

N.A.O. National Audit Office is the United Kingdom's independent spending watchdog, supporting parliament and holding the government spending to account

N.I.A.U.R. The Northern Ireland Authority for Utility Regulation

N.S.P.C.C. National Society for the Prevention of Cruelty to Children

O.C.C. Office of the Controller of the Currency regulates and supervises all U.S. banks and federal savings associations, as well as branches and agencies of foreign banks. The O.C.C. is an independent bureau of the U.S. Department of the Treasury

O.E.C.D. Organisation for Economic Co-operation and Development

Ofcom The Office of Communications is the communications regulator in the United Kingdom

O.F.G.E.M. Office of Gas and Electricity Markets are a non-ministerial government department and an independent National Regulatory Authority set up to protect consumers by working to deliver a fair energy system in the United Kingdom

Ofwat The Water Services Regulation Authority is the regulator for water services in England and Wales

O.R.R. The Office of Rail and Road is the rail and road regulator in the United Kingdom

Pandemic An epidemic occurring worldwide, or over a very wide area, crossing international borders and usually affecting a large number of people (epidemic: a widespread occurrence of an infectious disease in a community at a particular time)

Payment Services Regulator A subsidiary of the Financial Conduct Authority and the independent economic regulator for the payment systems industry in the United Kingdom

P.P.I. Payment Protection Insurance is a form of insurance which is designed to cover repayment obligations in certain circumstances where the policyholder cannot make them

Prudential Regulation Authority The Prudential Regulation Authority (P.R.A.) was created as a part of the Bank of England by the Financial Services Act 2012 and is responsible for the prudential regulation and supervision of around 1,700 banks, building societies, credit unions, insurers, and major investment firms

Regulatee The regulated party in a regulatory relationship; a person or organisation whose activities are overseen by a regulator

Regulation An official rule or the act of controlling something

Regulator A person or organisation whose job it is to ensure the activities of businesses or organisations are operating in accordance with official rules and laws

Regulatory Affairs Professionals Society R.A.P.S. is the largest global organisation and professional community in the healthcare and related products industry. It has a membership of more than 20,000 individuals in more than 80 countries

Regulatory Objectives The goals and aims of a regulatory authority that are usually defined in enabling legislation

Regulatory Relationship The conduit and connections between a regulator and the regulatee; the way in which people, groups, and organisations regard and behave toward each other. For our purposes, these include methods of interaction (e.g., meetings, submissions, requests), behaviours and approach (e.g., openness, transparency), content of interaction and drivers of outcomes (e.g., all a regulator should see), and perception and understanding

Regulatory Relationship Ecosystem The sum of information and insight used by a regulator to form its judgements and opinions

Regulatory Relationship Strategy The overall objective, scope, planning, and directing of activities, resources, and approaches dedicated to the regulatory relationship

Relationship Management The supervision and maintenance of relationships between an organisation and its external stakeholders, e.g., clients, regulators, partners, etc.

S.E.C. Securities and Exchange Commission is the organisation that aims to protect investors, maintain fair, orderly, and efficient markets, and facilitate capital formation in the United States

Section 166 A section 166 under the Financial Services and Markets Act 2000 relates to a skilled persons review, where a regulator will ask that a skilled person undertakes work on an organisation to understand issues or concerns the regulator may have

Social Engineering The use of deception to manipulate individuals into divulging confidential or personal information that may be used for fraudulent purposes

U.K.R.N. United Kingdom Regulators Network is a member organisation formed of 13 of the United Kingdom's sectoral regulators to enhance collaboration on issues of shared relevance

W.H.O. World Health Organisation has the role of directing and coordinating international health within the United Nations system, including preparedness, surveillance, and response

W.I.C.S. The Water Industry Commission for Scotland is the economic regulator for Scottish Water

INDEX